The Common European Constitutional Culture

Dia-Logos

Schriften zu Philosophie und Sozialwissenschaften
Studies in Philosophy and Social Sciences

Herausgegeben von / Edited by
Tadeusz Buksiński / Piotr W. Juchacz

Bd. /vol. 21

PETER LANG
EDITION

Roman Hauser / Marek Zirk-Sadowski /
Bartosz Wojciechowski (eds.)

The Common European Constitutional Culture

Its Sources, Limits and Identity

PETER LANG
EDITION

Bibliographic Information published by the Deutsche Nationalbibliothek
The Deutsche Nationalbibliothek lists this publication in the Deutsche Nationalbibliografie; detailed bibliographic data is available in the internet at http://dnb.d-nb.de.

Library of Congress Cataloging-in-Publication Data
Names: Hauser, Roman, editor. | Zirk-Sadowski, Marek, editor. | Wojciechowski, Bartosz, 1973- editor.
Title: The common European constitutional culture : its sources, limits, and identity / Roman Hauser, Marek Zirk-Sadowski, Bartosz Wojciechowski (eds.).
Description: New York : Peter Lang, 2016. | Series: Dia-logos, ISSN 1619-005X; v. 21
Identifiers: LCCN 2016000924 | ISBN 9783631659915
Subjects: LCSH: Constitutional law—European Union countries—Interpretation and construction. | International and municipal law—European Union countries. | Civil law—International unification.
Classification: LCC KJE5034 .C66 2016 | DDC 306.2/5094—dc23 LC record available at http://lccn.loc.gov/2016000924

This publication was financially supported by the Faculty of Law and Administration of the University of Łódź.

ISSN 1619-005X
ISBN 978-3-631-65991-5 (Print)
ISBN 978-3-653-05476-7 (E-Book)
DOI 10.3726/978-3-653-05476-7

Peter Lang Edition is an Imprint of Peter Lang GmbH.

Peter Lang – Frankfurt am Main · Berlin · Bruxelles · New York · Oxford · Warszawa · Wien

This publication has been peer reviewed.

www.peterlang.com

Table of Contents

Introduction

The fundamental postulate from Lisbon Treaty 2007 and other basic EU's acts is to make "an ever closer Union among the peoples of Europe" (Art 1) and empower its citizens to participate in processes of will-formation because the rule of law and the principle of democracy have the same source of their legitimacy, notably, public spheres. Thus unleashing normative premises of institutionalization of discourse occurs Janus-faced as it runs towards the human rights interpretation and recognition, that means, it results in the interplay between universalizable normative claims and their interpretation coloured with the ethical fibre – be it national, ethnic or cultural.

Nevertheless, processes of Europeanization have been proceeding on the legal level basically, wherein the prominent role was casted by the CJEU, and also on the level of intergovernmental decision-making. In the aftermath of such a proceeding the EU may be comprehended in terms of the rights-based union and problem-solving entity though the emergence of the values-based community has been stymied and the transnational public spheres are rather thin. In other words, the ethical fibre became crumpled up or at least huddled for the effective governance performance what caused a democratic deficit and gave rise to debates on the EU as a post democratic polity. There are disputes whether this oddity of the EU indicates its nobility or perversion, but the fact remains, that the Eurocitizens, in their post-sovereign states, became lost in the Hegelian extreme terms of the universal-formal rights (including the ECJ rulings in the *Viking* and *Laval* cases) and the individual interests what made them especially exposed on the economic crisis shocks.

The most important task carried out under the book is to undertake theoretical and jurisprudential research on the interrelations between the sense of the individual identity and the sense of national identity (including constitutional one) and the search for a common European legal culture. The outcome of the study in question will be a proposal of the foundation for a new paradigm of the EU law taking into account all of the said manifestations of identity. One of the main generators of the contemporary changes in the processes of globalization and legal integration is the specificity of constructing the law, namely its argumentative creation and application to specific situations, taking into account both the tradition and current claims to validity of one's national legislation and its national recipients, and then confronting it with the diversity of legal systems developed by other states, supranational or international institutions. This process may lead to some vital questions about the community and the nature of the political community whose rightful member one could become. The current paradigm of law, which has provided for civil rights in the Western tradition already since the times of Kant, has resulted in the vision of Europeanization only through legal and institutional integration. This, in turn, led to the collapse of civic integration, as manifested in the phenomenon of "democratic deficit" or a "crisis of public legitimacy" in the European Union. This generated the need for a new paradigm which will expressly take into account the widely discussed postulate (mostly in public institutional structures) of the empowerment of citizens and the requirement to provide national identity, while seeking and promoting a common legal culture. The proposed change of the paradigm of law recognizes the EU law through the prism of the references to the vision of the Roman republic, where the key role was played by the citizen. The condition for creating such a common legal culture is thus the development of the processes of formulating public justification for normative claims which is to be uniformly binding for us. The processes of formulating public justification will also possibly criticise the moral and ethical beliefs of all the creators and, at the same time, recipients of the EU law (i.e., those that come from all the EU Member States), as to arrive at such law and such an interpretation of the sources of common law which can be regarded as a common and thus unifying rather than separating cooperative goal of the EU citizens. The concept of the European citizenship will gain an actual content if the said European identity, and thus also the sources of the legal legitimation of the EU legal system, become actually "communitised", that is discursively determined in the processes of cooperative interpretation of the public politico-legal culture. This will perhaps allow, on the one hand, to overcome the contemporary crisis of the identity of the individual (understood as a rightful citizen having an actual influence on his or her rights and duties) while, on the other hand, to resolve and settle the emerging (or better yet – existing) conflict between the national identity and the European identity.

It seems like a considerably difficult task to speak of national identity and the sense of community with supranational structures (such as the European Union) and the international ones. In terms of the EU law, the national identity includes the constitutional identity of the Member State, and it is the responsibility of the European Union to preserve it. As a result, the Member States may require the protection of their own national identity and the required preservation of the constitutional identity of the Member State may constitute a legitimate interest which can give rise to the constraints of the obligations imposed by the EU law. Thus, the concept of the national identity manifests, besides the specifics of culture, language, customs or religion, the relationship with the national identity, reflected in the preservation of the basic state functions that condition the existence of the state as a separate entity. Moreover, national identity sensu largo is also treated as a requirement to consider the continuity of the existence of the Member States as sovereign entities, the respect for scientific cultures, the norms of national law, languages, ways of providing access to social security or the rules of the social – economic system of the state. In other words, national identity of a national community is understood as its collective self-consciousness, its self-determination, creating a self-image, as the entire content of the self-knowledge rather than the image of the national character constructed from the outside. In this context it is legitimate to treat the nation as a community-based group founded on the common understanding of certain values connected with the tradition of shared history, elements of culture and aspirations to preserve their identity. The foundation of the long process of unifying the European Union is a community of values which gave rise to the very process of the unification and continuous development. One of the pillars of this foundation is the existence of a common legal culture which is a source of the possible arguments legitimizing the EU law. Accordingly, the latter is seen not only as a universally valid system in the European Union, but also as the source of a shared knowledge about this world, what is of particular importance for the addresses of the law. However, it should be noted that the fundamental elements of the legal culture are rooted in a commonly shared world view and life of a given political community, and therefore they refer in some way to the broader concept of culture, namely to the public political culture and, at the same time, to the sense of identity of a specific political and legal community. Nevertheless, the identity of the values of a political and legal community, as the foundation of unifying the EU citizens, must also take into account the constitutional identity, understood as a recognition of one's national cultural identity through the reflection on the fundamental rights accepted in a given society and nation. The identity refers to a catalogue of fundamental rights contained in the Constitutions of the respective legal systems, yet as it turns out, the contents and limits of these rights cannot be determined only by examining the very text of the Constitution. We as if move naturally from the instrumental rationality, characteristic for the operation of the state institutions, to the understanding and interpretation of the constitutional rights. The fact of discovering the specificity of understanding these rights which we are able to identify with, stands for the discovery of the constitutional identity. In the case of the European Union, it is already the very conception of the integration that influences the relationship of the Constitutions of the Member States to the EU law as well as the possibility of creating the constitutional identity of the Member States. In other words, we assume that the Union does not accept federal aspirations. Although recently there have been discussions on the effectiveness of the so-called European governance, there is a strong conviction that the Union is to be merely a form of a cooperation between independent states that are united to jointly deal with selected issues. The Member States remain separate entities in the international relations and they preserve their powers. The cooperation does not have a supranational character. The respective decisions are therefore the reflection of particular state interests and not of the organization itself. The standpoints of the individual Member States are represented in the European Council and the Council of the European Union which, alongside the Commission, are the most important EU bodies. The European Council sets out the main directions of the EU development, while the Council of the European Union issues most of the legislation (alone or in cooperation with the Parliament). For this reason, the so-called democratic deficit in the Union, namely replacing the category of "European people" with "European public opinion" does not have a decisive influence on the effectiveness of EU operations. If one accepts the justification of democracy referring to the category of self-determination by the people, it is difficult to decide how to determine the place of the authorities that democratically set forth the rights and duties of the citizens so as not to interrupt the communication between these authorities and local communities. In other words, what comes as a problem is an authentic representation of particular interests and the possibility of articulating them in the central authorities of the Union.The empowerment contained in the new paradigm of law, developed under this grant, will be largely based on the Charter of Fundamental Rights of the European Union, thus demonstrating the possibility of creating the identity of EU's citizens by means of actively permeating human rights with content. In other words, the new paradigm of law will enable to generate a widely discussed, yet often neglected, public sphere in the European Union, understood as value-based community. The possibility of creating a value-based community, due to the proposed change of the paradigm of law, is of utmost importance for the further processes of Europeanization, since it constitutes a condition sine qua non for developing the European identity and for involving the EU's citizens in the processes of a valid law making by means of communicative articulation of citizens' will.It can therefore be assumed that the EU is currently dominated by anti-federalist approach, strengthened further by the financial crisis in the Eurozone. It therefore seems reasonable to consider the relationship of the Constitutions of the Member States with the EU law against the traditional conception of integration referred to as "the Europe of nations". In this perspective, the national identity, including the constitutional identity, is not in contradiction with the objectives of the

European integration. On the contrary, the multiplicity of legal languages, values and the sense of tradition are the qualities that build integration. What can be nevertheless perceived is a peculiar tension between the identity of the individual, the national identity and the European identity. Our task will be to demonstrate that it is possible to reconcile these identities without impinging on their essence and power. The latter will be achieved by showing that is it justified to speak of a formation of a common legal culture. Since the dawn of the history, Europe has been marked by a specific type of multiculturalism, though perhaps not the one that is widely discussed today, but rather the one related to the habit of integrating the central values and the characteristics of almost every new group encountered by the [European] dominant cultures. From the perspective of contemporary times, this phenomenon has resulted in a typical European cosmopolitan belief that the local or regional problems, such as those relating to Europe or the European Union, cannot be legitimately dealt with in a complete isolation from the claims made by the states, institutions or international organizations in the context of the issues that overwhelm the rest of the world, even those related with the processes of globalization. When searching for the answer to the question about our common identity, namely the identity of modern Europeans, it turns out that this concept is inherently problematic. Accordingly, it requires an understanding which refers us and our identity to the past. The answer to this question cannot be found in the future, possibly even not in the present, which is in many ways inscrutable. It plays a crucial role in the search for identity, tinged with self-understanding, which is [nevertheless] based on the solid structures of history, in our case, the history of Europe. The exploration of common aspects of history is meaningful and can be fruitful if we think and believe that it is possible to bridge the gap between the diverse cultures on the basis of a common tradition, which in some areas of values appears to us as a legal culture. It is undoubtedly a considerable bond in a shared vision of a normative world in which there is an axiological "hard core", manifested in the form of the catalogue of the so-called inalienable rights (human rights) as a part of either the text of law, judicial decisions, public administration decisions, or of the ordinary course of thinking of the recipients of law who participate in this culture and who think through the prism of this catalogue. The answer to the question about a common core of national and community-based identity can be given only from the perspective of the deepest layers of philosophical self-understanding characteristic of the European culture and its integrative core, namely legal culture. What merits a particularly profound philosophical reflection is the legitimacy of law whose justification allows to create the very concept of the legal culture and identity. Yet, the explanation that there is some solid belief of the individuals as to the need to comply with the law, namely with law making entities and with the interpretative findings of judges and other officials, proves to be a complicated intellectual challenge. The history of philosophical and legal thought shows that the reflection on the identity of the legal culture still remains in a dialectical conflict between the thesis on the existence of the fundamental elements of the possibility of legitimising this reality and nihilism, namely the thesis on the hopelessness of such exploration and the failure to hope for their discovery, i.e. the discovery of legitimising the identity of the legal culture. The issue is to identify the structures that justify not only the existence of the law, but also its content in the form of a specific catalogue of values, namely to provide such arguments which would be the reason for its existence as to the form and content, and therefore its acceptance. Such a cognitive procedure would be an important step in discovering the European identity and the national identity of the citizens of the member states of this community as well as a crucial step in understanding that the Member States of the European Union, as a common legal culture, can develop and implement "the best possible" catalogue of human rights. This is also very important from the practical (social) point of view. Experience shows that the most stable systems of social organization are those which gain inner acceptance for the rules that bind their members, namely for the identity. The argument of power and the likelihood of punishment or pain constitute a weak social bond. The need to justify – legitimise the law is typically manifested in the social crises that undermine the hierarchy of accepted values and, consequently, the whole social order. Yet, it turns out – as mentioned above – that this is not an easy task and the literature suggests that the answer to the question about the objective basis of legitimising law is far from being straightforward. It is neither the issue which is often discussed in the theoretical and jurisprudential literature, because the interests of the legal theorists and the philosophers of law focus primarily on the problem of the internal validity of the law, mainly for practical reasons. In turn, the question of determining the foundations of the axiological identity and the identity of the legal culture, both for the individual legal orders and for the European community, appears to be a difficult theoretical problem of the so-called external validity of the law. Literature indicates that the ultimate principle of the existence of law could be included in the analysis of the regulative idea, namely in a certain flagship model which can never be absolutely determined. We, however, claim otherwise. Axiological identity and the identity of the legal culture of the European citizens, as the foundation of values that provide the institutional basis for each state and, contemporarily, also for the European Union, have their pillars which are referred to as transcendental arguments, namely those which legitimise this culture due to their universal character. Each of these arguments is firmly and permanently inscribed in the constitutional identity of the individual Member States of the European Union, and thus – indirectly – in the very institution. These arguments can be found in the ontological conception of natural law, in the transcendental argument of practical reason and in the transcendental-pragmatic argument of communicative activities. The European legal culture has axiologically matured on these three pillars which now constitute the source of its legal identity. The latter allows to combine the diversity of other cultural elements of the national identity of its individual states that often differ from or even contradict one another, yet which always find their identity in the legal culture.

In fact, it concerns the well-known question "Who are we, the Europeans?" – Is there any "we" or simply an aggregation of interests, at most members states? Perhaps, the third possibility fits best: processes of the recognition of differences, recognition of the other in his/her otherness give rise to the emergences of the Europeans recognized in their *synthetic* constitution in the making – "in-between" the national and supranational or even international legal system. Drawing extensively on the idea of universalizable normative claims as the source of human rights recognized as the "general principles of the Union's law" shall we limit their understanding and claims to enforcement solely to the polity under construction (local constitutionalism) or become a visible and strong player on the international legal stage (global constitutionalism) – or rather should the EU remain the unsettled polity (soft constitutionalism)? Once again, who are we – the community of judges who are practicing philosophers? Or practicing politicians, perhaps? Finally, who *is* the "Master of the Treaty" and who *should* be? The CJEU's ruling in *Seda Kücükdeveci v. Swedex GmbH&Co. KG* opens up the sources of the constitutional traditions of the members states but the question remains to whom and to what purpose it is supposed to serve – to public debates in which citizens would be able to cooperatively rethink and re-examine the past in order to render their common future open and trigger off the processes of the emergence of the European constitutional demos – or simply to judicial decisions made behind the closed door. The idea is to investigate who constructs the future Europe, with what kind of resources and thus whether this construction is solid enough to undergo several crisis that the EU must face now and certainly will have to copy with in the future, if survives.

Roman Hauser, Marek Zirk-Sadowski, Bartosz Wojciechowski

Part I
The Common European Identity and the Idea of Self-Constitutionalisation

Antal Visegrády DSc
University of Pécs, Hungary

European Legal and Constitutional Cultures

Abstract: The article characterises the notion of European legal culture in context of the main difference between the English and continental legal systems which lies in the perception of the role of the judge and the recognition of the role of judge-made law as a source of law. In the next step it indicates the principal components of constitutional cultures and its relation to general legal culture. Finally, it responds to the problem how to understand a common European constitutional culture.

Key Words: a source of law, constitutionalism, the common constitutional values of Europe, the role of the judge

I.

There are two approaches to the notion of European legal culture: on the one hand, it may be used to describe the common features of the legal cultures of European states, and on the other hand, to denote the peculiar *sui generis* legal culture of the European Union.

European legal culture forms part of Western legal culture and, in essence, it may be regarded as its cradle. It is characterized by the secularized nature of law, in other words, law is formally distinguished from religious and moral rules. The values of these systems of rules are transformed into law through political law-making. Although European legal systems are secularized, they regard themselves as being rooted in Judeo-Christian traditions. Their scale of social-organizational and political values reflects parliamentary democracy, political pluralism, the rule of law and a commitment to human rights. Besides a professionalized law-making process, European legal culture is also dominantly characterized by the professionalized application of law, but the conception of the role of judges means a breaking point to some extent within European legal culture taken in the traditional sense: judge-made law is a natural part of the Anglo-Saxon (common law) legal culture, while in continental (civil law) legal cultures the law-making and law-developing role of the judge is debated. However, European integration has contributed to the approximation of legal cultures and the above-mentioned differences seem to be dissolving in the legal culture of the European Union.

According to Hesselink, the most important characteristic of European legal culture is legal formalism, the dogmatic, positivist approach to law, in other words, textual dependence and the dominance of formal-logical reasoning. Although the formalism of the English legal system is not so strong as that of the continental legal systems, in this respect – in Hesselink's opinion – there is still less difference between the English and the continental legal systems than between the English and American legal systems within the common law legal system, which means that there is greater coherence within European legal culture than within the common law family.

The European, and mainly traditional continental approach regards law as a coherent, logical system, in which the right (and only) answer to all arising questions may be found in the text of the statutes (codes) or by way of deduction. Jurisprudence is strongly positivist and the commentaries of legal scholars play an important role in the application of law, these commentaries are often relied on by the courts in their reasoning and in order to find the proper solution. Although the formalism of the 19th century was in due time mitigated by the spread of the method of teleological interpretation or the introduction of such general notions (e.g. good faith in private law) that broadened the judge's discretion, the task still fell primarily on the legislator to adjust the code serving as a basis for the administration of justice to the changing social conditions and requirements.

The main difference between the English and continental legal systems lies in the perception of the role of the judge and the recognition of the role of judge-made law as a source of law. According to the continental idea, the judge's role is solely to apply the law (this also flows from the principle of the separation of powers), legislation is the task of the legislator and the judge is merely the "mouth" of law. As opposed to this, the English legal system recognizes judicial practice or case law as a source of law, and judges may apply the law in the light of the changing requirements. As a matter of course, practice has shown that extreme formalism is untenable, and during the 20th century it was also recognized in several continental legal systems – to differing degrees and with phase delays – that judges make law in some way, which may become manifested in the guiding, orienting role of decisions in individual cases or in such legal institutions as the law uniformity decisions of the Hungarian Supreme Court.

At the same time, if one steps beyond the formalist approach and focuses not on differences between sources of law (as forms of manifestation of law), the difference between the English and the continental systems is reduced to the minimum and it is not greater than the difference between the individual continental systems. This difference is the most conspicuous on comparison with the American legal culture, which, in contrast with European positivism, places emphasis, during legal reasoning, not on sources of law, but on the consequences of the decision, in other words, it is rather pragmatist. Jurisprudence and legal training do not focus on the text either (be it statute or case law), but rather on its context and social correlations, the exploration of the roots and functioning of the law based on an interdisciplinary approach (in the disciplines of law and economy, law and society etc.).

As it is known the Romanistic-German legal systems could be divided into three legal groups.

European countries that belong to the *Romanistic legal group* are:

1. France (as the "cradle" of the legal family);
2. Belgium, Luxembourg, the Netherlands (that came to touch with French law as a result of French military expansion);
3. Italy, Spain, Portugal (that were also heavily influenced by the German and the Swiss codes which makes them representatives of an intermediary type)

The characteristic features of the Romanistic legal group could be summed up as follows:

a) The code of central significance is the *Code Civil* (1804) in the legal family. This code has a clear-cut structure, free of any feudal elements, any "compromises". It leaves almost no room for judicial discretion, its formulations are concise and simple. It is often called the "most *bourgeois*" civil code that laid the foundations for European codification.

The Code Civil is in force in Belgium, in four Italian regions, two Swiss cantons and with some modifications in Baden. Replicas of the Code Napoleon were enacted in the Netherlands (1838), in Sicily (1812), in Parma (1820), in the States of Sardinia (1837) and in Modena (1842). As an adapted translation of the original, it was instituted in Greece (1841), in the unified Italy (1865) and in Romania (1865). And finally, although not as the exclusive source but as primary inspiration, it influenced the Portuguese (1867) and the Spanish (1889) civil law codification, just like Louisiana and Quebec in North America.

However, the success of the Code Civil peaked in South America. It was took over in its original language in Dominica (1825), and later in translation in Bolivia (1831). The creative adaptation of European models (as mediated by French patterns) was first achieved in Chile (1825) that encouraged some countries to follow the lead (Ecuador 1861, Columbia 1873) and others to create their national code based on the Code (Uruguay 1867, Argentina 1869).

In Asia, the Code Civil made an impact on almost the same scale but in a far less homogenous way. Its principles are applied in Japan, and all four French codes were adapted in Turkey. In Egypt, the first codes (1867, 1883) were replicas of the Code Napoleon, the present code (1948) is a developed version based on it (which inspires Syria for adapted reception). The civil codes of Lebanon (1934) and Venezuela (1942) are also of French origin, although both are to be taken as significantly different to it.[1]

aa) The Code Civil regulates the relationship of the statute and the judge in a rather radical way. Judges are not allowed to interpret the statute "arbitrarily", in matters of legal interpretation they have to turn to the authority of *referé legislative* (established in 1970).

ab) The Code Civil is the code of the "owner". It was based upon the idea of a citizen who makes rational decisions, who is aware of the relevant information and the norms of law. The Code strives to guarantee the freedom of property and contract as much as possible.

ac) The Code finds a middle way between abstract principles and concrete (casuistic) norms. It determined the paradigmatic style for civil law codifications as well as codes on other fields of law for the future.

b) The Romanistic legal group (unlike the Germanic and the common law systems) is characterized by the prevalence of legislature. The influence of Roman law-quite paradoxically because of the early reception of Roman law – is much weaker.

The second is the *Germanic legal group*, its "members" are the following countries:

1) Germany;
2) Austria;
3) Switzerland;
4) the countries of Central Eastern Europe (especially the Chech Republic and Hungary).

As characteristics of this legal group, the following features are to be pointed out.

a) With respect to the development of the Germanic legal group, it proved to be a significant factor that, compared to other legal systems, *the influence of the Roman law* asserted itself rather late (only in the 15th century), although when came across *it was very strong*.

b) The code of central significance in the legal group is the *Bürgerliches Gezetzbuch* (1900) which is a conservative code (unlike the Code Civil).

1 See Varga Cs.: *A kodifikáció, mint társadalmi-történeti jelenség.* (Codification as a Social-Historical Phenomenon) Akadémiai Kiadó, Budapest, 1979. 117–118.

The BGB was used in the recodification of the Greek civil law (1940), and in the codification of contracts in Poland (1933). It provided the basis for the Brazilian (1916), the Mexican (1928), and the Peruvian (1936) Codigo Civil as well as the codification of civil law in Japan (1898), Siam (1925), China (1929), and Thailand (1962). It also inspired the Italian Codice Civil (1942) which is quite remarkable as the Codice Civile of 1865 was formulated in French spirit.

ba) The law of the BGB is the law of lawyers, it is characterized by a style that strives for accuracy, subtlety and abstraction. Its addressees are not citizens but primarily lawyers (of course, in the sociological sense of the world). Its institutional constructions and terms are artificial, its language is technical (only professionals can understand its true meanings). As its primary focus is not conciseness but accuracy, the code is often very complicated.

bb) The norms of the code are ordered in a specific way that more or less follows the structure of the Institutions of Justinian (personal and family law, the objects are types of property, the ways of acquisition of property, etc.).

Many think that the *Austrian Civil Code* (ABGB 1811) finds a kind of middle way between the lawyers' of law of the BGB and the application-oriented law of the Code Civil.

The famous *Swiss Civil Code* (ZGB, 1912) has distinguished position in the Germanic legal family. The ZGB is "deliberately vague" at certain points to allow the judge to search for the solution that is the most appropriate in the given case. The code is characterized by the extensive use of general clauses that are to be interpreted by the judges in the particular cases.

At last, the Nordic legal group consists of the following countries:

1) Denmark;
2) Finland;
3) Iceland;
4) Norway;
5) Sweden.

The legal group can be characterized by the following features.

a) This group is often regarded as *a kind of intermediate version between the common law and the Romanistic-German legal systems.*

It resembles the common law systems as it was hardly influenced by the Roman law and the wave of codifications in the age of the Enlightenment (e.g. the comprehensive codification of the civil law has not taken place yet). On the other hand, the similarity to the Romanistic-German systems can also be pointed out: judges do not have a central role in system and there is no normative precedent-doctrine.

The Nordic countries had lived in relative isolation for a long period. Their legal institutions were influenced by the French law in the 19th century, the German law at the beginning of the 20th century , and the common law (especially the law of the USA) mainly after World War II. However, despite all these influences, they kept their original character.

b) The co-operation of the Scandinavian countries is manifested in their laws as *they make efforts to integrate the content of their legal systems*. It could be exemplified by the Scandinavian Sales of Goods Act that was passed in every Nordic country (Sweden 1905, Denmark 1906, Norway 1907, Iceland 1922). The act is influenced by both the British Sales of Goods Act (1893) and the German BGB. The co-operation is facilitated by their common legal and linguistic traditions.

c) Last but not least, it should be mentioned that *judges of higher courts and jurists of high authority play an important role in Scandinavian legislatures.*

From this aspect the English legal system is really closer to the continental legal systems than to the common-law sister-system of American law, and the English and continental legal cultures may together be called European legal culture. As a matter of fact, behind the formalism of European legal culture – as opposed to the American – there is the ideological system of parliamentary sovereignty and supremacy, which implies trust in the legislator and the proper functioning of government (as opposed to the American lack of trust). As it is pointed out by Hesselink, the European approach is also less formalistic when the appliers of law do not trust other institutions, such as, for example, the institutions of the European Union.

The questions arises as to whether this lack of trust means the legal reflection of lack of political trust (the lack of trust in the institutional system of the EU on the part of the national political institutional system or, similarly to the American situation, the lack of trust in the political institutional system on the part of the legal institutional system), or the lack of trust of the appliers of law in other legal cultures, or it stems from both sources. From the aspect of our topic, it is worth examining whether lack of confidence in the EU may result from a lack of trust in "otherness", another legal culture, in other words, whether the European Union has a different legal culture from the above-analysed common European legal culture basically characterized by formalism.

II.

Constitutional culture is part of general legal culture

Constitutional culture is a certain system of values of the human community geared towards creative co-existence on the basis of common rules of social cohabitation acquired through mutual consent.

The principal components of constitutional culture comprise the intellectual absorption of social co-existence, the existence of fundamental values for organic subsistence, of social accord around them, the reproduction thereof through universal behavioral rules of living and acting, a rendering of a certain systemic legal nature thereto, and a particular attitude towards them within the society. In social practice these components are historically expressed in their systemic integrity, as well as in a more fragmented manner.

Constitutional scholars often use the notion of "constitutional culture" in the plural. When talking about constitutional cultures the emphasis is put on the systemic properties of their formation. For example, the notion "Verfassung" in Germany acquired broad usage in the 17–19th centuries, when it was used to denote laws of fundamental importance, containing norms, which aimed at sustainable and lasting perspective. The term applied to the "Capitulation Act" of King Ferdinand III in the elections of 1648; the Peace of Westphalia,

1803; the Final Act of the Principal Royal Standing Committee etc.

Professor Cheryl Saunders, in turn, singles out the constitutional systems of the United Kingdom, the USA and France Robert Goodin stresses the existence of features that are common to constitutions of various countries.

Each country and nation has gone through its individual path of formation of constitutional culture and establishment of constitutional realities, borrowing to this or that extent the experience of others, making additions and amendments emanating from its own system of values. The essential and fundamental aspect is that constitutional culture and the Constitution itself can not be a commodity that is imported or exported. These realities are formed upon the basis of a particular society's system of values.

Constitutional culture is determined by a number of factors:

1. trends in the development of the society and the degree of social validation of man;
2. the nature of relations between an individual and the society;
3. value system priorities of the social community;
4. the level of development of production relations;
5. the level of social protection of an individual;

6. the level of legal and philosophical perception of social phenomena and patterns;
7. the level of political culture and legal awareness within the society;
8. the existence of socio-economic prerequisites for the establishment of social accord;
9. the ideological orientation of state authorities and the level of their understanding of the responsibility for the society's future;
10. the nature of impact of universal values and the degree and possibility of harmonization thereof with the qualities of national identity;
11. the nature of impact by exogenous and endogenous factors on systemic stability, etc.

Constitutional culture is a continually developing phenomenon, which acquires a qualitatively new essence and sub- stance in conditions of a democratic state and civil society. The latter is determined by the role and significance of the Constitution in these societies. The constitutionalization of social relations is an important accomplishment of democratic civilization in the sense that such societies are characterized by non-discrimination, pluralism, tolerance, solidarity, respect toward human rights and freedoms and protection there-of, clear-cut and reliably guaranteed separation of powers, and the administration of justice prevails.

In a society like this the following become the main descriptors of constitutional culture:

1. the place and role reserved to an individual within social relations, recognition of and respect towards his dignity, guaranteeing rights and freedoms as ultimate values with direct effect:
2. restricting authority by law;
3. separation and balance of powers:
4. establishment of the power of the people, elected nature and accountability of government;
5. optimal decentralization of political, economic and administrative powers, guaranteeing free economic competition;
6. the existence of a judiciary system endowed with functional, structural, material and social independence;
7. harmonization of domestic legal system with international legal norms and principles;
8. assurance of a dynamic equilibrium in the chain functions-institutions-competences;
9. the degree of assuring Constitution's supremacy and stability. These principal descriptors may be expressed differently in various constitutional systems.

Constitutional culture is not an abstract notion; it is manifested in all aspects of the existence of social organism. It reveals, first and foremost, the system of values that underlies social interaction and the operation of state machinery. The level of constitutional culture determines particular constitutional solutions, and the progressive nature of a Constitution as a country's Fundamental Law. Constitutional culture is incarnate in the laws and statutes enacted, the political organization of a state, the operation of and relations between political institutions and branches of government, the social substance and the legal capacity of an individual. Lessons learnt from history invariably indicate that, after all, the main yardstick for gauging the level of constitutional culture in a country is the degree of constitutional democracy, and raising it is the foremost requirement of constitutional culture.

III.

The formation of a common European constitutional culture is not therefore the product of an arithmetic summation, nor of a progressive geological stratification, but rather of the process of communication and reception between the divergent interpretations of different constitutional cultures.

According to the constitutional basis of member states of the European Union, the principle of integration of the Union forms the legal order of the Union as a constitutional order.

The constitutionality of European integration in the relation to constitutions is (was) always certified and a lot of changes in the constitutions was needed for the development of integration. The acceptance of communitary law (its criteria) usually does not interfere with the sovereignty of states. It however has no "supranational" authority in the typical sense of word.

The legal order of the European Union belongs still to the international order, it experiences however a process of special centralisation. It however still does not have the qualities and values of a positive law of state, it is a "special constitutional order".

The process of integration has caused from the start constitutional legal adaptation of member states. Generally it does not cause transcribing of texts of constitutions and follows pragmatically and peacefully. It of course depends on the nature of national constitutional system. The effect of constitutional integration is: the execution of competences and activity of european institutions influences the inner separation of powers. The transition of competences has made and is making the executive power of state stronger, that can influence the position of national parliaments, so the inner separation of powers.

The constitutional systems, especially those of the member states of European Union, are becoming the so-called open systems, when the constitutions reflect not only the supranational law, but also the creation of common supranational institutions. The constitutions have not lost the character of national document, which captures (in fact conserves) the system. The ruling of a process is slowly asserting into the texts of constitutions of countries of the European Union, through which the country applies for the new supranational power, including the possible transition of sovereignty.

From the viewpoint of constitutional law, the constitutions of member states are still describing the communitary law more as an international law than their own law, even when they accept it as a directly acting law, which is prefered before the laws.

The states are traditionally basing their political identity upon the constitutional culture, which can be called constitutionalism: this culture has elements of stability and durability. It sets up an order and constitutional institutions.

The European Union tries to define its own constitutional culture according to its identity. The new constitutional order is based upon national constitutional cultures. The constitutional value of national states is considered to be a basis of the value of integration, because it is also created by law (principles).

There is a mutual impact among the EU and the member states' constitutional cultures. Let see two examples. The doctrine of the "separation of power" has traditionally proposed that the states is divided into the separate and distinct arms of Executive, Legislature and Judiciary, whereby each arm acts as a "check and balance" on the others.

However, until 2009 this doctrine was not observed in the UK, with the Executive (the Government) drawn exclusively from members of the Legislature (Parliament), while in the office of the Lord Chancellor the three arms were fused: the Lord Chancellor was a Cabinet Minister, a member of the House of Lords and head of the Judiciary.

In July 2003, the Government announced plans to abolish the post of Lord Chancellor (making the Lord Chief Justice head of the judiciary, as "president of the Court of England and Wales"); abolish the system of Law Lords sitting in the House of Lords and replace it with a separate Supreme Court; and to establish a new Judicial Appointments Commission.

The Constitutional Reform Act 2005, which came into force in April 2006, considerably modified the role of the Lord Chancellor and in so doing, strengthened the independence of the Judiciary.

The judicial functional of Parliament ended in 2009, when an independent UK Supreme Court was established. The court assumed the jurisdiction of the Appellate Committee of the House of Lords and the devolution jurisdiction of the Judicial Committee of the Privy Council. It is an independent institution, presided over by twelve independently appointed judges, know as Justice of the Supreme Court.

Of course, this reforms were the results of the impact of EU.

At the same time the United Kingdom also have had an impact for the EU constitutional culture. Namely the European Court of Justice in Luxemburg become a precedent court.

The communitary law in its international legal nature also has ties to the natural sources of international public law, which contains legal constitutional values. It concerns mainly the long-term development of human rights and democratic principles.

At the same time the human rights become a part of international law and especially in the way of custom law and on this basis as a law recognized by civilised nations. It does not mean, that the common international law would include all components of human rights, but it includes the relations to humanitarian norms and to the international criminal law.

The internationalisation of the concept of the rule of law and democracy is another source of the norms of constitutional nature.

The international European system is represented strongly by the "dominance" of the European Court for Human Rights, the organs of the Court themselves have spoken out in the sense, that "Court aims to be considered a constitutional tool of European order". Legally, the matter and content of the activity are classifiable as constitutional legal ones. The whole European treaty is inspired by national texts of founding states. The Court contributes to the homogenisation and to the fixing of the normative European space. The Court has practically defined the minimal standard of the protection of human rights. Mostly it happens so in the relation to the communication between the national constitutional courts and the Court. The Court in Strasbourg contributes to the development of judicial monism and to the federalisation of Europe.

The decisions of court can lead to the nullifying or to re-interpretation of laws, jurisdictional decisions, especially those of constitutional courts. Generally one can say, that the time after the World War II is typical for its convergence of the constitutional sources of the single european states and the EC/EU. Especially the treaty of Amsterdam strengthens the nature of European Union. One can also speak about a "common european constitutional culture", also about a legal property, heritage. This culture is common to the member states, it has formed itself and it was formalised.

The common constitutional values of Europe are based on the philosophy of the values of liberal democracy, which consists of a certain "triarchy" of this philosophy: the democratic system, rule of law and basic rights. Upon these values the so-called western democracy is built.

Recently there is a tendency to sort human rights into a system of hierarchy. "Thus international law agrees on fundamental human rights that are ius cogens, for example the right to life, prohibition of torture, slavery and legal penalty with retrospective effect. These fundamental norms are obligatory without exception, contradicting international legal norms are invalid (ineffective) placing human rights on top of the hierarchy. More numerous are the so called erga omnes rights, that are obligatory to all parties. Respecting these rights so essential for the international community serve the interest of all states.

During the highly complex process of globalization, human rights development has been heavily influenced and human rights themselves have had their own wide range of effects on globalization. Along with intensifying international cooperation, basic human rights have become primary subjects of international law, several brand new rights emerged in response to global challenges and also universal human rights initiations have stimulated globalization.

Globalization has always had negative effects on the realization of human rights in many aspects of everyday life, but particularly so with increasing disparities. Globalizing economies have produced a number of rights abuses, arousing only slow-motion reactions – which are also controversial ever since – from the economic and financial bodies of global government. Instead of helping to solve problems, economic sanctions imposed on human rights violators only worsened the situation caused by the violations. It is now widely believed, that although human rights abuses cannot be overlooked, instead of or along with economic sanctions alleviated with a combination of programs promoting human rights are to be implemented.

The establishing of constitutional judiciary in the majority of states of continental Europe is an important phenomenon of the development of constitutionality after the World War II in Europe, but it is also an important article, which influences the inner relations in the European Union of that states, which are its members and have established the institutional court. The phenomenon of the activity of those constitutional courts demonstrates itself in that they had to separately sort out the relation of their own constitutional system to the system of communitary law, to the organs of EC/EU and also to the judicature of the

European Court of Justice. The constitutional courts have so decided about their role during the control of compatibility of their own laws with the constitution, but also about the character of "superiority" of communitary law to the own constitutional order.

Last but not least on a terminological problem.

Harmonization of law in the EU is a normative concept, i.e. a process of creating common standards across the internal market. For many thinkers it means a total uniformity.

This is why I find better the descriptive concept of *approximation*, which means that the member states must align their national laws, rules and procedures in order to give effect to the entire body of EU law contained in the acquis communautaire.

Bibliography

Antal *Visegrády:* Jogi kultúra, jogelmélet, joggyakorlat (Legal Cultures, Legal Theory, Legal Practice) Budapest/Pécs, 2003.

Kondorosi F. – Visegrády A.: *Európa: az állam- és jogfejlődés irányai* (Europe: the directions of state and legal development.) Hvgorac, Budapest, 2011.

Constitutional Cultures, Ed. by M. *Myrzykowski*, Warsaw, 2000.

Gagik *Harutyunian*: Constitutional culture: The Lessons of History and the Challenges of Time. Yerevan, 2009.

Francis *Snyder*: Modelling of EU constitution, http://www.eurozine.com/articles/2004-02-19-snyder-en.html

Karel *Klíma:* The Costitutional Legal Nature of the European Union, http://www.enelsyn.gr/papers/w4/Paper by Prof. Karel Klima.pdf

Multicentrism as an Emerging Paradigm in Legal Theory, Eds. by M. *Zirk-Sadowski*, M. *Golecki*, B. *Wojciechowski*, Frankfurt am Main, Berlin, Bern etc. 2009.

Morton E. *Winston:* The Philosophy of Human Rights, 1989.

Karolina M. Cern
Adam Mickiewicz University, Poznań, Poland

Bartosz Wojciechowski[1]
University of Łódź, Poland

The Holy Grail as the Heritage of the Future – on the Search for a Common Legal Culture in Presources of the EU Law

Abstract: Firstly, the articles investigates the key components of what is contemporarily perceived as the sense of common (European) legal culture. Secondly, it analyses one of the most characteristic judgments of the Court of Justice of the European Union, namely the decision of 19 January 2010, issued on C-555/07 *Seda Kücükdeveci v Swedex* GmbH & Co. KG. Finally, it argues why and in what sense the answer to the question about a common core of national and European identity may be given only from the perspective of the deepest layers of philosophical self-understanding characteristic of the European culture and its integrative core, namely the legal (constitutional) culture, in other words – from the perspective of *the future*.

Key Words: multicentricity, constitutional identity, European self-constitutionalisation, discursive competencies of Euro-citizens, tradition that opens up the future

Introduction

Modern man, differently than within the last few thousand years, experiences the phenomena of time and space, both in the individual, socio-cultural and institutional perspective. The changes in the surrounding social reality that take place under the influence of broadly understood processes of globalization and European integration imply the disappearance of the old ways of life. As a result of these divergent processes we typically experience a variety of feelings. On the one hand, we experience greater freedom, various possibilities of being and acting that were previously reserved only for the elites, or that even remained in a dream world or fiction. On the other hand, these rapid and multiple changes generate frustration,

---

1 The following text was prepared by Bartosz Wojciechowski as a part of a research grant financed by National Science Center (Poland), No. DEC-2012/05/B/HS5/01111.

disappointment, a sense of uncertainty and instability, or even a sense of the loss of the ability to understand the world and a membership to the community.

One of the main generators of these transformations is the specificity of the construction of laws, namely their argumentative development and application to specific situations, taking into account the tradition or the current claims to validity of the national legislation and its national recipients as well as supranational or international institutions confronted with the divergent legal systems of other states. This process can lead to the inquiry about the community and the nature of the political community that one could be an eligible member of.

Legal and institutional functioning of the European Union, including Poland as its Member State, has generated worldwide unique phenomenon of multicentricity or in other words, multifaceted polycentricity of the legal system. Multicentricity, understood as the division of powers *quo ad usum* between national and EU authorities, stems from adopting the principle of supremacy of EU law and the primacy of the principle of effectiveness (*éffet utile*) of that law in relation to the national legal systems. The said polycentricity of the sources of EU law (the level of various EU institutions, the level of national institutions and the level of multilateral agreements between Member States) undoubtedly drives the debate about national and European identity as well as about the alleged common roots of supranational law, like EU law.

Part I

Multicentric system is based on a logic far different from the one adopted both on the basis of Member States' systems, as well as within the EU law whose hierarchy of the sources of law, issues of legal validity or the hierarchy of law enforcement bodies are still regarded as crucial research issues[2]. This entails the change in the paradigm of understanding law and its operation as a system, particularly in its vertical structure. What is being challenged here is the view on the monistic perception of law

---

2 The issue of the ambiguity of the hierarchy of EU sources of law has been recently pointed out, among others, by A. Całus in the article "Hierarchia w prawie Unii Europejskiej" [Hierarchy in European Union Law], in: *Współczesne wyzwania europejskiej przestrzeni prawnej. Księga pamiątkowa dla uczczenia 70. urodzin Profesora Eugeniusza Piątka* [*Modern Challenges of the European Legal Space. Memorial Book to Commemorate the 70th Anniversary of the Birthday of Professor Eugeniusz Piątek*], A. Łazowski, R. Ostrihansky (eds.), Kraków, 2005, pp.47–56.

presented by Hans Kelsen or Herbert L. A. Hart in favour of multicentric[3] or even global legal system[4]. It turns out that the classical dynamic – static relations between the norms are not sufficiently adequate to describe the current system (systems) of law, both with regard to the reconstruction of the types of systems as well as a specific system. This is mainly due to the recent emergence of many different and mutually independent lawmaking centres. In this context, we can talk about multicentricity of the legal system[5] from the perspective of 'the geometry of the three planes'[6]: national law, EU law and the law created under the Council of Europe.

---

3 G. Falkner, M. Hartlapp, S. Leiber, O. Treib, *Democracy, Social Dialogue and Citizenship in the European Multi – Level System*, paper for the 1st Pan-European Conference on European Union Politics, Bordeaux 26 – 28 September 2002, http://www.mpi-fg-koeln.mpg.de/socialeurope/downloads/BordeuxCitizenship.pdf; W. Kerber, "An International Multi – Level System of Competition Laws: Federalism in Antitrust", *German Working Papers in Law and Economics*, 2003, no 1. The term 'multicentricity of the legal system' was coined by E. Łętowska, "Multicentryczność współczesnego systemu prawa i jej konsekwencje" [Multicentricity of Modern System of Law and its Consequences], *Państwo i Prawo* [*State and Law*], 2005, no 4, pp. 3 – 10; idem, "Między Scyllą a Charybdą – sędzia polski między Strasburgiem i Luksemburgiem" [Between Skylla and Charybdis – Polish Judge between Strasbourg and Luxembourg] *Europejski Przegląd Sądowy* [*European Judicial Review*] 2005, no 1, pp. 3 – 10. As the author notes, the Polish accession to the European Union caused a different perception of the participation of citizens and public authorities in the legal culture, what is directly manifested in the fact that *corpus iuris polonicum* became genetically heterogeneous, as it includes the system of national law and *acquis communautaire*.

4 See, inter alia, M. Kerchove van de, F. Ost, *Legal System. Between Order and Disorder*, London 1994, *passim*; R. Voigt, „Globalisierung des Rechts, Entsteht eine ‚dritte Rechtsordnung'?", in: R. Voigt (ed.), *Globalisierung des Rechts*, , Baden – Baden 1999, p. 13ff.; W. Cyrul, B. Brożek, "Globalny system prawa" [Global System of Law] *Studia z filozofii prawa* [*The Studies in the Philosophy of Law*], (ed.) J. Stelmach, Kraków 2003, vol. 2, pp. 94 – 109. The global system is understood as a pluralistic conception of law, in which several legal systems coexist at the same time. Pluralistic conception of law was touched upon by Neil MacCormick in *Questioning Sovereignty. Law, State, and Nation in the European Commonwealth*, Oxford University Press, New York 2001, p. 94, p. 115.

5 The scope of this essay is too modest to thoroughly analyse this important, yet extensive issue. Consequently, we will narrow down our discussion only to a few – as we believe – most important comments. We would like to note that the multicentricity of the legal system is manifested in at least three areas: the creation of law, legal validity and law application.

6 The concept used by M. Safjan during the Conference „Pozycja sądów konstytucyjnych w następstwie integracji z UE" ["Position of Constitutional Courts Following Integration with the EU"] Bled – Slovenia 30 September – 2 October 2004, quoted after

As aptly noted by Wiesław Lang, in the case of multicentricity we deal with such a situation that 'in one legal order there are many equivalent sources of law which do not form a hierarchical system (the hierarchy of norms)'[7]. The thesis about a hierarchical and pyramidal ordering of the legal system was a widely accepted one so far[8]. Generally speaking, in the monocentric system, a higher-level norm is the basis of the validity of a lower-level norm, as long as it was established by a competent authority on the basis of a higher norm (dynamic relationships indicating institutional and lawmaking dependencies) and a lower norm is related with a higher one like a specific claim is related with a general one (static relationships indicating the differences in the validity of the norm on account of its content). It does not mean that such relationships do not exist at present, but rather that not all relationships between norms can be arranged in an obvious vertical or horizontal manner, since they are contemporarily replaced by the so-called circular or looped hierarchy of norms[9].

In this approach, even though the legal system becomes clearly reflexive in nature, it is at such a high price that in its framework the existing conception of validity, based on the principle of legality, is displaced by the procedural programs based on the idea of regulation[10]. The analysed problem touches upon the displacement of the idea of *government* (the existing normative idea of a democratically legitimized mode of the exercise of authority) – widely discussed in the literature in the field of European integration – by the idea of *governance* (the new idea of the effective exercise of authority where the normative core is clarified through a series of mainly operative rules of action tailored to specific political

---

P. Mikłaszewicz, "Pozycja sądów konstytucyjnych w następstwie integracji z Unią Europejską (Konferencja w Bledzie – Słowenia 30 IX – 2 X 2004)", *Państwo i Prawo* [*State and Law*], 2005, no 3, p.120. See also A. Kustra, "Wokół problemu multicentrycznosci systemu prawa" [The Issue of the Multicentricity of the Legal System], *Państwo i Prawo*, 2006, no 7, p.87ff.

7 W. Lang, "Wokół problemu 'multicentryczności systemu prawa'" ["The Issue of the "Multicentricity of the Legal System"'], *Państwo i Prawo*, 2005, no 7, p.95.

8 In the literature the hierarchy is presented in the form of an ordering relation, while the nature of the relations is one of superiority and equivalence. See K. Płeszka *Hierarchia w systemie prawa* [*Hierarchy in the Legal System*], Kraków 1986, chapter 4.

9 M. Kerchove van de, F. Ost, *Legal System…*, *op. cit.*, p.69. F. Ost believes that a looped hierarchy can be regarded as an interaction between levels in which the relationships occur in all directions, namely the highest level is directed back to the lower level, affecting the latter, and yet it is at the same time determined by the lowest level.

10 Wojciech Cyrul, Bartosz Brożek, *Globalny system prawa* [*Global System of Law*], *op. cit.*, p.103.

and economic areas). This new vision of government as governance, rather enthusiastically perceived in the eighties or even nineties of the twentieth century, is contemporarily quite critically discussed and often seen as one of the causes of democratic deficit in the EU in the framework of the separation of powers (i.e., both in terms of legislative, judicial and executive power)[11]. The groundwork for these reflections is intra-European discussion on good governance by the EU bodies and on good administration. A representative example here is the issue of the so-called judicial governance, i.e. the assessment of a well or badly governed court, which includes an assessment of the administration of the courts and the so-called governance of adjudication[12].

In other words, the tendency of the modern legal system is its network arrangement, including mono-centric structure for each of the respective levels or 'subsystems', which is particularly evident in the relation between the EU law and the laws of particular Member States. In this sense, these systems are complementary, i.e. they mutually coexist, thus creating a complex system which manifests a peculiar hierarchical consistency.

It should be noted that although the phenomenon of multicentricity does not in itself determine a conflict of norms, the risk of such collisions is undoubtedly greater in a multicentric system than in a monocentric one[13]. The problem here concerns mostly the aspect of law application, which is connected with competency disputes, namely the mutual competition of many decision-making centres taking place at the abovementioned levels. Multicentricity indeed requires the acceptance of the fact that the external bodies my take binding and effective decisions regarding the application and interpretation of law in a given state. In other words, as a result of the European integration in the legal dimension, although we deal with one legal order of a Member State, it has a multicentric character in the sense that it provides the grounds for *quoad usum* division of powers between national and EU authorities[14].

Multicentricity of the legal system involves actual issues of the conflict of laws rules, emerging at the level of the *harmonious quoad usum* functioning of both subsystems (national and European one) that, after all, create one *legal space*. These

---

11 Compare Karolina M. Cern, *The Counterfactual Yardstick. Normativity, Self-Constitutionalisation and the Public Sphere*, Peter Lang Edition, Frankfurt am Main, 2014, Chapter II. 1.

12 See more on that issue: M. Zirk-Sadowski, "Interpretation of law and judges communities", *International Journal for the Semiotics of Law*, 2012, Volume 25, No. 4.

13 W. Lang, *Wokół problemu ...*, *op. cit.*, p.97; A. Kustra, *Wokół problemu ...*, *op. cit.*, p.91.

14 E. Łętowska, *Multicentryczność współczesnego systemu prawa ...*, *op. cit.*, p.6ff.

changes specifically affect primarily the application of the law by the courts, and as it turns out, they give rise to the most serious problems. The latter is due to the fact that in the face of the obligation imposed on the national judge to apply national law, the EU law, and the international law, namely national, supranational and international standards, rules and principles, s/he should be able to identify the legitimate and appropriate elements of the legal system necessary to adjudicate a given matter. The judge should be able to resolve the conflict between colliding principles or standards. This task is undoubtedly complicated by unclear, questionable and 'sensitive' political bonds and relationships between national law and EU law as well as competence disputes between the national and European courts that give the impression of 'jurisdictional chaos'[15].

Systematic reflection on the contemporary law, the process of its creation and application, ensuring legal certainty and security, its purpose and justice are further complicated by the assumption of deeply rooted cultural connections of law. The concept of legal culture brings forth numerous methodological and research issues. Contemporary scientific reflection on law, and especially the legal anthropology, comparative studies and sociology of law deal largely with confronting cultural spheres of different legal communities and societies treated as a system of institutions that operate through the processes of socialization, in order to ultimately compare *humanum* that can be observed in different cultural systems and, in addition, at different times. This is due to the generally accepted belief that every legal order has its mystical, ontological and functional origins in culture. Thus, the analysis of law is not free from the cultural studies, in which it operates or will operate. This raises the further question as to what is meant by the concept of culture.

Unfortunately, the latter is considered a difficult task, subject to endless disputes, as demonstrated in particular by anthropological research[16]. Maria Borucka – Arctowa indicates that what proves most compelling and useful for *the reflection on law* is the normative concept of culture in relation of which the legal culture can be defined as "all normative patterns of behaviour and values connected with these norms, socially accepted, learned (or rather acquired through interaction

15 A. Wróbel, „Globalna wspólnota sądów?" [*The Global Community of Courts?*], *Europejski Przegląd Sądowy* [*European Judicial Review*], 2006, no. 3, p. 1.

16 See, inter alia, A. Kroeber, C. Kluckhohn, "Culture: A Critical Review of Concepts and Definitions", *Harvard University Peabody Museum of American Archaeology and Ethnology Papers*, 1952, vol. 47, no. 1; C. Jenks, *Kultura* [*Culture*], Warszawa 1999, p. 19ff.; A. Kłoskowska, *Kultura* [*Culture*] in: *Encyklopedia Socjologii* [*Encyclopaedia of Sociology*] vol. 2, Warszawa 1999, p. 100.

and mutual relations between individuals and groups of individuals), passed through the symbols of meaning within one generation (diachronically) or from generation to generation (synchronically), i.e. when this process is characterised by a certain permanency"[17]. This normative approach to culture allows for a fairly clear indication of the importance of the constitutional culture in the context of currently controversial problem of national identity. The 'constitutional culture, one might say, mediates between universal norms and particular contexts. One might also say that the constitutional culture itself is then formed through what could be envisioned as a circular process, in which constitution, constitutional culture and cultural (including national) self-understandings in a more general sense come to influence and, ideally, reinforce each other'[18].

Due to the current research on the concepts of nation, or on different forms of nationalisms, what becomes increasingly recognized in the scientific centres is a historical-cultural thesis about constructing these concepts, especially in the medium of the Enlightenment humanist and social reflection which is contemporarily strongly manifested. Therefore, talking about the national identity and about the sense of community with supranational structures (such as the European Union) or international ones, not only proves considerably complex but, above all, socially 'sensitive'. In accordance with the first sentence of article 4 paragraph 2 of currently binding Treaty on European Union (TEU), 'The Union shall respect (...) national identity (of the Member States), inherent with their fundamental political and constitutional structures (...)'[19]. In the context of EU law, national identity involves, above all, the constitutional identity of the Member States and the preservation of the latter constitutes the obligation of the European Union, although as a result of this responsibility, the Member State may require the protection of

17 M. Borucka-Arctowa, "Kultura prawna na tle myśli filozoficznej i społecznej o kulturze" [Legal Culture in the Context of Philosophical and Social Thought about the Culture], *Studia Prawnicze* [*Legal Studies*] 2002, No. 1, p.14. In turn, Roman Tokarczyk presents the following view on the distinction of legal culture: 'Each of the known units of law – norm, institution, branch, system, family, tradition, type, culture – contains the elements of culture and it stems from culture. (...) Some units of law demonstrate this content in cultural retrospectives (e.g., family, tradition, type), and others – in cultural perspectives (e.g. norm, institution, branch, system). The category of legal culture combines both these perspectives, placing law among other components of culture (...).' Idem, *Współczesne kultury prawne* [*Contemporary Legal Cultures*], Warszawa 2008, p.87.

18 J.-W. Müller, "A European Constitutional Patriotism? The Case Restated", *European Law Journal*, 2008, Vol. 14, No 5, pp.542–557; here p.548.

19 Consolidated Version of the Treaty on European Union (OJ EU C 83, of 30 March 2010).

its own national identity. However, the required preservation of the constitutional identity of the Member State may constitute a legitimate interest, which could give rise to the restrictions of the obligations imposed by the European Union law[20].

Thus, the concept of national identity includes not only the specific culture, language, custom and religion, but also the identity of the state, which manifests itself in the behaviour of the basic state institutions and functions that determine the existence of the state as a separate political entity. In addition, a broadly understood national identity can be also treated as a requirement of taking into consideration the continuity of the existence of the Member States as sovereign entities, respecting scientific cultures, norms of national law, languages, the ways of providing access to social security or the principles of socio-economic development of the state[21].

All the above phenomena complicate our understanding of what is contemporarily perceived as the sense of common (European) legal culture which takes into account the sense of national identity, or more precisely, constitutional identity. What comes to the fore here is a momentous role of the Court of Justice of the European Union (CJEU)[22]. On account of the scope of this essay it is not possible to present a detailed analysis of its case-law; therefore we simply aim at indicating one of the most characteristic judgments of the Court of Justice, namely the decision of 19 January 2010, issued on C-555/07 *Seda Kücükdeveci v Swedex GmbH & Co. KG.* which concerned the problem of outlawing discrimination on grounds of age. The decision in this case is of particular interest for the analysis of the Court of Justice views on the question of the direct effect of EU directives. What is characteristic for this decision is the fact that the CJEU recognised that the principle of non-discrimination does not stem from Directive 2000/78/EC[23].

---

20 See: the Opinion of Advocate General – Miguel P. Maduro delivered on 8 October 2008 in Case C 213/07, *Michaniki*, ECR 2008, I-9999, 31–33.

21 Cf. J.- H. Reestman, "The Franco-German Constitutional Divide. Reflections on National and Constitutional Identity", *European Constitutional Law Review*, 2009, no 5, p.376.

22 Interesting analyses of the of the idea of importance of some (chosen) CJEU's rulings deliver Mattias Derlén and Johan Lindholm in "Good bye *van Gen en Loos*, Hello *Bosman*? Using Network Analysis to Measure the Importance of Individual CJEU Judgements", *European Law Review*, Vol. 20, No. 5, September 2014 (pp.667–687).

23 Council Directive 2000/78/EC of 27 November 2000 establishing a general framework for equal treatment in employment and occupation (EC OJ L 303 of 27 November 2000, p.16) adopted on the basis of the previous article 13 of the Treaty establishing the European Community, which in paragraph one established the legal basis for adopting

The Court noted that this principle belongs to *the general principles* of the EU, and thus it constitutes a category which does not belong to the secondary legislation (e.g. EU legislation, such as the regulation or directive; international agreements entered into by the EU etc.) but to the primary legislation, that is to the law established by the founding treaties (or amending treaties), general principles of law or – importantly – common law.

What proves to be of utmost interest from the perspective of our discussion is the implication of the above court decision which opens the possibility of a broadly understood reference to 'non-written' and 'non-EU' sources rather than a mere EU law. It should be indeed noted that non-discrimination principle in respect of age was considered as a *general principle* of EU law, which should have its origin in *the common constitutional traditions* of the Member States and the international agreements that bind them[24]. The Court: a) when pointing to 'pre-sources' of non-discrimination principles (i.e., recognizing that such sources exist), b) which can be also found in non-EU public international law (its principles and the Universal Declaration of Human Rights as well as in the constitutional traditions of the Member States), c) concluded that non-discrimination principle 'permeates' from the said legal orders to the European Union law which, after all, constitutes a part of the *international* legal community. CJEU therefore considerably enlarged the sources of EU law to axio-normative references. Two issues stand out to the fore here.

Firstly, it can be assumed that the adjudication with the use of *general principles* was presented by CJEU as a particularly legitimized method that complies with the rule of law of the applied EU law, because – as the Court intends – it is to provide the grounds of the normative unity and axiological pluralism of the EU law harmonised with the international law and the laws of the Member States. Normative unity must be therefore understood here as deontologically perceived *threshold weights* for the harmonised pluralism of values in the sense that they never exceed the said burdens[25].

---

by the EU Council 'appropriate action to combat discrimination based on sex, racial or ethnic origin, religion or belief, disability, age or sexual orientation'.

24 Point 21 of the judgment in *Kücükdeveci* case.

25 On the subject of *threshold weights* and the concept of political morality see: Karolina M. Cern, *Jürgena Habermasa koncepcja sfery publicznej – komunikacyjne kształtowanie opinii oraz woli obywateli, czyli idea samokonstytucjonalizacji* [*Jürgen Habermas' Concept of the Public Sphere – Communicative Opinion- and Will-formation of Citizens, i.e. the Idea of Self-Constitutionalisation*], in: P. Orlik, K. Przybyszewski (eds.), *Aktualność*

Secondly, the problem also concerns the legitimacy of EU law, i.e. the fact that the possibility of justifying common norms and shared values and giving reasons in their favour is of fundamental importance for a reflective development of historically formed national identities and for jointly constructed community identities of the European citizens. What comes to the fore here is the principium of democracy. Justifications are designed to shape the area of normative activity. Although these activities are designed, on the one hand, by sovereign legislators (understood as political and legal institutions of the Member States) and, on the other hand, by the EU institutions, in the area of mutually acceptable claims and justifications, they each time encounter the European citizens as an elementary and, at the same time, fundamental factor that legitimises their decisions. Without identifying those reasons, nor without the justifications approved by three parties, the compliance with law cannot fully rely on the respect resulting from it being worthy of respect and the authority of law can only be the authority of coercive sanctions (power). These reasons can be restored (reconstructed) only when adopting a reflective attitude to tradition, especially the tradition of legal culture, understood as a constitutional culture embedded in the public political culture (i.e. the culture of public justifications).

The authors of this article believe that the judgment of CJEU in Case C-555/07 *Seda Kücükdeveci v Swedex GmbH & Co. KG* provides a real chance to undertake a project – widely discussed recently on the basis of the social sciences – concerning self-constitutionalising Europe. This chance can be understood in a narrow sense as an institutional task, engaging the so-called strong public spheres of the EU, i.e. both EU as well as national legal and political institutions. However, in our view, there is also the chance of particular importance, namely the possibility to address the issue of the EU law sources also by general public spheres of the EU. The latter option would create a real legitimacy of the EU law, implying its strong role in integrating European citizens. In other words, the judgment of CJEU is here interpreted as an expression of institutional recognition of the thesis – commonly presented by researchers – about the democratic deficit of the European Union and, at the same time, as an attempt or the initiative to provide – at least institutional – chance of compensating for the said deficit. It merits emphasising, however, that the answer to the question whether that opportunity will also be taken on a large scale depends not only on policy makers and the media, but also

filozofii [*Topicality of Philosophy*], Wydawnictwo Naukowe Instytutu Filozofii UAM, Poznań 2012.

on the citizens themselves, because 'democratic institutions of freedom disintegrate without the initiatives of a population *accustomed* to freedom'[26].

Our task is to clarify this possibility from the philosophical – legal perspective and to identify its reasons and scope in the sphere of public political culture, with particular reference to the constitutional culture. Changes in a deep institutional and legal dimension indeed require profound cultural changes and their medium may only be a democratic civil space, i.e. critical and reflective attitude of the citizens taking a major challenge to be not only the addressees of law but also its authors. However, in order to meet this ambitious and so far unique task, one needs a special kind of civic education that provides and strengthens *moral and democratic*, i.e. *discursive* competence of every citizen of the European Union.

Part II

According to Aulis Aarnio who seeks the answer to the question about our collective identity, namely the identity of contemporary Europeans, the analysed concept has an intrinsic and irremovable problematic nature[27]. The latter primarily requires understanding which – in the author's opinion – refers us to the question of our identity in the past. 'The answer to that question cannot be found in the future, possibly not even in the present, which is in many different ways impenetrable. It plays a large part in the search for identity, coloured with self-comprehension, which take place on the solid building blocks of history, in my case the history of Europe'[28].

The search for that which is common in history makes sense and can be fruitful only when we think and believe that it is possible to bridge the gap (whereby there is not always a chasm) between the different (legal) cultures – only or primarily – on the basis of common tradition, for the understanding of which the basic point of reference is, according to Aarnio, the past, i.e. the history of Europe.

Legal culture in terms of the Finnish philosopher of law would undoubtedly constitute a binding element for a shared vision of the normative world in which there would be a 'hard axiological core' expressing the abovementioned

---

26 Habermas Jürgen, *Between Facts and Norms. Contributions to a Discourse Theory of Law and Democracy*, trans. William Rehg, The MIT Press, Cambridge, Massachusetts, 1999, p. 130.

27 A. Aarnio, "Who are we? On Social, Cultural and Legal Identity", in: (eds.) T. Gizbert-Studnicki, J. Stelmach, *Law and Legal Cultures in the 21st Century. Diversity and Unity*, Warszawa, 2007, p. 134.

28 *Ibidem*, p. 146.

self-understanding in the catalogue of the inalienable rights (human rights) as a part of either the text of law, or court rulings and decisions of public authorities, but also the current thinking of the recipients of law participating in this culture, i.e. thinking through the prism of this catalogue. Accordingly, legal culture, understood in such way, implies the specific public culture in which political consensus would stem from axiological and cultural – or in the broader sense – fairly homogenous base, and not only from the procedures so abstract that they comply with the universal laws that form threshold weights for harmonized axiological pluralism and integrate citizens not through cultural socialization, but through the practice of joint constitutionalisation of legal and political reality.

Yet, when holding a discussion on a common legal and political culture of the European citizens one can also take a different view. In our opinion, the answer to the question about a common core of national and European identity may be given only from the perspective of the deepest layers of philosophical self-understanding characteristic of the European culture and its integrative core, namely the legal (constitutional) culture, in other words – from the perspective of *the future*. Let us not forget that according to Jürgen Habermas who followed the considerations of Max Weber, Western culture owes its highly innovative potential to the active attitude towards the world, whose current form is continually negated[29]. Moreover, as noted by Mark van Hoecke, despite the fact of choosing a different direction to seek the answers to the question of the European legal culture and the European identity, 'legal cultures are generally based on a long tradition and even aim at keeping it unchanged for as long as possible. Nevertheless, also in law there are recent cultures that lack such a tradition. This, for example, is the case with European Union law and European Human Rights law'[30].

In other words, it is possible to provide the examples of such legal orders of the European Union law (understood as the system of action) which are to such extent considered 'new legal phenomenon' that the possibility of a reflective reconstruction of the underlying reasons which legitimize them (the knowledge which belongs to the very legal culture) by means of a reference to the tradition understood as respected history, can be a task so challenging and disputable on the basis of the various cultures of the EU Member States that its implementation will

---

29 Jürgen Habermas, *The Theory of Communicative Action,* Volume I, *Reason and the Rationalization of Society*, trans. By Thomas McCarthy, Beacon Press, Boston 1984, pp. 186–215.

30 Mark Van Hoecke, "European Legal Cultures in a Context of Globalization", in: T. Gizbert-Studnicki, J. Stelmach (eds.), *Law and Legal Cultures in the 21st Century. Diversity and Unity*, Warszawa, 2007, p. 83.

render vain the noble ideas which guide it, thus leading to undesirable conflicts in the search for common legal culture of the European Union. The reason is that certain modern elements of EU law simply lack tradition.

The second important observation made by van Hoecke is such that we are currently facing 'the tension (…) rather between old and new ideas than between different traditions'[31]. What requires understanding, and thus internal reconciliation, is the tension between what is past and covered by a respectable tradition, and what is contemporary and proactive, oriented towards the future which is deeply believed in by both individual people as well as nations in the sense that it will provide them with the possibility of choosing such life which is contemporarily worth the endeavour. The problem that merits reflective thinking is therefore not so much – or perhaps not *only* – the necessity of finding common elements of 'a diverse and newly developed' legal reality, so that due to this common root of the tradition it was possible to trace back the basis legitimizing it and giving it a certain reasonable form, but rather to demonstrate that such a root of justification for newly flowering tree of the EU law can be found and that from the perspective of legitimization, the latter can carry a number of new ideas and legal systems, thus acting as the source of public legal justification. It needs to be emphasised that at this point we do not pose a question – riddle about the most sophisticated justification of a general norm which can provide basis for any lower-level norms but rather about a serious matter, possibly requiring a laborious answer, namely about the issue of reconciling the rule of law within the multicentric – i.e. reflexive legal system – with the government of EU citizens, focused on various public spheres, sadly with the dominating element – from the perspective of the issues related to the legitimacy of EU law – of domestic spheres.

What seems much more fruitful and necessary from the presented perspective is the development, the analysis and discursive construction of the idea of the common future of Europe, its constitutional self-determination, and thus the creation of the legal culture shared by the Europeans by means of an increased civic participation, influencing on the construction of identity, rather than simply by heading towards the past or the legacy that, after all, has been the source of conflicts in the course of the centuries of shared history. We do not have in mind here any reductionist, revisionist, or revolutionary steps. We strongly say NO to *3 Rs*. The development of the idea of the common future of Europe, namely the idea that would, after all, guide our construction of the social world, inevitably implies the use of language which is deeply rooted in historically and culturally

31 *Ibidem*, p.95.

defined concepts, in cultural patterns and traditions in the broad sense of this concept. What is more, prospectively oriented development of the idea of a common Europe involves, to some extent, the reference to the past, though perceived not so much as a specific *dogmatic* authority or a 'monumental structure', but rather as the solid material for a critical reflection facing the future.

To our mind, a reflection on the tradition should therefore be perceived from the perspective of the processes of constructing the future as crucial and – in some sense –*emancipatory*. What proves essential in the context of the analysed issues are the comments made by John Stuart Mill. Though they were presented more than150 years ago, they seem to be still topical like peculiar lodestars.

> But it is the privilege and proper condition of a human being, arrived at the maturity of his faculties, to use and interpret experience in his own way. (…) The traditions and customs of other people are, to a certain extent, evidence of what their experience has taught *them;* presumptive evidence, and as such, have a claim to his deference: but, in the first place, their experience may be too narrow; or they may not have interpreted it rightly. Secondly, their interpretation of experience may be correct, but unsuitable to him. (…) Thirdly, though the customs be both good as customs, and suitable to him, yet to conform to custom, merely *as* custom, does not educate or develope in him any of the qualities which are the distinctive endowment of a human being. The human faculties of perception, judgment, discriminative feeling, mental activity, and even moral preference, are exercised only in making a choice. (…) The mental and moral, like the muscular powers, are improved only by being used. (…) If the grounds of an opinion are not conclusive to the person's own reason, his reason cannot be strengthened, but is likely to be weakened, by his adopting it (…)[32].

Mill points to at least three reasons for which *a mature man*, that is, independently minded man, should reflectively approach the tradition. At the same time, the concept of reflectivity in the quoted essay *On Liberty* stands for the search for the rationale behind the binding legal or social rules, and – possibly – moral norms in the public space[33]. In turn, the concept of tradition refers both to certain experience treated as a source of knowledge, as well as to an inherent reflection on them. According to Mill, one cannot speak of tradition as the basis of knowledge about ourselves, if we do not interpret its meaning and the significance of its constituent experience, taking into account the prospect of increasingly different experience, either synchronously or diachronically understood. The interpretation of tradition – significantly based on experience – is thus constantly open to

32 John Stuart Mill, *On Liberty*, available at http://www.bartleby.com/130/ [20-01-2015; 16:26].

33 *Ibidem*, Chapter II.

future processes of its reflective interpretation and critical adaptation. Understood in such a way, *tradition that opens up the future* undoubtedly deserves respect, as emphasised by Mill.

Therefore, Mill believes that, firstly, "experience [which constitutes the basis of tradition] may be too narrow; or (...) wrongly interpreted". This finding points to the need for realising the randomness (i.e., the lack of historical necessity) of the experience comprising all traditions. What can be therefore implied is a certain (almost inevitable) possibility of a peculiar one-sidedness and particularity – in other words a limitation in experiencing certain phenomena. In this sense, we can also speak of a certain amount of indelible arbitrariness contained both in the processes of the reflection on history, which are inevitably doomed to limited material, as well as in the processes of constructing collective self-understanding, based on (collective) emotions and on the needs that arise from the random historical constellations. Accordingly, 'incorrect' interpretation of the experience that creates the tradition of a certain community may also result from the lack of suitably rich spectrum of experience that constitutes interpretative material (in the sense of the said limited experience), but most of all, the assumption that the relevant spectrum of experience provides a profound and varied interpretive material, points out their improper interpretation.

In turn, incorrect (improper) interpretation of experience that provides the basis for the tradition may represent a number of possibilities on account of intersecting institutional, social and methodological factors. Having in mind the scopes of this essay, it is unfeasible to analyse all of the latter or even more so – to do it thoroughly enough. Therefore, relying on a critical reflection of the readers, we point out – to our mind – most crucial possibilities of improper interpretation of tradition.

A) The bias resulting from the interpretive patterns – widely socialized, so one even say that 'embedded' in the society – of the past experiences that at the same time constitute the reflective immutability and stability of the self-understanding and the tradition of a given social and political community. The idea of this essay does not allow us to systematically analyse all possible reasons of this phenomenon, therefore, we will indicate the most obvious ones. The said interpretive bias may be treated as a response to external threats (such as the seizure of the state by its neighbours or terrorist attacks) or to internal threats (such as the illegitimate, or despotic public authorities), and as we know from sociology, the identification of the enemy strongly integrates societies (Simmel-Coser theory). This bias can be also understood as an attempt on the part of the authorities having social or political power to undertake transculturation and in such case the social and institutional power used by them aims at creating bottom-up mechanisms of authority approval, namely of the engineering implementation of its justification. However, the reverse process can also take place and the bias in interpreting past experiences can function as a mechanism for generating power on the part of those who are at a given moment fighting for (a more extensive) social recognition. In short, the said bias can be both the form of defence as well as of cultural, social or political 'attack'.

B) The incorrectness or inappropriateness may also result from a narrowed or even low methodological awareness which in order to be constantly developed requires an open access to the independent world of knowledge, i.e. the world of researchers. Any ideological interventions in (normatively) independent scientific world in some way generate conditional results. Political and economic formulas – commonly provided in contemporary times – of practising science are not normatively innocent[34].

Nonetheless, the tradition is not shaped merely or even primarily by scientists, but by the citizens. Lancet blade of reflection oriented at the analysed incorrectness is manifested in the questions about the openness and independence of public opinion, freedom of exchange of views by the citizens, ideological independence of the media, ideological circles etc. In other words, what is analysed here are the communication structures that primarily allow flexible and free exchange of ideas on the largest scale possible as well as the opportunity of in-depth, thorough and systematic reflection.

C) 'Incorrect interpretation' of the tradition may also stem from the complexity of historical and political experiences of specific communities that are related to the institutional 'distortion' of the meaning and the sense of certain experience. After all, fiction may someday prove to be a part of the tradition, just as claiming that something is an element of tradition – respected so highly that no one bothered to question it – may one day turn out to be fiction.

Secondly, Mill notes that while 'interpretation of experience may be correct [yet it may still prove] unsuitable' for a certain mature man. What seems to come to the fore here is a specific particularity of experience that is a characteristic feature of the entire experience treated as one's own experience. This particularity stems from the inevitable limitations of knowledge (in this sense: tradition) based on the random material of experience. The problem concerns mostly methodological and epistemological issues, namely specific limitations – of time or space – encoded

34 Johan P. Olsen, *Governing Through Institution Building. Institutional Theory and Recent European Experiments in Democratic Organization*, Oxford University Press 2010, p.168, p.192.

in human cognition as well as the construction of the world correlated with them. After all, there constantly take place social, cultural and political changes which result in the change of the very political community, not just due to the change in its constituent elements, but rather on account of the fact that the next generation has already a different education, knowledge and picture about the world and sometimes even different geographical origin (as a result of migration processes of various scope). Legal and political framework in which they live also significantly influences the process of shaping the awareness of what comprises tradition. Finally, spatial framework of the community may also be subject to changes.

World cognition which always stands for the reflection on the tradition is the more accurate and objective, the more it is based on the communicative inclusive structures of a temporal dimension (as compared to the past, present and future generations that are entitled to voice their opinion, i.e. to undertake their independent interpretation) and a spatial dimension (the voice of others, namely those who are 'on the other side' of our subjective experience). The tradition constructed on the basis of such communication (that is, inclusive) structures is regarded – let us once more repeat it – as *the tradition that opens up the future*.

Thirdly, Mill stresses the importance of critical reflection, aimed at justifying rules and norms for intellectual and moral development of every human being, which is of utmost importance here and thus influences the concept of the very tradition. A mechanically repeated custom ceases to have the character of a custom of major importance because its symbolic embedment disappears and becomes a mere convention which can be without any inhibition rejected at any time by anyone who finds that it is ineffective or it prevents the effective implementation of other meaningful or significant social tasks. Reflectively preserved customs, namely those for which the modern rationalized world is looking for momentous reasons and a justification for their continuation and those which allow the possibility of conscious modification (special non-random adjustments) may, contrary to popular fears, strengthen the tradition and its awareness in a given group.

In other words, reflective attitude towards tradition may even revive the collective consciousness of a given group and focus on the common search for the justifications of certain practices – acceptable by all members of a particular group. The search for those justifications that would be approved by all members of a given group and, additionally, would be opened in time and space to the reasons of others is somehow perceived as a filtering process which provides a critical analysis of at least three types of beliefs. The first type comprises the moral beliefs of a definitional and universalist character of claims (related to the moral, i.e. normative self-determination of a given community). The second group involves ethical beliefs, crucial for the self-understanding (self-realisation) of a given group and a common answer to the question of an authentic way of life. Finally, the third type comprises customs, construed as numerous yet scattered ways to coordinate daily activities which, although they themselves are not particularly profound, their rational harnessing is of utmost importance, since due to the latter the world is perceived by the people as understood, well-known and predictable, what allows them to rationally plan their actions in this world, thereby effecting their numerous interests.

It appears, therefore, that according to Mill, a reflection on the tradition is an important contribution to develop one's critical reflective attitude towards the surrounding reality and to search for the possible justifications of its specific form and character. Such critical – reflective attitude to seek justifications for rules and norms which we should comply with, allows to differentiate between the various types of claims (moral, ethical, pragmatic) which are made by us or by the society, and on this basis only – to approve or reject them. Mill thus indicates the basic elements of moral and democratic competence, namely an active attitude towards the present reality, where the concept of activity stands primarily for a critical exploration, understanding and providing justifications which constitute the basis for an approval (or lack thereof) for different types of claims that differ from each other both in their scope and validity, as well as in their implied argumentative openness, namely both to claims to validity, made by others, their unencumbered articulation, as well as the cooperative construction of a common world where every person has an equivalent voice.

Mill's vision of a 'mature man' seems to largely meet the contemporary requirements imposed by democratic societies on its citizens who need to develop their moral and democratic competence as long as they want to live autonomously. Due to them the reflection on the tradition may become an actual incentive to reflectively form social solidarity in favour of universal and harmonized pluralistic particular claims as well as universally recognized individual claims.

Part III

It should be therefore noted that only targeting towards *the future* in which the world can be our joint product, continuously released from the existing inherent limitations, would allow to cooperatively develop such understanding of our *past*, that it would be manifested in such categories which have always reinforced the *possibilities* of our existence in the social *milieu*. As noted by John MacCormick, the specific nature of Europe has always been a peculiar type of multiculturalism, though perhaps not the one that is widely discussed at present times, but rather the one related to 'a Europeanist habit of integrating core values and features from almost every new group with which its dominant cultures have come into contact'[35]. In modern times it gave rise to a typically cosmopolitan European conviction that local or regional problems, such as those relating to Europe or the European Union, cannot be validly dealt with in complete isolation from the claims made by the states, institutions or international organizations in the context of the issues absorbing the rest of the world, for example those connected with the processes of globalization[36].

At this point there arises the question concerning the relationship between the release of the sources of the European Union law by the Court of Justice of the EU and the cosmopolitan attitude of the European culture touched upon by MacCormick. The answer to this question can be given from the perspective of the deepest philosophical layers of self-understanding, characteristic of the European culture. To this end, let us return to the 'core' problem of exploring the common elements in the legal and political European culture. We therefore face the following problem: Do we decide to search for a substantive determination of common pre-sources of legal culture in the past, taking the archival effort to find common European legal contracts, cultural or political events or international institutions? Or do we find this element only in *the future*, what has according to the EU Treaties *already formed* the basis of the European integration. The latter would be achieved by undertaking the task on the general cultural level, namely on the level of 'existential construction' corresponding to the question posed by Aarnio, i.e. 'Who are we, the Europeans?', or in other words 'political legal construction' of our truly common legal culture.

The strategy outlined by the reasoning presented in this essay may seem to be uncertain. After all, one can notice that if we were to undertake the latter task, i.e. political and legal construction of our common public legal culture, wouldn't we fall into ideologically permeated justification of the goals set on the basis of ad hoc policies pursued by international or pan-European institutions or intergovernmental agreements? Wouldn't we then justify the goals 'imposed from the above', i.e. emerging from the discussions of political and economic elites, and

35 John MacCormick, *Europeanism*, Oxford – New York 2010, pp.169–170; see also Patrizia Nanz, *Europolis. Constitutional patriotism beyond the nation-state*, Manchester University Press, Manchester and New York 2006, p.52.

36 J. MacCormick, *Europeanism*, *op. cit.*, p.66.

thus satisfy the will not so much of the Europeans but the mighty of the world[37]? What proves to indicate the contrary trend is the direction of the legitimisation processes implied by the abovementioned decision of the Court of Justice of the EU[38]. This decision seems to satisfy the requirements of modern democratic societies, which, above all, submit legal and political justifications to the public debate[39].

The concept of political and legal construction of the common legal culture presupposes the application of the idea of deliberative democracy, which is, in turn, based on the application of the issues related to democratic societies of discourse theory that, having as its basis the underlying concept of Habermas' autonomy[40], in some way forces the public debate on the arguments providing possible justification of legal solutions of the EU legal system. In other words, the essence of the strategy of legitimising the EU law, as presented in this essay, is neither arbitrariness nor randomness of its perception, nor ideologically permeated adaptation of legal justifications to political objectives or to collective interests of the Member States of the European Union. On the contrary, the essence of the matter is to release (*Abhebung*) to the level of public and institutional consciousness (i.e., rational in the analysed perspective) the need to incite the cooperative powers to create communicative justifications for the most basic principles of the European coexistence.

We therefore believe that the main problem here concerns a simultaneous stimulation of two dimensions: on the one hand, the institutional orders related with the establishment of the EU law and the law in the Member States and the orders relating to the application of law inherently connected with its rational justification, i.e. with the level of national judiciary that forms the core of the idea of

---

37 Jiři Přibáň, "Multiple Sovereignty: On Europe's Self-Constitutionalization and Legal Self-Reference, *Ratio Juris*, Vol. 23 No. 1, March 2010 (pp.41–64), p.48. Cf. also: J. MacCormick, *Europeanism*, Oxford 2010, p.4.

38 On the initiating (and contributing in) the constitutional dialog by the CJEU compare Mark Dawson, "How Does the European Court of Justice Reason? A review Essay on the Legal Reasoning of the European Court of Justice", *European Law Journal*, Vol. 20, No. 3, May 2014 (pp.423–435); especially pp.428–430.

39 Karolina M. Cern, Piotr W. Juchacz, Bartosz Wojciechowski, "Whose Reason or Reasons Speak Through the Constitution? Introduction to the Problematics", *International Journal for the Semiotics of Law*, Vol. 25, No. 4, 2012 (pp.455–463).

40 On this topic see: Karolina M. Cern, Bartosz Wojciechowski, "Postmetaphysical approach to moral autonomy and justification of the thesis of the necessary relations between the legal and moral discourse", in: Bartosz Wojciechowski, Piotr W. Juchacz, Karolina M. Cern (eds.), *Legal Rules, Moral Norms and Democratic Principles*, Peter Lang Verlag, Frankfurt am Main, 2013.

the harmonization of EU law. On the other hand, it is important to give an inducement to debates in public spheres, both national and pan-European ones, on the basis of which the existing legal cultures and the justifications of (national) legal order embedded in the latter could be subject to the reflection of the EU citizens.

When clarifying the position on the decision made by the Court of Justice of the EU, it can be even noted that the latter satisfies the requirement of searching for legitimate reasons of the legal system on the part of the citizens being both authors and recipients of the said law. There is nevertheless something more to this, when we pay attention to the thesis made by Mattias Kumm under which 'competing methodological accounts of how courts should interpret constitutions are grounded in competing conceptions of the role of institutions charged with enforcing the constitution. In this sense, questions of legal methodology are questions of institutional design or questions concerning the interpretation of an institutional role. Debates on legal methodology are typically debates about what courts should do. They are closely connected to arguments about the appropriate function of courts in their relationship to other actors within a particular scheme of institutional division of labour[41].

According to this idea, methodological issues of law, including undoubtedly the analysed decision of the Court of Justice of the EU also apply to the vision of the institutional role of the courts and judges in the perspective of their relation to other institutional actors in the legal system, or even to the role of the courts and judges understood in a broader perspective of political and legal culture, as proposed by the conception of Marek Zirk-Sadowski[42].

From the jurisprudential perspective of the latter author, the analysed decision can be rightly interpreted as recognising the community of judges as one of the communities that co-create legal and political culture and on that basis it can be assumed that it opens the discussion on the pre-sources of the EU law for other communities, namely for the national courts as well as for the national and EU *strong* public spheres. It is feasible, provided that this idea is further 'picked up' (i.e., it gains recognition) by different institutions operating in the chain of the legal system, taking into account 'an institutional pattern of the division of labour' associated with certain moments of making or enforcing law.

41 M. Kumm, "The Jurisprudence of Constitutional Conflict: Constitutional Supremacy in Europe before and after the Constitutional Treaty", *European Law Journal*, Vol. 11. No. 3 May 2005 (pp. 262–307), p. 283.

42 M. Zirk-Sadowski, "Rządność sądów a zarządzanie przez sądy" [Judicial Governance and Governing through Courts], *Zarządzanie publiczne* ["Public Governance"], 2009, no. 1, pp. 45–65.

Understanding the significance of recognising the community of judges as *only one of the communities that interpret law* – as expressed in the analysed decision of the Court of Justice of the EU – constitutes an important step towards implementing the vision of *self-constitutionalisation* of Europe, based on the idea of constitutional patriotism, as presented by Habermas[43]. The development of this conception whose sources can be discerned already in *Between Facts and Norms* (or even a bit earlier), where the abovementioned redefinition of Kant's concept of autonomy has taken place, has led Habermas to take a position on the basis of which it is possible to construct the European political community[44] based on reasonable *public justifications* of its political and legal, and thus moral framework.

In order to create such a public legal culture it is crucial to ensure the processes of reasonable formulation of public justifications for normative claims that are to bind all of us. Provided the processes of formulating public justifications are undertaken both by the strong public spheres, as well as by weak public spheres, namely by spontaneously organized EU citizens, they will form the basis of criticising moral and ethical convictions of all (i.e. coming from the EU Member States) authors and addresses of EU law, so that the final result will be such law, namely such an interpretation of the sources of EU law, that can be regarded as a common cooperative product of all EU citizens.

It is only due to the analysed process or, possibly, even to the entire sequence of processes that a highly criticized superficiality of the idea of EU citizenship[45] – on account of founding it on the concept of the citizenship of the EU Member State – can be transformed into a significant concept, key to determining the identity of the Europeans. The concept of EU citizenship will gain real meaning only when

43 On this subject see Karolina M. Cern, "On the Constructivist Premise of Constitutional Patriotism as a Normative Idea", in: Marek Zirk-Sadowski, Bartosz Wojciechowski, Karolina M. Cern (eds.), *Legal Recognition of Minority Groups in Light of Social Sciences*, Ashgate, Farnham, 2014.

44 It is potentially possible, i.e. when taking the legal and political perspective, to postulate the construction of even a global community, however, in order to meet this demand, the missing link turns out to be real relationships of the so-called positive civil solidarity – Jürgen Habermas, *The Postnational Constellation*, The MIT Press, Cambridge, Mass. 2001, p.65ff. On the notion of constructivist communities see: Bartosz Wojciechowski, *Interkulturowe prawo karne. Filozoficzne podstawy karania w wielokulturowych społeczeństwach demokratycznych* [*Intercultural Criminal Law. Philosophical Foundations of Punishment in Multicultural Democratic Societies*], Toruń 2009; as well as *Philosophical Approach to the Interculturality of Criminal Law*, Frankfurt am Main, 2010.

45 J. MacCormick, *Europeanism*, *op. cit.*, p.66, 75, 78.

the said European identity, and therefore the sources of the legitimacy of the legal system of the EU law, are actually 'communitaurised', namely commonly and discursively established in the processes of cooperative interpretation of public political and legal culture, open to thorough critical (emancipatory) reflection on individual particularistic traditions and a common future whose source has already indicated its presence in these traditions.

Conclusion

The analysed issue of the decision of the Court of Justice of the EU is not detached from the observations made by the English philosopher whose views have been touched upon in the heart of this essay. On the one hand, the release of the pre-sources of the interpretation of EU law can be perceived as the symbol that one of the most important institutions of the EU legal system recognised the community of judges as one of the many communities interpreting the EU law and invited other communities and citizens to co-operative discourse, which in fact concerns our European identity, thus complying with the self-constitution of the European Union. On the other hand, this decision expresses the appreciation – being a peculiar constraint of rationality – that we, Europeans are 'mature people' who have already developed or recognized the inevitable need to develop moral and democratic competencies aimed at public formulation of the justification of our claims, or meta-competences of differentiating and qualifying these claims, which proves necessary in the process of justifying the extent of their validity. The problem in fact relates to the recognition of moral and democratic competencies that enable our autocratic and reflective attitude in the context of a common European order of justice.

Tadeusz Biernat
Andrzej Frycz Modrzewski Krakow University, Poland

From the Community of Law to the Community of Principles

Abstract: The articles attempts to formulate a new respond do the problem of the future of Europe. The future of Europe and the creation of the conditions for the observance of human rights require not only political will, but also very good theoretical basis for decision-making processes. The scope of the considerations presented in this essay applies to the discussion on the construction of the European system and the mode of taking the most important decisions. It is argued that it is crucial to agree on and share the contents of two principles, namely the rule of law principle and legitimacy principle.

Key Words: the future of Europe, features of the European legal system and its construction, the principle of the rule of law and the legitimacy principle

1. The problem

When discussing the future of Europe we are in fact facing two questions. Firstly, whether the adopted model for shaping the European system can be considered as relevant in the context of current challenges and whether it is a form of the guarantor of peace, thus ensuring the respect for human rights and tackling crises? If not, then what is the direction of development? The organizers of the International Conference "The Common European Constitutional Culture – Its Sources, Limits and Identity" have precisely formulated one of the key issues of the debate on the EU as a democratic polity by writing:

> "The idea is to investigate who constructs the future Europe, with what kind of resources and thus whether this construction is solid enough to undergo several crisis that the EU must face now and certainly will have to copy with in the future, if survives. This issue is inextricably linked with the role of human rights within the internal and external perspective of the European legal system and further processes of European democratization focused on empowering citizens. The third factor indicates institutions that are in need of questioning their self-reflectivity if the "Grand Experiment" is supposed to give voice to the "Normative Power Europe".

The problem is not new , but, it seems, it requires a new approach. The previous considerations were based on two premises. The first was a reference to the history of the European integration and the effectiveness of the solutions adopted. The main motive of the implementation of the idea of the European integration, in the form of the European community, was to secure peace and ensure the respect for human rights. The effectiveness of the adopted legal and institutional solutions has been to a large extent positively verified, as confirmed by the European history during the last sixty years. The second condition can be presented in the form of the thesis that the European system should be adapted to the changes, resulting from a "natural" development, taking place both inside and within this system.

The current threats to a stabilized European order, however, are too serious to be able to rely merely on the concept of adapting only the existing solutions to the requirements of contemporary times. One example of such a risk may be the political situation in Ukraine and its conflict with Russia.

The attempt to join the discussion proposed by the organizers of the Conference requires the precise determination of the respective levels of the analysis. The following statement is crucial from the point of view of the proposed considerations. The future of Europe and the creation of the conditions for the observance of human rights require not only political will, but also very good theoretical basis for decision-making processes. The practice requires the involvement of politicians, a close international cooperation, the adoption of legal regulations and the creation of new organizational and institutional forms. Politicians need to obtain relevant tools or proposals, developed in the form of theoretical findings, in order to take appropriate decisions.

As a part of the scientific discourse, a key element of the analysis is the attempt to determine the dominant trends that occur within the studied phenomena and on this basis to search for the relevant solutions. These solutions should be effective and useful in the discussion on the construction of the European system and the mode of taking the most important decisions. The scope of the considerations presented in this essay applies to this very problem. What constitutes a visible trend is an increasingly difficult process of working out a form of a compromise between the representatives of the Member States on key issues concerning the EU and its members. In this situation, any attempt to identify the basis of a more stable, yet at the same time flexible and, importantly, viable system is of crucial significance. These bases should be provided in the form of agreed and shared contents of the principles which are considered as most important for the legal system and the European Polity . It is crucial to agree on and share the contents of two principles, namely the rule of law principle and legitimacy principle. Interdependencies between these principles and the semantic (symmetric) relationships cause that they play the most important role as determinants of the discussion on the construction of the system that would be adequate for the future of Europe. Combining the content of the said principles allows effective control of not only the implementation of human rights standards, but also allows to verify the real capacity of the system and the actions undertaken by the European actors both in the internal relations as well as in the international environment.

An academic discourse that results in determining the conditions for agreeing on and sharing the contents of the abovementioned fundamental principles needs to take into account two conditions. Firstly, it needs to consider the current shape of the European system, its history and the attempts of its modernization. The fundamental question is whether and to what extent the construction of the European system determines the scientific debate on its modernization. What can be inferred from the analysis of their respective stages of development? What conclusions can be drawn from the decisions taken at the crucial moments? The second premise is provided by jointly shared values, common legal culture and the chance to build on that basis the "new agreement" about the content of the principles, more functional and useful for solving the most important problems.

2. The structure of the system and its impact on the created solutions. The community of law

The structure of the EU system, on the one hand, limits the applicability of the conventional modernization solutions and, on the other hand, it indicates the possible directions. The main structural limitations arise from the essence of the system encoded at the time of its creation. The system was created as a sui generis organization, based on the law, in which legal decisions were to replace political decisions.

The formulation of the thesis that the Community has been based on law as its foundation, as well as that this basis constituted an original and unique solution in comparison to the previously known forms of social organisation, provokes a question whether the establishment of the Community was an undertaking limited to the economic sphere, or it was expected from the very start to expand its scope of interest from purely economic to a political one .

It is, thus, a very specific kind of system-making process, which begins to develop and expand, comprising more and more spheres of, firstly, economic and then social life from the very moment of its creation in the form of the European Coal and Steel Community. The change that took place in 1957, that is the creation of the European Economic Community, was to a certain extent a "forced" revolutionary change. Further development of the European Community also bears this very specific character. A discussion of this phenomenon must take into consideration the confrontation of a whole range of parallel processes. Since a detailed and well-documented presentation of these processes would require particularly extensive analyses, let us point only at the fundamental issues pertaining to the above-mentioned unique feature of the system.

Shaped in a way which denies any sort of definite classification (it is neither a state, nor an international organisation), the system manifests a range of exclusive characteristics. Apart from the position of law as its basis, other significant features are the character of the legal system itself, the legal sources that create this system and the law-making procedure. However, the most important quality results from the fact that the system is created not only by states but also by nations. Consequently, there is no central source of political authority. Power execution varies according to the sphere of activity, clearly determined on the basis of the issues pertaining to economics, foreign politics, security and justice. There is also a lack of integrating factors, such as common European identity of the communities that create the system, of the sort of national identity. The system comprises a unique structure of institutions characterised by very complicated inner relations, as well as equally complex relations with regard to the Member States. Another significant element is the phenomenon referred to as the deficit of democracy, also manifest through the European Union citizens' opportunity to participate in its political sphere of life. As a result, there appears a problem of lack of sufficient legitimisation in regard both to the whole system as well as particular EU institutions and decision making processes.

However, the essence of the problem is contained not only in the above-mentioned features of the system. There were two processes not less important in the context of the development of the system. The first can be described as expanding the sphere of legal intervention which, since the mid-seventies, began to cover a wider range of social relations, thus transforming the economic community into the political community. The second concerned the extension of the community which steadily included a broader range of states. The latter process made the political community more complicated and requiring an adequate legal and institutional infrastructure that would allow making the most important decisions.

The Laeken Declaration was, beside the Declaration on the Future of Europe, annexed to the Final Act of the Nice Intergovernmental Conference , a corner stone of the discussion on the process of modernization. Justification of the assumed activities has been given the label: 'Europe at the crossroads'. The steps, which were taken, seemed as a proper choice of direction. In the end of 2004, the European Constitution was ready .

I do not carry out a detailed analysis of the content of the Treaty establishing the Constitution for Europe from the point of view of the changes implemented to the European Union's legal order, but the opinion about a stabilizing and modifying function has been manifested in the legal solutions included in the document submitted to the Member States for ratification. It should be noted that a number of solutions, if not perfect but positively modifying the current state by its clarification, have appeared in this document. The examples of such solutions are, first of all, clarification and classification of the Union's powers, simplification of the Union's legal instruments.

Deep constitutional crisis in the EU was caused by rejecting the Constitution which was accepted and signed by 25 Member States and on the account of stopping the process of ratification, took place in May 2005. I refer to what took place as a paradox. On the one hand, we deal with an accepted system, developing naturally, in which a successful economic integration, turned systematically into more extensive unification that concerns political aspects of the social order, has become a self-constituting process. On the other hand, the attempt to order a legal basis of the existing system without implementing revolutionary changes was blocked in French referendum . If we look at this problem from the perspective of the EU system, the question is close to the issue of political power. The essential problem, including the difficulty with denoting detailed characteristics of political power, and possibly pointing at the "centre" of political power, is based on the fact of "power diffusion" among the institutions of the Community and the EU, as well as the Member States and the institutions or organs of those States' authorities. The key question is clear: the concept of the constitution is closely associated with monolithic sovereign political power but the monolithic system of power is not suitable for such polity as the European Union.

The conclusions that can be drawn from a failure of the existing modification of the European system, conventionally defined as the attempts of its constitutionalization (at the legal level in the form of adopting the constitution as the supreme legal act and at the political level in the form of creating a sovereign centre of authority in the EU), suggest two possible solutions. The first points to a particular type of action, namely gradual changes in the law of treaties, and "smuggling" constitutional solutions, but without the use of the concept of the constitution, which should facilitate the ratification process. The Lisbon Treaty is an example here. The second entails forcing the discussion towards working out a method of consolidating the EU and its conversion to a federal state model. For various reasons, both approaches are ineffective.

There is no doubt that the formation of the European system considerably affects the possible variants of its transformation or change. It is also clear that these changes are necessary to ensure its efficiency, effectiveness and functionality attributed to it in the economic and political sphere. This situation provokes to look not so much for a "third way", but rather for some proposals to redefine the approach to the essence of the system. Such a redefinition takes into account the current level of the development of the European system and, simultaneously, promotes the introduction of decision-making mechanisms relevant for the contemporary challenges that stabilize the system and guarantee the implementation of the core values. What can be considered as such an attempt "to redefine the system" may be the creation of its specific foundation understood as "Community of principles".

When formulating such a thesis, we ought to examine the fundamental issue. In the structure of the European system, principles are not merely present, but they play a key role. This follows simply from the nature of the legal system. The problem is that the current possibilities of using the existing principles in practice are clearly limited. This is due to the lack of the agreed scope of their content. Due to the institutional and procedural reasons, the interpretation of the content of these principles is embroiled in a fundamental dispute over political powers. Building the "community of principles" consists in breaking this deadlock. This is made possible by agreeing and accepting the essential content of the principles. Agreeing to the content of the principles stands for making their application independent of the economic approach of decision-making bodies, motivated by the political interests, regardless of whether they are the authorities of the European Union or of its constituent Member States.

3. Positive premises of forming the community of principles (common legal culture and shared constitutional values)

Shaping the community of principles understood as the basis of the modern European governance and the principal point of reference of the undertaken activities is regarded as the process that synthesizes two forms of activity. The first is the search for the full and expanded contents and their articulation in a synthetic form. The second is the process of agreeing and determining, in the form of a political compromise, which ones can be regarded as a declaration of recognition and acceptance. This is possible because, in either case, we have a very solid base at our disposal, namely a common legal culture and shared fundamental values, often characterized as constitutional ones.

The thesis about the influence of legal culture on law and legal principles is commonly acknowledged and exploited. What is stressed in these researches is also the fact that legal culture has very strong bonds with tradition. As Mark van Hoecke writes:

> "Culture is often linked to a more or less long-lasting tradition, during which all this has been created, developed and fixed. (…) Legal cultures are generally based on a long tradition and even aim at keeping it unchanged for as long as possible".

It is worth pointing at the consequences of such interdependence between tradition and culture generally and tradition and legal culture in particular. Such interdependence allows both for inferring the thesis that a diverse tradition of legal institutions, legal solutions, and generally speaking law within the state, is the basis to distinguish diverse 'cultures of law'. We can then talk about French, German, Spanish, or Polish legal culture. If we, however, take into account such legal institutions, such solutions or such rulings, which share common features occurring in the traditions of various countries, it seems proper to draw the conclusion concerning their common legal culture. Pointing at such thesis, which is more proper, does not depend on subjective judgement but on what significance common or similar legal solutions have for a proper functioning of legal and social system. The latter can be illustrated on the following example. A legal solution which occupies a particular position in the tradition of European constitutionalism is the one, which is included in Article 16 of the Declaration of the Rights of Man and of the Citizen of 1789:

> "Any society which the protection of rights is not guaranteed and the separation of powers is not established, has no Constitution".

According to the abovementioned article, such solutions as 'the separations of the state powers', which are well known from the tradition of European political thought and the tradition of legal doctrine, have become the basis of commonly binding patterns of legally oriented social attitudes. This process was also seen as:

> "(…) the development of the paradigms that embody the relationship between the formulation of human rights and approaches to their achievement, the relationship between participation and representation, as well as the relationship between norms and hermeneutic".

The process of popularising this solution in many European countries, manifested by the appearance of similar legal solutions, has become not only the basis of a common, European tradition but it has also constituted the basis of the principles fundamental for every legal system.

> "This paradigm consists of basic views on the concept of law, legal sources, the methodology of law, legal argumentation, the legitimization of law and, more generally, some common values and world views. Such views may change over time, but only slowly. Legal rules may be changed from one day to the other, but the way these rules will be handled, interpreted, and applied will still be governed by the unchanged, legal culture".

The factors, which contributed to the creation of sui generis legal culture, were as follows: the process of shaping legal tradition in Europe as a result of enacted legal acts, implemented solutions, the development of legal doctrine and the philosophy of law and the influence of numerous centres promoting the ideas connected with law, including such significant ones as universities. Its characteristic feature is, among others, to attribute special position to law in shaping social order. It is manifested in commonly accepted constitutional principles. The examples, which have been chosen, and which could be easily supported with further ones, constitute only an illustration of the phenomenon in question. When discussing them I referred to the world's second, in the terms of the time of creation, after the constitution of the USA, modern constitution which was Polish constitution of 1791. This constitution, known as the Constitution of May 3, was an expression of revolutionary approach to the shape of social order, introducing as a principle codification and writing down the fundamental rights. It shaped the principles of a democratic system and it introduced political rights, though only for a part of citizens, about 10% of the whole population, but it was nevertheless a very progressive solution compared to other countries.

Only these few above-mentioned observations on the common legal culture and shared values fundamental for the development of the social order indicate that there are good reasons to build a community of principles. This applies particularly to scientific discourse, namely such as a result of which there should be indicated fundamental principles as well as presented their content articulated in a synthetic form.

4. Towards the creation of the community of principles. On the content of the rule of law principle and legitimacy principle

The real role of these principles is dependent on the precise definition, acceptance and respect for their content. If one traces the undertaken actions and the ongoing scientific discussion, it is easy to see that more attention is paid to the rule of law principle. This applies to both institutional activities as well as scientific analyses. There are a number of initiatives and proposals that can be indicated in the circle of institutional and pragmatically oriented activities. In this area there can be also traced the activities undertaken by the Council of Europe and the existing initiatives led to presenting the results which were the canvas for an interesting scientific discussion.

In November 2007, the Council of Europe adopted a Resolution "The principle of the rule of law". The premise for adopting this Resolution was the statement that the legal thinking in many countries supports the understanding of "the rule of law" as the supremacy of "the superiority of positive law". In this way one understands the idea of the rule of law in the states where both in the theory and in practice there are present totalitarian traditions. Such a formalistic approach and the interpretation of the concepts of "the rule of law" and Etat de droit (as well as Rechtsstaat) are contrary both to the essence of "the rule of law" and the primacy of law. At the same time, in section 6.2 of this Resolution it was adopted that the issue at hand merited further development by the European Commission for Democracy through Law (Venice Commission).

As indicated by the content of the adopted Resolution, the clarification of the meaning of the analysed concepts is of utmost importance from the perspective of the functioning of the modern political systems. This fact was often pointed out and the said Venice Commission has taken a number of measures in this area much earlier . The documents adopted by the Venice Commission contain valuable findings that significantly orient the discussion on the problem of the scope of the content of the rule of law principle .

The findings which were made in the Report adopted by the Venice Commission in March 2011 are interesting for two reasons. Firstly, they constitute a kind of summary of previously developed views on the essence of the principle of the rule of law (Rechtsstaat) and in a number of points they refer to the latter.

Secondly, it was for the first time that there has been developed a set of characteristics that allows to undertake the evaluation of specific countries in terms of verifying whether they comply with the principle of the rule of law .

As highlighted in the Report, the aim of the study was to find a compromise definition. The contemporary legal thinking undertakes a unification of the meanings of the concepts of law and the rule of law. It is emphasized that the concepts of "the English rule of law, the German Rechtsstaat and the French Etat de droit, if we consider the three most important legal traditions in Europe, provide similar answers to similar questions" .

It was necessary because "'The divergences of the meanings given to the notion of the rule of law – as well as of Rechtsstaat – may lead to doubting its usefulness as a fundamental concept in public law. However, it needs to be understood and therefore be defined, both because it appears in many legal texts, and because the rule of law is accepted as a fundamental ingredient of any democratic society" .

Such a definition has been presented together with the identification of the basic elements of the principle of the rule of law. A reference has been made to the definition proposed by Tom Bingham in his book "The Rule of Law", London (2010), which, as stated, covers most appropriately the essential elements of the rule of law:

> "all persons and authorities within the state, whether public or private, should be bound by and entitled to the benefit of laws publicly made, taking effect (generally) in the future and publicly administered in the courts".

Drawing on that definition and on others based on very different systems of law and the state, it seems that a consensus can now be found for the necessary elements of the rule of law as well as those of the Rechtsstaat which are not only formal but also substantial or material (materieller Rechtsstaatsbegriff). These are:

(1) Legality, including a transparent, accountable and democratic process for enacting law, (2) Legal certainty, (3) Prohibition of arbitrariness, (4) Access to justice before independent and impartial courts, including judicial review of administrative acts, (5) Respect for human rights, (6) Non-discrimination and equality before the law.

It has been stated in the Report that:

> "The aim of the present report has been to find a consensual definition which is outlined above, together with an identification of the core elements of the rule of law. Its object has been that the Council of Europe, the international organisation which has defined the rule of law as one of its three pillars, may contribute, among other organisations and institutions, to the practical implementation of this important principle through its interpretation and application vis-à-vis and in its member states".

A further development of the abovementioned work was the annex attached to the Report, which included the checklist for evaluating the rule of law in single states. In this annex there were formulated nearly 50 points which provided the content of the principle of the rule of law that form the development of the abovementioned "necessary elements of the rule of law".

It should be emphasized that, regardless of the findings presented above, the authors of the said Report perceive the need not only of a relevant discussion on the content of the principle at issue, but also its detailed description in the legal regulations. The report stated that:

> "The notion of rule of law has not been developed in legal texts and practice as much as the other pillars of the Council of Europe, human rights and democracy. Human rights are at the basis of an enormous corpus of constitutional and legal provisions and of case-law, at national as well as at international level. Democracy is implemented through detailed provisions concerning elections and the functioning of institutions, even if they often do not refer to this concept", as well as that: "Legal provisions referring to the rule of law, both at national and at international level, are of a very general character and do not define the concept in much detail". As a consequence, "This has led to doubting the very usefulness of addressing the rule of law as a practical legal concept".

Legal usability of the rule of law principle, both in the sense indicated above and as the basis of forming the system, is dependent on the development of its content. In the introductory part of this essay, I have pointed out that in this respect it will be necessary to agree on and to adopt correlated contents of two basic principles: the principle of the rule of law and the principle of legitimacy. Full justification of the standpoint according to which the abovementioned principles combined together play a special role in forming and functioning of democratic systems that respect as completely as possible human rights, requires a separate study. The primary reason for the necessity of their correlation stems from the fact that these principles, combined together, allow to determine a certain procedural minimum, subjective and material for modern democratic systems. They determine the direction of the discussion on solving the problem which K. Tuori refers to as Rechtsstaat paradox that can be formulated as follows: how can the law limit and discipline the exercise of state power, if the law itself emanates from this very state power, as it according to the dominant positivist understanding does.

Combining the principle of the rule of law with the principle of legitimacy also stems from the need for the legitimacy of law . The basic dilemma for legitimacy processes arises from the relationships between the state authority, politics and law. Law is created by the authority. Regardless of the existing constraints and forms of control, such as judicial control over constitutionality, the authority cannot acquire full legitimacy from the source produced by it. On the other hand, legal principles and regulations must acquire legitimacy on the basis of political and moral arguments. It is not only possible but even crucial to raise the question about the legitimacy of law, including the legitimacy of the principles, constitutional norms which are often regarded as the basis for legitimacy of authority.

The main problem of a combined determination of the content of the principle of the rule of law and the legitimacy principle consists in defining the scope and the level of the analysis and in identifying the adequate starting point that would perform the role of the axiom. In the previous concepts there seemed to be committed an error, as indicated by R. Dworkin in the following words:

> "It is often said that we must first understand the nature of law before we can consider what the Rule of Law means. That might seem natural. But I'm suggesting the opposite: our opinion about the nature of law depends on the more obviously political question of what we should take the Rule of Law to be. The Rule of Law is the fundamental question; your concept of law turns on what answer you give to that more fundamental question".

Dworkin's position makes it clear that the discussion on the determination of the content of the rule of law concept is a discussion in the field of political theory and political philosophy and concerns the central topic, namely political legitimacy. At the same time, Dworkin's standpoint indicates the most important prerequisite for defining the direction of reflections, namely the protection of human dignity. In this respect, human dignity has a dual role. In the context of democracy and the observance of human rights respecting the dignity requires only a "fair warning" when the government intervenes in human affairs. At the same time, however, the dignity of the individual poses higher requirements for the operation of the system. It should lead to what Dworkin refers to as egalitarian integrity.

The indicated direction of considerations and the emphasis on the importance of the protection of human dignity as the most crucial reference point for controlling government actions that interfere in the affairs of men, and consequently, the legitimacy of state authority and statutory law, corresponds well with the legitimacy model proposed by me. Under the proposed model, legitimacy is understood as a kind of game of social actors within the delineated aspects of the political and legal system, if the actors are willing and able to participate in this game and when they meet proper conditions to be involved in it. In this game we use commonly known patterns which determine what is legal, correct, righteous, fair, just, moral, etc., yet we are not informed of what are the conditions under which a "comprehensive" legitimacy is possible. The game can take place by means of a discourse, both the traditionally understood one as well as the one that applies specific legal decisions and facts. The discourse is not only a directive or a postulate. It is a potentially possible and significant fact – when it actually takes place – whose effect and significance come down to creating legitimacy.

What proves essential for the proposed solution is to treat this dimension of legitimacy differently from the dominant approaches. The differences boil down to a dynamic rather than a static approach, and to challenging the possibility of a "comprehensive" legitimacy, arrived at somehow a priori, in favour of a "fragmentary" legitimacy, relativized to individual actions, objects, etc. In such a situation, human dignity as a 'basis' of human rights, is a fundamental reference point not only for shaping legitimacy discourse but also to provide the content of the principle of legitimacy.

José Manuel Aroso Linhares*
Faculdade de Direito da Universidade de Coimbra, Portugal

The Political Contingence of Constitutional *Voluntas* and the Practical *Continuity* of Law's Cultural "Project". A *Conversation Piece* Concerning a "Narrative" of *Discontinuity*

Abstract: The articles addresses the problem concerning the critical and reflective relationship between contemporary European identities, their practical and cultural legacy in general and their shared constitutional culture in particular. It analyses in-depth the diagnosis made by Jürgen Habermas who states that Europe is a 'constitutional project' and reviews what he calls 'the precarious relation between law and power'. Further it responds to the problem which autonomous role we can expect from law as a key element of the said legacy and as a plausible answer to the issue of inclusion.

Key Words: Jürgen Habermas, constitutional project, post-conventional stage of legal development, decontextualized morality, juridification of a political system

In his essay *Zur Verfassung Europas*[1], Habermas alludes to the «detachment» or «differentiation» *(Ausdifferenzierung)* of law or «the *medium* of law» *(das Medium des Rechts)* «from the *ethos* of society» *(aus dem Ethos der Gesellschaft)* as a specific acquisition of the «Roman Empire» (allowing for some autonomous «rationalizing effects» concerning the exercise of authority-*potestas*)[2]. However, he immediately adds that the «juridification» *(Verrechtlichung)* which is «relevant in our present (our contemporary) context» *(die in unserem Zusammenhang relevant*

---

* linhares@fd.uc.pt.

1 More precisely in «Die Krise der Europäischen Union im Lichte einer Konstitutionalisierung des Völkerrechts» (2011), the central piece of the collectanea *Zur Verfassung Europas. Ein Essay*, Frankfurt am Main, Suhrkamp Verlag, 2012 (4. Auflage), pp. 39–96.

2 « Das Recht und die rechtsprechende Gewalt des Königs bezogen die Aura des Heiligen ursprünglich aus der Verbindung mit mythischen Gewalten, später aus der Berufung auf religiöses Naturrecht. Aber erst nachdem sich das Medium des Rechts im römischen Kaiserreich aus dem Ethos der Gesellschaft ausdifferenziert hatte, konnte es seinen Eigensinn zur Geltung bringen und schließlich, über die rechtliche Kanalisierung der Herrschaftsausübung, eine rationalisierende Wirkung entfalten » (Ibid., p. 44).

ist)[3] presupposes other (much later) acquisitions, due to *social* and to *cultural* European modernity[4], namely the «secularization» of political authority (of «state *potestas*») and the «throughout pursued» positivation of law *([f]reilich musste die Staatsgewalt säkularisiert und das Recht durchgängig positiviert werden*[5]*)*, both conditions that make a *new* «civilizing force» possible (not only a «*rationalizing* but also a *civilizing* force») which, freeing «the concept of the political» from its «sacral aura», provides the opportunity for a new kind of legitimation (dependent on legally institutionalized consent)[6].

In order to address some of the main topics of this meeting[7] — and very specifically the problem concerning the critical and reflective relationship between contemporary European identities, their practical and cultural legacy in general and their shared constitutional culture in particular — I think it may be productive to concentrate on this diagnosis or piece of diagnosis — in which Habermas, in attempting to understand why, more than ever, Europe *is* today a «constitutional project»[8], briefly reviews what he calls «the precarious relation between law and power»[9].

From this exercise we may, in fact, compose two different ensembles-*cores* of possible questions and answers, the first a more closed and integrated one, constructed within the horizon of reflection and categories of intelligibility which Habermas' proposal directly justifies, and the second constituting a more

---

3 Ibid., p. 45.

4 As we know, Habermas explores *cultural modernity* and *social modernity* as autonomous irreducible dimensions (inscribed in the rationalising process which distinguishes *Lebenswelt* and *Welte*, *Lebenswelt* and *System*): an eloquent use of this *cultural/social* counterpoint is developed by Habermas in «Neoconservative culture criticism…» , in Richard *Bernstein* (ed.), *Habermas and Modernity*. Oxford, Blackwell, 1985, pp. 81 ff.

5 *Zur Verfassung Europas*. cit., pp. 44–45.

6 «Diese entfaltet nämlich eine nicht nur *rationalisierende*, sondern eine *zivilisierende* Kraft in dem Maße, wie sie der staatlichen Gewalt den autoritären Charakter abstreift und dadurch den Aggregatzustand des Politischen selbst verändert.» (Ibid., p. 45).

7 This text was written *de toute pièces* for a presentation at the International Conference «The Common European Constitutional Culture - Its Sources, Limits and Identity» (Warsaw, 6–8. March 2014).

8 «Warum Europa heute erst recht ein Verfassungsprojekt ist» is the title of the first chapter of «Die Krise der Europäischen Union…», *Zur Verfassung Europas…*, cit., pp. 39–47.

9 « Ich möchte zunächst mit einem kursorischen Rückblick auf das prekäre Verhältnis von Recht und Macht daran erinnern, worin die zivilisierende Kraft des demokratisch gesetzten Rechts besteht…» (Ibid., p. 44).

open and complex ensemble, not only because it discusses (albeit briefly) some a-problematical components of the former, but also because, in explicitly aiming to determine the autonomous role we can expect from law as a key element of the European legacy, it considers the *urgency* of an alternative path. As the first of these ensembles of answers leads us to well-known and well-trodden common ground, a short concentrated account may suffice to identify its claims. The same cannot be said of the second and since I cannot aspire here to more than a rough outline of the reflections that the quest for this *alternative path* demand, I will try to concentrate as clearly as possible (with some unavoidable simplification) on its primary (indispensable) *requirements*.

1. Let us begin with this small piece of Habermas' «narrative» — a narrative, as we know, about Europe, but also, inseparably, about law's unfinished *constitutionalization* project, a project which, under the constructive challenge of cosmopolitism, finds itself unavoidably extended to the challenge of a politically constituted world society *(in Gedanken zu einer politisch verfassten Weltgesellschaft*[10]). As I have said, the fragment in question has to do with a brief review of the *law/politics* coupling and it is precisely the reconstitution of this coupling (concentrating on the problem of legitimation) that gives Habermas the opportunity to identify two different historical processes in which a *differentiated* (isolated, autonomous) *law* apparently emerges. The counterpoint that he outlines does not, however, appear to consider the relevance of possible *continuities* relating both processes: it is, instead, concerned with eloquently accentuating the irreversible *discontinuities* (if not the abyss) that separates them. All the features significantly assigned to the first of these processes — doubtless not by chance displaced from the experience of the Roman Republic to the legacy of an indiscriminate Roman Empire *(römisches Kaiserreich)*! — seem, in fact, to be considered in negative terms, or at least selectively reconstituted from the perspective of the second — whose conditions are certainly inseparable from the *cultural* and

10 Ibid., p. 40 (and note 49, identifying the three key texts in which Habermas attempts to reinvent Kant's *Idee des Welbürgerrechts*). I have synthetically explored some of the implications of Habermas' reconstruction of *cosmpolitism* in «*Jus cosmopoliticum* e civilização de direito: as "alternativas" da tolerância procedimental e da hospitalidade ética», *Boletim da Faculdade de Direito* 82 , Coimbra, 2006, pp. 135 ff.

social «decentring» (*Dezentrierung*)[11] of Modernity, and also from the (progressive) institutionalization *of Rechtstaat* [12].

Having established that the *discontinuities* between these two processes involved in the differentiation of law are considered exclusively *from the perspective of the second one,* it is essential to add that this, at least in terms of the present narrative, intervenes less as a contingent historical (more or less achieved) ensemble of performances (shaping different *constitutional realities*), than as an irreversible opening and promise of new rationalizing possibilities. These are possibilities that not only become fully recognizable as civilizational acquisitions when we identify certain stabilizing practices or the tentative *paradigms* that these practices constitute (from the *formalist liberal paradigm* to the *policy-driven social paradigm* and the *procedural communicative paradigm*), but in particular when we understand that the common level (or platform) which makes these paradigms possible (and which drives the relentless institutionalizing and conquering impetus that generates them) represents, in itself, the highest step in a dynamic progression (a progression which was historically acquired and culturally situated, whose *acquisitions* may, however, be reconstructed using an *onto-genetical* analogy[13], thus granting them an *a-culturally* conceived[14] *claim to universality*).

Within this brief narrative concerning the detachment of law from the *ethos* of society, which *rationalizing* and *civilizational* acquisitions (characterizing the *second* process of *differentiation*) should be highlighted[15]?

---

11 For a reconstitution of this «decentring», see in particular *Theorie des kommunikativen-Handelns*, Frankfurt am Main, Suhrkamp, 1981, volume I, pp. 164 ff., 441 ff., 455–460, volume II, pp. 179 and ff., 209 ff., 225–227, 270 ff., 413 ff., 571–593.

12 The indispensable reference is obvously *Faktizität und Geltung. Beiträge zur Diskurstheorie des Rechts und des demokratischen Rechtsstaats*, Frankfurt, Suhrkamp Verlag, 1992, pp. 151–166 («Diskurstheoretische Begründung der Grundrechte: Diskursprinzip, Rechtsform und Demokratieprinzip»), 166 ff («Die Prinzipien des Rechtsstaates»), 349–398 («Deliberative Politik – ein Verfahrensbegriff der Demokratie»), 468–537 («Paradigmen des Rechts»), 632 e ss («Staatsbürgerschaft und nationale Identität»).

13 See mainly *Moralbewußtsein und kommunikatives Handeln*, Frankfurt am Main, Suhrkamp, 1983, passim.

14 In the words of Charles Taylor: «Inwardness and the Culture of Modernity», in Honneth/ McCarthy/ Offe/ Wellmer (Hg.), *Zwischenbetractungen im Prozess der Aufklärung. Jürgen Habermas zum 60. Geburtstag,* Frankfurt, Suhrkamp, 1989, pp. 601–623.

15 For a less crude consideration of the following synthesized *acquisitions* and their connection with a conclusion-claim of universality (including essential bibliographic references), see my essay «O *homo humanus* do direito e o projecto inacabado da modernidade», in Canotilho/Vital Moreira (coord.), *Da virtude e fortuna da*

1) The first is certainly the possibility of a *post-conventional (principled) judgement* — a possibility which, as we all know, requires differentiating clearly between a *contextualized substantive ethics* (immersed in concrete *forms of life*) and a *decontextualized autonomous morality* (freed from a substantive world-view and capable of assuming the structures of an undistorted *intersubjectivity*)[16].
2) The second, no less important, specifically concentrates on the possibility of recognizing *post-conventional (post-metaphysical) decontextualized morality* and *post-conventional (post-metaphysical) positivated law* as irreducibly parallel and reciprocally complementary practical worlds, both detaching (separating) themselves simultaneously and irreversibly from a fragmented *traditionale Sittlichkeit* to assume a generative preoccupation with *autonomy.* It is an autonomy which, as a concept, is offered to us in abstract terms, thus enabling the first of these worlds to precipitate its claims in an internal *Moralprinzip* (related to the autonomy of moral subjects) and the second in an external *Demokratieprinzip* (related either to the autonomy of the *socius-Gesellscahftsbürger* or the autonomy of the *citizen-Staatsbürger* and, as such, granting an indispensable *private/public,* if not *suum/commune,* dialectic and the corresponding fundamental *legal rights*)[17].
3) This key presumption of equality and complementarity — attributing a genuine *Gleichursprünglichkeit* to (*deontologically* conceived) moral rules and legal norms — acquires its decisive meaning in a third step in which the counterpoint between internal moral and external juridical *constitutions* acquires its definitive transparent metadiscursive intelligibility *(während das Moralprinzip auf der Ebene der internen Verfassung eines bestimmten Argumentationspiels operiert, bezieht sich das Demokratieprinzip auf der ebene der aüßeren*[18]*).* This is the intelligibility that only the perspective-paradigm of communicative action is able to provide, presenting the *principle of morality* and the *principle*

repúblicaaorepublicanismopós-nacional, Casal de Cambra, Caleidoscópio, 2011, pp.91 ff. [also in *Boletim da Faculdade de Direito* LXXXVI (2010), pp.505 ff.].

16 See for example Habermas, «*Moralbewußtsein* und kommunikatives Handeln», *Moralbewußtsein und kommunikatives Handeln,* cit., pp.169 ff.

17 See mainly *Faktizität und Geltung,* cit., pp.135–151 (II). However, the *Gesallschaftsbürger (-socius)/ Staatsbürger* counterpoint is only considered in the indispensable «Zur Legitimation durchMenschenrechte», *Die postnationaleKonstelation. Politische Essays,* Suhrkamp, Frankfurt am Main, 1998, pp.173–174.

18 *Faktizität und Geltung,* cit., p.142.

of law, the latter a-problematically identified with the *principle of democracy*, as two autonomous specifications of the general *principle of discourse*[19].

4) A final comment is necessary, simply to highlight the way in which law, as an autonomous practical world, should respond (or is able to respond) to the «decentring» challenge of modernity, namely the process of rationalising the *life-world* (or, alternatively, the possibility-claim of distinguishing between *Lebenswelt* and *Welte*, and *Lebenswelt* and *System*). It is sufficient to say that this response involves defending a claim for universality and, with this, the institutionalization of an internal argumentative distinction (if not a split) between different uses or levels of practical reason[20] i.e. the institutional possibility of demanding that pragmatic-strategic arguments (connected with the material reproduction of the economic and political systems) and ethical substantive arguments (fed by particular forms of life and their concepts of «good») — both in their ineradicable particularity, plurality and contingence — should be submitted (from the perspective of a universal norm-*ratio* and its *künstliche Charakter*) to the rationally selective integration (and symmetrically responsive inter-connection) that only the *principle of discourse* specified as the *principle of democracy* (mobilizing an autonomous process of statutory prescription, as well as an effective system of fundamental rights) is able to grant, with the certainty that in our present context the demand in question involves extending the reason-giving processes which only the principles of *deliberative democracy* are, in turn, able to precipitate[21].

In the light of all these *acquisitions* and the *level* of evolution to which they correspond (justifying, as previously stated, an *acultural* understanding of Modernity), how can the reference to the «detachment» of «the medium» of law in Roman

19 Ibid., pp. 138 ff. «In meiner bisher veröffentlichtenUntersuchungen zur Diskursethik habe ich zwischen Diskurs und Moralprinzip nicht hinreichend differenziert…» (Ibid., p. 140). «Das Moralprinzip ergibt sich nämlich erst aus einer Spezifizierung des allgemeinen Diskursprinzips für solche Handlungsnormen, die allein unter dem Gesichtspunkt gleichmäßiger Interessenberücksichtigung gerechtfertig werden können.Das Demokratieprinzip ergibt sich aus einer entsprechenden Spezifizierung für solche Handlungsnormen, die in Rechtsform auftreten und mit Hilfe pragmatischer, ethisch-politischer und moralischer Gründe —und nicht allein aus moralischen Gründen — gerechtfertig werden können…» (Ibid., p. 139).

20 See in particular «Vom pragmatischen, ethischen und moralischen Gebrauch der praktischen Vernunft», *Erlaüterung zur Diskursethik*, Frankfurt am Main, Suhrkamp, 1991, pp. 100 ff.

21 *Faktizität und Geltung*, cit., pp. 153–154.

civitas be understood? Certainly not as if such a practical-cultural isolation meant a significant rupture (or fragmentation) of the so-called *global social ethos (Gesamtgesallschaftsethos)* and even less as if this could signal any deterioration in the vertically integrated overlapping of *Lebenswelt*! In Habermas' understanding, this *vertical* interpenetration (shaping *cultural axiological patterns* and *communitarian institutions* respectively as *motives* and *orientations* for personal actions and their structures) constitutes the basis of pre-modern conventional judgment[22]. Without damaging (*wounding*) this *ethos* and vertical *Klammer*, is it possible, however, to identify a horizontal autonomization of law that is capable of freeing its practices from (or at least distinguishing them within) a holistic global normative *continuum* (shared with ethics and politics)? Habermas' narrative does not address these questions explicitly. All we are told is that this first *Ausdifferenzierung* has a certain *rationalizing* practical effect directed towards power (although not yet a *civilizational* one) and that we should await modernity's reinvention of *Lebenwelt* (and the corresponding process of rationalization) to recognize an authentic *break* with the previous integrative *overlapping* i.e. the possibility of exposing action and inter-subjective processes to separate modes of coordination, integration and reproduction. However, which rationalizing effect is this one, which does not «divest state violence of its authoritarian» sacred «character»[23]? And how does this accentuation of *auctoritas* unfold before the factual domain of *potestas*? Should the expression «the *medium* Law» *(das Medium des Rechts)*, explicitly chosen by Habermas, have a strict meaning i.e. the understanding granted by the *retrospective* projection of the (modern) binomial *law as a factual medium/law as a normative institution* (the first corresponding to a norm-free systemic integration and the second to a communicatively achieved social integration[24])? If so, it may be concluded that the so-called «detachment» of law's *auctoritas* (preserving an instrumental connection to the exercise of *potestas* or at least a holistic reference to the communitarian validity that legitimizes this power) only enacts a semblance of isolation. This conclusion may ultimately help us to understand why the experience of «detachment» exemplified in this present narrative has been inexplicably

---

22 Ibid., pp.124 ff.

23 *Zur Verfassung Europas*, cit., p.45.

24 A *retrospective* projection, undoubtedly because the *Recht als Institution/ Recht als Medium* counterpoint is one of the essential structural resources in the understanding of Law developed in *Theorie des kommunikativen Handelns*, albeit completely losing its relevance (certainly not by chance) in the *Faktizität und Geltung* proposal: see *Theorie des kommunikativenHandelns*, cit, vol. II, pp.522–547 («Tendenzen der Verrechtlichung»).

transposed from the republican *civitas* to an indeterminate moment in the Imperial cycle: if we exclusively consider the problem of the *law/power* coupling, this highlighting of law's *auctoritas* seems, in fact, to have no other plausible meaning than the one that may be recognized retrospectively in the (Janus-like) *ius respondendi ex auctoritate principis* (an honourable distinction conferred by the *imperator* on selected jurists, which could also function as a devious, irreversible domestication of the *auctoritas prudentium*)[25].

2. *If we exclusively consider the law/power coupling…* This formulation provides me with the essential cue to continue exploring Habermas' narrative, both *with* and *versus* Habermas! What I mean to say is that it is not difficult to admit the plausibility and productivity of this narrative and its diagnosis of *discontinuities* if we *exclusively* consider the problem of the normative *rationalization of power* or certain core aspects of this problem (at least in our specific civilizational horizon, committed to a certain *Idea of Europe*), but that this same narrative and diagnosis would prove drastically inadequate (if not unacceptably reductive) if our aim was to infer from this concentrated (if not *concentrationary*) experience of *juridification* (and from the conditions of equilibrium available to the corresponding problem) the exclusive features which, in our present context and under the same civilizational horizon, may identify law's problem or law's answer (i.e. its specific ways of creating and institutionalizing communitarian meaning).

2.1 Accepting the plausibility of this narrative within the limits of the first problem undoubtedly means confirming that the process of *juridification* of a *political system* is today (in our cultural and institutional context) practically and normatively inseparable from modernity's experience of *societas* (as an unequivocal human invention) and from the *constitutional turn* which, since Kant's *fin de*

---

25 At least if we a-problematically accept the two traditional versions, today the subject of intense debate: «The research on *ius respondendi* has basically wavered between two opposing stereotypes, of the benevolent and the malevolent Augustus. The kind Augustus supported the jurists with altruistic motives and did not use the *ius respondendi* as a means to interfere with the law. In contrast, the corrupt Augustus usurped the free Roman jurisprudence and used it as a tool for his political aim, the total dominance over Roman society. (…) During the latter half of the 19th century the discussion on the *ius respondendi* began to reflect the debate about codifications. Puchta saw in the *ius respondendi* a parallel to all rulers who attempted to deviously terminate the freedom of jurists and to take control over the law. Similarly Mommsen envisioned how Augustus destroyed independent jurists by terminating the freedom to give response…» [KaiusTuori, «The iusrespondendi and the Freedom of Roman Jurisprudence », *Revue internationale des droits de l'Antiquité,* 51 (2004), pp.295 ff. (excerpts quoted from pp.317 and 319)].

siècle (in a «founding, re-founding or revolutionary way»[26]) gave (or has been giving) this *artefact* (in different stages and under different paradigms) its macroscopic normative statutory corpus[27].

Moreover, accepting the plausibility of this narrative may even signify admitting, already in Habermasian terms, that the *quest* for the stabilization of democratic constitutionalism in general and the *quest* for the institutionalization of a post-national Europe (if not *European-ness*) as a *constitutional project* in particular, should today pay particular attention to the devastating colonizing effects that current policy-making (responding to the urgency of the economic crisis), albeit rejecting the explicit mask of systemic-functional assimilation or material reproduction, imposes on the *life-world* communicative context and symbolic reproduction (relentlessly threatening the socially integrative power of *solidarity* indispensable to the present development of these projects and trends towards juridification)[28].

It is, however, one thing to be aware of the eloquent and productive power of this diagnosis and another to unconditionally follow all its components, namely those determined by a decisive understanding of the claims of universality or universalizability — i.e. those which aim to make the *life-world* «general structures» and all «existing life-world historical totalities»[29] compatible, or which admit to submitting every cultural pattern of (flesh and blood) communication or participation to the perspective of *ideal-role taking*.

---

26 In the words of Castanheira Neves, «O direito interrogado pelo tempo presente na perspectiva do futuro», in Avelãs Nunes / Miranda Coutinho (ed.), *O direito e o futuro. O futuro do direito*, Coimbra, Almedina, 2008, p. 52.

27 Needless to say, this normative *statute* (pursuing an effective institutionalization of the *will of the demos*) is expected to include not only a second-order cluster of structuring and legitimizing rules (creating *organs*, conferring competences, conforming *offices* and limiting *functions*), but also a *first order fundamental* core of *rights- and duties-conferring* norms (inseparable from the legacy of human *rights*).

28 Undoubtedly because this policy-making has mainly been allocated to professional politicians and economic elites as well as scholars subordinated to individual interests, drifting away from the open arenas of public discussion. See the developments proposed in *Zur Verfassung Europe...*, cit., pp. 48 ff. («Die Europäische Union vor der Entscheidung zwischen transnationaler Demokratie und postdemokratischem Exekutivföderalismus»), but also and very specially in *Ach, Europa*, Frankfurt, Suhrkamp Verlag, pp. 77 ff., 138 ff.

29 Habermas, «Questions and Counterquestions», in Richard *Bernstein* (ed.), *Habermas and Modernity*. pp. 214–215.

Following these components would certainly mean defending the discursive-democratic structures of constitutionalism as *culturally neutral acquisitions*, emancipated from the specific historical configuration that made them possible, if not *crystallised* beyond (and independently of) the *civilisational* horizon that created them. It would also (and more specifically) mean responding to the *European constitutional project* and the danger of a «post-democratic executive federalism» with a democratic constitutional project for *world society* and a «cosmopolitan community», conceived of not as a *world republic* but as a supranational association of *citizens* and *peoples*[30].

2.2 Rather than discussing the meaning and the limits (or even the ambivalence) of this *constitutional juridification* (i.e. rather than considering the several possibilities it is able to pursue) in terms of its specific relationship to the political system, it is necessary to clarify why I have stated that the diagnosis of *discontinuity* or *discontinuities* presented in Habermas' narrative — reducing law's contemporary identity (or at least the final *foundation* or horizon of this identity) to the recreation of the constitutional project, but also concluding that a relevant process of differentiation only happens in the post-conventional cycle — seems to be exemplarily refutable.

The answer lies certainly in an argument of *continuity*, whose *warrants* and *backing*, doubtless not by chance, would be more or less explicitly rejected if exposed to Habermas' concept of modernity. It is an argument which claims that the invention of law (as an autonomous practical world) in republican *civitas* — which created the «name» *humanitas*[31] (and its *intention to validity*) as a context and as a correlate of a concrete praxis of *respondere* (a *respondere* which presupposes the cultural *artefactum* of a specific kind of *problem*)[32]— should be taken seriously (and reconstituted reflexively) in our present circumstances as the bright *initium* (the first significant expression or step) of a cultural-practical *project*, a project-*proicere* whose pursuit

30 *Zur Verfassung Europe...*, cit., pp. 82 ff. («Von der internationalen zum kosmopolitischen Gemeinschaft»).

31 «Unter ihrem Namen wird die Humanitas zum ersten Mal bedacht und erstrebt...» (Heidegger, *Über den Humanismus*, Frankfurt, Vittorio Klostermann, 1947, p. 19).

32 In fact, the emergence of law's cultural project needed more than the Aristotelian secularization of *praxis* and the (relative) emancipation of *phronêsis*. It needed a specific problem of inter-subjectivity to be invented which, distinguishing the juridical specifications of *phronêsis* from those which would be assumed through ethics, morality, philosophy and politics, could free the experience and treatment of controversies *related to past events* from its holistic *continuum* (and create a *new world* of significations and discourses and also a new specification of communitarian validity).

(institutionalizing an authentic *form of life*) has played (and is still destined to play) an indisputable role in constructing European identity[33].

Why an argument of *continuity* (if not *iterability*[34])? Obviously because it admits that some major *signs* or *traces* recognizable in this *initial* step — even though permanently recreated and transformed (and as such inscribed-*immersed* in a *productive circle* of construction, reproduction and realization[35]) — persist as more or less explicitly constitutive *features of identity* in the subsequent trajectory, significantly experienced as performative elements of a *non universal* (culturally plausible and civilizationally conformed) answer to the *universal* (anthropologically necessary) problem of institutionalization of a *social order*[36]. It is precisely this tension between persistence and change (and the reciprocally constitutive intertwinement it generates) that enables us to understand why the critical-reflexive deciphering of such *signs* or *traces* should simultaneously (and without paradox) be conceived of here as an exploration of *difference* (even though not necessarily *différance*). It would not, in fact, be possible to experience the *continuity* of the claim for an autonomous law — questioning, as radically as possible, the plausibility of its contemporary pursuit (in its inseparable bounds with Europe's heritage) — if one were allowed to forget the *differently* demanding cultural and social

33 See the synthesis I have proposed in «Law's Cultural Project and the Claim to Universality or the Equivocalities of a Familiar Debate», *International Journal for the Semiotics of Law*, Vol. 25, no. 4, November 2012, pp. 489 ff.

34 *Iterability* in Derrida's *deconstructive* sense (*itérabilité générale*): see the indispensable «Signature événement contexte», *Marges de la philosophie*, Paris, Éditions Minuit, 1972, pp. 365 ff.

35 I have attempted to explore the meaning and limits of this explicitly Heideggerian understanding of the *circle* in «Phronêsis und Tertialität: Die Behandlung des Neuen als Kern des "geworfenen Entwurfs" des Rechts», in Lothar Philipps und Rainhard Bengez (Hrg.), *Von der Spezifikation zum Schluss: Rhetorisches, topisches und plausibles Schließen in Normen- und Regelsystemen*, Baden-Baden, Nomos Verlag, 2013, pp. 39 ff., and especially in *O direito como mundo prático autónomo: "equívocos" e possibilidades. Relatório com a perspectiva, o tema, os conteúdos programáticos e as opções pedagógicas de um seminário de segundo ciclo* in Filosofia do direito, mimeo, Coimbra 2013, pp. 157 ff. (3.3.2.).

36 This is one of the most fruitful and challenging lessons of Castanheira Neves's philosophy of law: see in particular two key essays — «Coordenadas de uma reflexão sobre o problema universal do direito ou as condições da emergência do direito como direito» and «O problema da universalidade do direito ou o direito hoje, na diferença e no encontro humano-dialogante das culturas» (both now included in *Digesta*, vol. 3°, Coimbra, Coimbra Editora, 2008, pp. 9 ff., 101 ff.).

environments which, as essential contexts for its realization, have been *(en)framing* its project (and, as such, characterizing the successive steps in its trajectory)…

> Concerning these steps, we may add that the particular attention paid to the complex layout of the different contexts of realization (and the way in which they intertwine with the projected communitarian meanings) certainly does not exclude the reflexive *need* to concentrate their features within a sequence of broader historical cycles or stages (that may be used as integrative open references). This means recognizing that the ultimate permitted exercise in concentration will obviously be the one which distinguishes three other plausible stages and their corresponding arcs from the initial jurisprudential *Isolierung*: the first corresponding to the stabilization of an (axiological and hermeneutical) translation of the mediaeval *respublica Christiana*, the second emerging from the irreversible *turn* in modernity (and Enlightenment) acquisitions, and the third exposing the legacy of the second and the impressive return of the rationalizing possibilities enshrined in the first to address the paradoxical contemporary challenges of homogenizing globalization and self-celebrating plurality (if not *incommensurability*).

Even though it is not my intention here to continue exploring this argument for continuity, some brief comments would appear indispensable in order to clarify its main *claim* and *reflexive opportunity*,

1) The previous allusions have made it clear that the said *continuity* (constitutively related to a conclusion-claim of autonomy) only makes sense when considering a *non universal* experience of law (and legal thought), significantly *inscribed* in the deployment of what may be called the *Idea of Europe* (or the *heritage* of European civilization). This acknowledgment is perhaps sufficient to enable us to understand why every problematized conscious attempt to *universalize* such an experience (accomplished under the aegis of *cosmopolitanism about justice*[37]) faces insurmountable difficulties, condemning us to a differentiated spectrum of more or less persuasive *weak answers* (from Rawls' *overlapping consensus* to Nussbaum's *cosmopolitism of capabilities* and from Habermas' *procedural tolerance* to Derrida's *ethics of hospitality*)[38]. However, more relevant than this diagnosis is the alternative it opens up: rejecting the plausibility of a meta-discursive equidistant

37 In the words of Samuel Scheffler, «Conceptions of Cosmopolitanism» (1999), *Utilitas* 1, pp.255 ff., which means counter-posing *cosmopolitanism about justice* and *cosmopolitanism about culture and the self.*

38 Why *weak* answers? Undoubtedly because they aim to go beyond (overcome) the material commitments of a historically constituted practice, whilst paradoxically remaining bound to a certain *texte de l'Occident* (since only rethinking different plausible balances between the legacies of Athens and Jerusalem were permitted). I have attempted to partially explore this argument (concentrating on the opposition in Habermas and Derrida) in «*Jus cosmopoliticum* e civilização de direito: as "alternativas" da tolerância

perspective in this context in fact means accepting the challenge of a horizontal inter-discursive counterpoint between *internal* perspectives (if not exploring the possibilities of *translation*), and it is precisely the *mapping* of this counterpoint (with the reflexive concentration, if not reduction of complexity it demands) that enables us to distinguish *one* (necessary) problem — the problem which emerges from the *need* to institutionalise a social order — and *two* different kinds of culturally plausible (major) *answering axes.* Moreover, this is achieved with the first axis enacting a *response* to this problem which develops law as an *autonomous practical world*, whilst the second finds the required response in a kind of a practical (holistic) *continnum*[39]...

2) Concentrating explicitly now on the conclusion-*claim* of autonomy and the order-*ordinans* it generates, how should we understand the reflexive opportunity to reconsider its *project* which the explosion of multiculturalism and globalizing *deterritorialization* imposes on contemporary European societies? Doubtless not *only* as an opportunity to confirm that the institutionalization of a social order (or the production of stabilizing social outcomes) faces, in this practical context, a disquieting problem of *efficiency* (emerging from a growing lack of integration or a severely damaged integrative performance)...

> This is surely a first step, indispensable to *diagnosing* the tensions between plurality and unity (between the hermetic radicalisation of difference and the renewal of promises of identity), which is insufficient, however, if its meaning is exhausted in the global or indiscriminate (trivial) confirmation (regardless of questions of content) that we need an *efficient* social order.

How then? As the need (already associated with a spectrum of explicit content commitments!) to rethink the balance (or to invent new balances) between possible *communities of ideas* or *communities of memory*[40] (the former invoking the

---

procedimental e da hospitalidade ética», *Boletim da Faculdade de Direito* 82 , Coimbra, 2006, pp.135 ff.

39 I mean a *continnum* in which morality, religion, shared narratives and other social criteria are experienced as constitutively inseparable and *law* is not a specific *identifiable* (separable) voice (determined by an explicit claim to autonomy) but the only effective institutionalizing regulative (if not coercive projection) of the content (a selective content!) of this *continnum* i.e. that *law* is able to *name* when invoking the culturally unique normative nucleus of the Islamic order, Hindu *dharma,* Jewish *halakhah* or indigenous *beehaz'aanii.*

40 In the words of Robert Booth Fowler, «Community. Reflections on Definition», in Amitai Etzioni (ed.), *New Communitarian Thinking. Persons, Virtues, Institutions, and Communities*, Virginia, University Press of Virginia, 1995, pp.88 ff.

universalizability, if not the cultural-neutral quality of modern or Enlightenment acquisitions and the latter celebrating the particularism of *mores* and traditions)? This would ultimately be *the* plausible route (or at least the step or the stage *to pursue*!) if we could understand law's *projection* of intersubjective meanings as a pure assimilation or reception (albeit an authoritarian-prescriptive selective one) of the values, standards or rules produced and stabilized in the practices of *political morality*...

> When we consider the relevance of those practices we are, in fact, identifying two different possible fields (to be taken as separate alternatives or overlapping possibilities), the first concerning *critical (tendentially universal and procedural) morality*, and the second reproducing *positive or conventional (substantive) morality (or ethicity)*[41].

This understanding of law as an explicit *sancire* of moral resources is, however, very far from necessary. In order to conceive of law, in our present context, as a *project* or as a *projection* of communitarian meanings — simultaneously clarifying that this *proïcere* is neither a *plan* in its onto-teleological pre-modern sense[42] nor a *programme* in its modern finalistic intelligibility, but a historically constitutive (circularly reinvented) *form of life* (presupposing the treatment of *communitas*, in its juridical relevance, as a *self-transcendentally* conceived *artefactus*) — leads us, as a matter of fact, to another (more demanding) thematic level which enables us to defend a kind of (non positivistic!) *separation thesis* between *political morality* and *juridicalness*. Why a *separation thesis* (to be justified in the light of the western canon)? Undoubtedly because *law* and *morality* (or more exactly, *law* and *moralities*), without excluding convergences and overlaps, are confronted here as distinct

---

41 In the words of Habermas (distinguishing between *procedural morality* and *substantive ethicity*), but also (simultaneously!) in the words of Hart and Waldron (underlining-clarifying a distinction which was introduced by Austin and made habitual through the dialogue with utilitarianism). See Hart, *Law, Liberty and Morality*, Stanford, Stanford University Press, 1963, pp. 17–24 («Positive and Critical Morality») [«... "positive morality" [as] the morality actually accepted and shared by a given social group...»/ «..."critical morality" [referring to] the general moral principles used in the criticism of actual social institutions including positive morality...» (p. 20)], Waldron, «Particular Values and Critical Morality», *California Law Review*, vol. 77 no. 3, pp. 561–589 [«the moral culture of a particular community [as a] (...) body of distinctive mores, norms, and standards / a critical [reflective] (...) general account of what a society must be like if it is to accommodate the sort of beings we are...» (pp. 561, 562, 563, 582, 587)].

42 In the words of Heidegger: «Das Entwerfen hat nichts zu tun mit einem Sichverhalten zu einem ausgedachten Plan, gemäß dem das Dasein sein Sein einrichtet, sondern als Dasein hat es sich je schon entworfen und ist, solange es ist, entwerfend» [*Sein und Zeit*, 18th ed., Max Niemeyer Verlag Tübingen, 2001, p. 145].

languages or different sets of «occasions and opportunities for the creation of meaning» (if not practical-existential resources)[43], with different leading problems and unmistakably distinct understandings of communitarian *validity* (determining, as such, experiences and concepts of autonomy and responsibility that are *not to be* reciprocally *confounded*). To defend this separation thesis means *on the one hand* avoiding a common misunderstanding about law's validity[44], and *on the other hand* opening up, more or less adventurously (and almost always without a safety net!), a new and radical sequence of questions, such as the following. Is the *form of life* institutionalized through law — as a specific way of constituting and performing substantive communitarian meaning (irreducible, as such, to other plausible constructions of *praxis* and practical rationality and certainly to other forms of collective identity) — capable of enduring (and being reinvented) in our present situation? Does our experience of plurality and fragmentation favour an alternative promise of integration pursued *outside law* (under the challenges of a celebratory singularity and incomparability)? And if it does, can it be said that we need another *homo humanus*? Should we dive into a *quest for the humanitas* (or *dignitas*) *of man* developed beyond the *limits of humanism* (or the already known forms of humanism)? [45]

None of these indispensable *interpellations* directly concern us here. The allusions that have been just made are, however, enough to return us to Habermas' narrative. We have seen that the conclusiveness (or the justifiability) of the said

43 The formulations quoted are from James Boyd White, *From Expectation to Experience. Essays on Law and Legal Imagination*, Michigan, The University of Michigan Press, 1999, p.52.

44 This misunderstanding is the one which defends that the attribution of sense (or validity) claims to law depends entirely on the conceptual relevance of a moral perspective. I have attempted to offer some critical reflections on this misunderstanding in *O direito como mundo prático autónomo: "equívocos" e possibilidades*, cit., passim (and also, very briefly, in «Law's Cultural Project and the Claim to Universality or the Equivocalities of a Familiar Debate», cit., passim).

45 I have partially addressed these questions in a sequence of dialogues with Levinas and Derrida: see «Autotranscendentalidade, desconstrução e responsabilidade infinita. Os enigmas de *Force de loi*» (2004), in Figueiredo Dias, Gomes Canotilho, Faria Costa (ed.), *Arsiudicandi.Estudos em homenagem ao Prof. Doutor António Castanheira Neves*, I, cit., pp., pp.551 ff., «O *dito* do direito e o *dizer* da justiça. Diálogos com Levinas e Derrida» (2006), in *Themis – Revista da Faculdade de Direito da Universidade Nova de Lisboa*, VIII, no. 14, 2007, pp.5 ff., «Dekonstruktion als philosophische (gegenphilosophische) Reflexion über das Recht. Betrachtungen zu Derrida» (Maio 2005), *Archiv für Rechts- und Sozialphilosophie (ARSP)*, Band 93 / 2007, Heft 1, pp.39 ff.

argument of discontinuity — placing the two selected moments of *juridification* in separate compartments — depends on an understanding of law (or law's rational acquisitions) which, based on a culturally neutral understanding of *progress* (as discursive rationalising progress), may be said to concentrate on (or even be inferred from) the second of those two moments. Exploring the counterpoint with our *argument of continuity*, it is now certainly possible to add that the plausibility (or the correctness) of this (or other similar) diagnoses of discontinuity demands (argues for) a representation of law's *answer*, enabling us to abstract from the constitutive (or the generative) relevance of controversy *as perspective* and from its unique (microscopically conceived) jurisprudential *tertialité*. More precisely, it presupposes a representation of a relevant legal *societas* (inscribed as a decisive macroscopic component in a certain *Projekt der Moderne*) which, in contrast to the proposed understanding of *juridicalness* as a *form of life*, allows us to treat the experience of *comparability* in its specific *concreteness*, as a rationally assimilable subordinate (more or less negligible) dimension (whose importance as an autonomous rational resource should today be treated as a historically overcome contingence). This presupposition means not only privileging a *normativistic* (purely deontological) account of *universality* and *practical reason* — attributing to *norms-ratio* a discursively self-constitutive *validity* (which transforms *statutes* in *Gesetze der Freiheit*[46]) — but also rejecting the relevance of a (dialectical) counterpoint whose outlines we have already confirmed as reflexively indispensable to understand the *argument of continuity* (and the productive intertwinement that this argument attributes to the different historical cycles). This is the counterpoint which emerges when distinguishing the *core* of law's project — identified as a continuous attempt to institutionalize a specific kind of *intersubjectivity* (between *relativized*, *comparable* and *limited* spheres of *autonomy* and *responsibility* and the corresponding *masks* of subjects-*persons*) — from the different cultural, political and economic *environments* in which this tentative institutionalization has been (and continues to be) pursued — and where we may recognize a situated context of questions and problems (conditioning the criteria and the balances of *comparability*, whilst not preventing us from identifying the autonomous sense of «this» specific *comparability* as an unmistakable task of *ius suum cuique tribuere*)[47].

46 *Faktizität und Geltung*, cit., p.285.

47 Defending this argument for continuity in fact means concluding that, even though the heritage of modern *societas* should undoubtedly be qualified as a dimension of the *institutional environment* of our present *quest for law* (with decisive acquisitions such as *rule of law*, human rights, separation of powers, exclusion of arbitrariness, social certainty, tolerance, respect, solidarity, protection against violence, freedom from want), we should

Rejecting the relevance of this counterpoint in fact means avoiding that democratic constitutionalism may be reflexively treated only as a component (albeit a key component) of the *institutional environment* in which our present *quest for law* is pursued, paving the way for a celebration (as an irreversible *progress*) of the identification between *juridicalness* and *constitutionality* (or between law as an autonomous discourse and the rational claims of a certain *external constitution*[48])...

With this return to Habermas, my purpose is not, however, simply to confirm an irreducible *litige* between the arguments concerning *continuity* and *discontinuity* about law (or *western* law). In order to clarify the relevance of the *difference* that separates those arguments, I would like to allude, albeit briefly, to another piece of Habermas' narrative, this time a more significant and complex one, constituting the core of another well-known essay («Das Konzept der Menschenwürde und die realistische Utopie der Menschenrechte»[49]). Corresponding to the promises of its title, this second narrative (internally admitting exemplary trends in *continuity* and *discontinuity*) relates to the category of intelligibility «human dignity» and explores the following «circumstance» *(Umstand)*: even though already «existing as a philosophical concept in Antiquity» and having «acquired its current canonical expression in Kant», the category in question (not considering «human dignity» exclusively but also «people dignity») «has found its way into texts of international law and into national constitutions» only in the *post-Holocaust* context (as a «clear response to the mass crimes committed under the Nazi regime and the massacres of Second World War»)[50]. In Habermas' point of view, the reflexive challenge which we should face here is precisely the one concerning the «conceptual bond» that connects the two categories (*Menschenrechte / Menschenwürde*), i.e. which claims that the «*temporal* asymmetry» drawn between the «history of human rights» (dating from 17th century) and the recent legal *juridification* of the concept of

---

equally be able to argue that law's cultural project (in its unmistakably practical identity) is *irreducible* to this *environment*. This evidently means avoiding the shortcomings of all answers which *reduce* law's cultural project to one of its major cycles (or which at least consider that the relevant autonomy of law began with modernity's «decentring of world conceptions» and «perspectives» and the consolidation of the Enlightenment) [The quoted formulations are evidently by Habermas: see *supra*, note 11].

48 See *supra*, note 18.

49 An essay published for the first time in *Deutschen Zeitschrift für Philosophie* (2010) and included (with substantial revisions) in the collectanea that mainly interests us: *Zur Verfassung Europas...*, cit., pp. 13–38.

50 Ibid., pp. 14–15.

«dignity» (systematically imposed in the second half of the 20th century)[51] should be corrected (if not overcome). This means claiming that the latter concept, instead of being treated as an «*a posteriori* classifying expression» *(nachträglich klassifizierende Ausdruck)*, should be understood as the «moral "source" from which all basic rights derive their substance» *(die moralische "Quelle", aus der sich die Gehalte aller Grundrechte speisen)*[52].

Without continuing to explore Habermas' persuasive reconstitution, but also without questioning (or even diminishing) the importance of his *argument of continuity* (as a *continuity* that we may say is *internal* to the *Projekt der Moderne*), I believe this is the opportunity — *beyond* Habermas and certainly also *versus* Habermas! — to consider another (no less relevant!) *argument of continuity*. As a specification of the first argument that I have introduced — which attributes a practical-cultural *continuity* to the «western» experience of law and which *includes* the referred *Moderne* only as *one* of the historical stages to be taken into account — this present narrative exercise returns us to the invention of *controversy* as a specific *artefactus* due to the Roman *rise of the jurists*, and more directly and specifically to a certain structural element essential to this controversy. I refer here to the element which concerns the *position of the subjects-parties* in relation to the situation-*event* and the dogmatically presupposed context-*order*. We may, as a matter of fact, argue that the identity of the masks of *rights and duties* — masks that, as practical and cultural artefacts, are constitutively *assumed* (*buckled*!) by those subjects — depends on the *chance* and the *legitimacy* (which is also an institutionally consecrated *opportunity*) that such subjects have to consider *the*

51 Ibid., p.15.

52 Ibid., p.16. Even though the observation made by Habermas in note 19 (pp.22–23) introduces new (and certainly not negligible) elements concerning the *morality/law* relationship — namely those which come from the consideration of a certain «conceptual bridging» between «the moral content of the equal recognition of everyone» and «the legal form of Human Rights» *(die statuserzeugende soziale Anerkennung der Würde des Anderen [bietet] eine begriffliche Brücke zwischen dem moralischen Gehalt der gleichen Achtung für jeden und der Rechtsform der Menschenrechte)* —, I shall avoid discussing here the important differences concerning «human rights» (defending its «moral» and «juridical» *nature* respectively) which separate Alexy and Habermas [I have already reconstituted these differences in «O *homo humanus* do direito e o projecto inacabado da modernidade», cit., passim]. The truth is that Habermas himself recognizes that the new elements introduced in «Das Konzept der Menschenwürde...» (inspired by Georg Lohmann's analysis) do not seem sufficiently significant to demand a «revision» of his «original introduction of the system of rights» in *Faktizität und Geltung* (chapter III).

same concrete situation and to invoke *the same dogmatically enforced context-order*, building, expressing or defending *distinct* nuclear understandings of *the masks* in question and of the reciprocal connections that *inter-subjectively* relate them. This observation is less trivial than it sounds. In this possibility and the opportunity for *attention* or care that it institutionalizes (opening up a process of assimilation-treatment and submitting this to a *contradictory* dynamics), we should, in fact, acknowledge two basic (foundational) dimensions which help us to understand the experience of the problem-controversy and the recognition of the subject-person as two genetically *indistinguishable* components — to the point where perhaps we can say that it is this inseparability that provides us with the key to differentiating or autonomising that experience (of the problem) and this recognition (of the subject) in terms of their *strict juridical relevance* (identifying the meaning and limits that the *practical world* of law imposes on them).

Which basic dimensions are these? *On the one hand*, the dimension which corresponds to the reciprocal *pragmatic respect* between the subject-parties (and to this *pragmatic respect* as a requirement for *hearing the other* and his or her arguments) and, *on the other hand*, the dimension which, mobilizing a promise of univocity and comparability, enables these arguments (and also the impartial third's *adjudication*) to be taken seriously as plausible situated experimentations or realizations of a certain context-*order* (of common *warrants* and *criteria*) — a context which will later be significantly identified with the objectivation of a *legal system*.

Should this pragmatic respect and its claim for equality (as a microscopic claim inseparable from the structure of *controversy* and from the possibility of a *rational prudential comparability*) be treated as a specification of *human dignity*? I would say it should. More precisely, I would say that, on account of this inseparability — on account of the relevance conferred to a microscopically experienced *thirdness* (granted by the adjudicator-*third* and the presupposition of a *tertium comparationis* called the *legal system*) — this is precisely the specification of *human dignity* which law´s cultural project invented *as its own* (even though in its initial consecration this meant exploring an implacably *closed* circle of inter-subjectivity) and which has been continuously pursued and permanently reinvented (not only *expanded* in its circle!) as an indispensable identifying claim. With the unsuspected help of Jeremy Waldron, I would even add that this *pragmatic of respect* (as a source of juridical normative claims) in fact has much more relevant affinities with the experience of *dignity as rank or status* (which, according to Waldron, is an «intrinsic», *non contingent*, «legal idea»[53]) than with the claim for *dignity as value* (the political-philosophical and moral idea which has found its culminating canonic expression in Kantian *Menschenwürde*!)[54]. The said pragmatic and *relativizing* mask (which this pragmatic consecrates) are, as a matter of fact, inseparable from the principle of *audiatur et altera pars* and as such represent the invention of an autonomous and responsible *subject* — the inter-subjectively *relativized* subject who, (implicitly or explicitly) invoking an order of *warrants* and *criteria*, addresses himself simultaneously to the other party and to the judge, demanding a hearing (as well as expecting a rationally *judicative* treatment of the controversy)[55] ...

---

53 «When you hear my definition, the sense in which law inherently promotes dignity begins to become apparent. For it is easy to get the impression from the way I set this out of a person appearing in their own behalf before a public tribunal (say) and demanding to be listened to, demanding indeed that their view of things be taken account of before any public decision is made (for example, any public decision about what is to be done with them). This is evidently a legal idea, and it is arguably non contingently so—in the sense that it is not a matter of the law-maker having just decided to promote dignity (...). Dignity seems to hook up in obvious ways with juridical ideas about hearings and due process and status to sue...» [Waldron, «How Law Protects Dignity: the 2011 David Williams Lecture at the University of Cambridge», available (as working paper no. 11–83) in *Public Law & Legal Theory Research Paper Series* da New York University School Of Law, http://papers.ssrn.com/sol3/papers.cfm?abstract_id=1973341## (accessed in February 2013), pp.4–5].

54 This emphasis certainly does not exclude the idea that the political-philosophical and moral idea of *dignity as value*, autonomously introduced in the modern cycle, has not been assimilated into law's practical world: it *has* (translated into an immediate claim of equality), first of all formally, due to a decisive understanding of *statute law* as *norm* (as the Rousseaunian *loi encore à faire*, constitutively identified with an intrinsic expression of rational universality), then substantively, following a progressive (more or less contingent) conformation of the proposed legal-politic prescriptive solutions (and the corresponding justification).The normative *dimension* or *level* in which these claims to equality are incorporated (macroscopically referred to as a self-sufficient or, at least, autonomously conceived context-order, even when predominantly understood as a system of individual rights) is, however, significantly different from the normative dimension or level (intrinsically related to the problem-case) in which the said microscopic pragmatic and its experience of dignity (albeit in some historical cycles significantly hidden or apparently reduced to a subordinate place) grows and has been growing since Roman *civitas*.

55 It is important to add that Habermas considers Waldron's contribution (*Zur Verfassung Europas...*, cit., pp.27 ff.) and, through his reconstitution of *dignity as rank or status*, also the «direct precursors» of the concept of *dignitas humana* in «Greek philosophy» («especially in the Stoa») and «in Roman humanism» (namely in Cicero), decisively

3. The allusion to these two irreducible (and, as such, for once compatible!) *stories of continuity* — one exploring the internal trends of the *project of modernity* and the other considering the much more extended *route* of «western» law's *form of life* — leads us to a final clarification. In defending the accuracy of an understanding of law's *continuity* as a cultural project and as a constitutive process of reinvention and growth — emphasizing that this process of institutionalization (of a specific order of inter-subjectivity) is irreducible to a mere «expanding circle view», or at least that it should be experienced without the *pathos* of progress or the *providentialist teleology*[56] which, by giving it an acultural conformation, misunderstands this expansion — the intention is certainly not to problematize the decisive acquisition (made possible through the modern cycle) of an «idea of law» or «of a legal system» embodying «the assumption that everyone in a society ruled by law is treated as *sui juris*» (i.e. «as having full legal dignity»)[57], even less to devaluate the absolutely indispensable role played in our present circumstances by democratic constitutional objectivation— it being certain than the problem that this objectivation faces is precisely the *juridification* of the political system, if not the normative institutionalization of the global relationship between *communitas* and *societas*

accentuating the context-*horizon* of an *ontological understanding* of the «superior value» of man as «species» (the «ontological status of human being in cosmos») but also (certainly not by chance) neglecting the (no less relevant connection!) between *dignitas* and the (specifically juridical) *contradictory principle* (as a source of normative claims). This certainly does not prevent Habermas from giving all the due relevance to the invention of *individuelle Person* in the context of the *respublica christiana* discussion of *Gottesebenbildlichkeit* [Ibid, p.28], but allows him to conclude that there is no authentic «semantic bridge» between «those direct precursors» and the modern experience of *dignitas.* «Aber trifft das den Sinn der gleichen Menschenwürde eines jeden? Auch die direkten Vorläufer, die der Begriff der Menschenwürde in der griechischen Philosophie, vor allem in der Stoa und im römischen Humanismus - etwa bei Cicero - hat, bilden keine semantische Brücke zum egalitären Sinn des modernen Begriffs. Damals erklärte sich die *dignitas humana* aus einer ontologisch ausgezeichneten Stellung des Menschen im Kosmos, aus dem besonderen Rang, den der Mensch aufgrund von Gattungseigenschaften wie Vernunftbegabung und Reflexion gegenüber „niederen" Lebewesen einnimmt. Die Höherwertigkeit der *Species* kann vielleicht einen Artenschutz begründen, aber nicht die Unantastbarkeit der Würde der einzelnen Person als Quelle normativer Ansprüche...» (Ibid., pp.27–28).

56 The formula is by Michael Rosen, «How Law Protects Dignity. Replies to Jeremy Waldron: Dignity, Rank and Rights...», http://scholar.harvard.edu/files/michaelrosen/files/replies_to_jeremy_waldron.pdf (accessed in February 2013), p.2.

57 The formulations quoted are by Waldron: «How Law Protects Dignity...», cit., p.17.

(both understood as cultural *artefacts*). It is rather to inscribe the experience of constitutionality as an authoritarian-prescriptive one within the practices of legal system (i.e. the practices involved in stabilizing an open multi-dimensional legal system[58]), so that its unavoidable (more or less explicitly ideological[59]) political-social contingence[60], as well as the temporal dynamic that characterizes

58 I allude here to the specific concept of the *legal system* proposed by Castanheira Neves' *jursiprudentialism*: see, in particular, *Metodologia Jurídica. Problemas Fundamentais*, Coimbra: Coimbra Editora, 1995, 78–81, 152–157, 188–196, 278–283 (ßß) and «A unidade de sistema jurídico: o seu problema e o seu sentido» (1981), in *Digesta*, Coimbra: Coimbra Editora, vol. II, 1995, pp. 95 ff.

59 This unavoidable ideological identity is certainly more explicit in constitutions which may be called revolutionary (corresponding to an authentic intention of rupture) than in those which mobilize a consensual political basis and the compromises that this requires. It could be said, however, that the latter («constituições de consenso») do not «eliminate» (they only «elude» or «circumvent») the problems (relating to this ideological characteristic) which the former («constituições de rupture e revolucionárias») expose in all their crudeness and gravity. In this sense, but also exploring the limits of *extension*, *intension* and *validity* that should be recognized in constitutional prescriptions, see Castanheira Neves, «A redução política do pensamento metodológico-jurídico», *Digesta*, cit., vol. II, pp. 406 ff. and «O direito interrogado pelo tempo presente na perspectiva do futuro, cit., pp. 51 ff.

60 This political-social contingence is *unavoidable* even when the paradigmatic programme is a procedural or relational one, or even when we admit answering the challenge of *cosmopolitism* with a *constitutionalisation* of International Public Law, if not directly with the project of a *Mehrebenensystem* (and the possibility of a *Weltinnenpolitik ohne Weltregierung*) [Habermas, «Hat die Konstitutionalisierung des Völkerrechts noch eine Chance?», *Der gespaltene Westen. Kleine politischen Schriften X*, Frankfurt, Suhrkamp Verlag, 2004, pp. 133–137 («Weltinnenpolitik ohne Weltregierung»)]. Although the leading (not only regulative, but also constitutive) perspective here is procedural rationalization — a rationalization that only universal pragmatic reference to the *ideal speech situation* and its *counterfactual* power can justify (and institutionalise) — it should not, in fact, be forgotten that, beyond the abstract formulation of the rules of *ideal consensus*, contingence remains unavoidable whenever these procedural rules are used (enacted) in their rationalizing task, i.e. whenever decisions about substantive normative content are effectively and authoritatively taken (in a institutionalizing step still performed *within* constitutional *juridification* or already developed beyond this, in ordinary statute law). This contingence is still emphasised if we recall that the mask of *ideal speech* is, in itself, a historically situated construction, appearing to be unavoidably compromised with a certain *idea of Europe* (if not with cultural modernity) even when it is reduced to its most undifferentiated or indefinite nucleus (with its performative strength concentrated on an almost nominalistic appeal).

its (*fragmentary*, *extensionally* limited) programming and its (more or less deliberate) *open texture* — confirming it as an unmistakable component of the *stratum* of statutory law[61] — may be *confronted* with the experience of the other autonomous *strata* that compose the multilayered legal system (and with these strata reconstructed in correspondence with the «multicentric nature» that the experience of European institutionalization today imposes[62]). This, in fact, means that constitutional prescriptions should not only be determined (specified, integrated, developed) from the perspective of *other* (systemically incorporated) jurisdictional and dogmatic *criteria* (if not within the possibilities of an authentic European *jurist's law*), but also experienced (and transformed) under the challenges of *constitutional reality* (for its part, inscribed in a much broader *legal reality* and, as such, facing the possibilities of multiple *protestant* practices[63] and fragmented *interpretative communities*). Last but not least, it also means that these prescriptions (independently of the discussion of their political-social legitimacy and the problematization of their efficacy and efficiency as policies, involving a certain *ratio legis*) should be critically reconstructed in their *juridical validity* or *ratio juris*[64], precisely under the normative claims of an autonomously re-thought *community of principles* (taken seriously as *jus* and *foundational*

---

61 Which means benefitting it globally with a presumption of political pedigree and authority-*potestas*, but also particularly with the undisputable hierarchical condition of *lex superior* or *Grundgesetz*.

62 In this sense, see Bartosz Wojciechowski, Piotr Juchacz, Karoline M. Cern, «Whose Reason or Reasons Speak Through the Constitution? Introduction to the Problematics», *International Journal for the Semiotics of Law*, Vol. 25, n. 4, November 2012, pp. 455 ff..

63 In the words of Levinson, in his well-known understanding that relates *constitutional Protestantism* to the need to consider the interpretations and practices of the constitution developed by social movements and individual citizens (in counterpoint to *constitutional Catholicism*, which attributes the task of an authentic unitarian interpretation exclusively to the Supreme Court judicial review): see the synthesis proposed by Levinson in «Constitutional Protestantism in Theory and Practice: Two Questions for Michael Stokes Paulsen and One for His Critics», *Georgetown Law Journal*, vol. 83, 1994, pp. 373 ff.

64 I allude here to another indispensable distinction proposed by Castanheira Neves: see, in particular, *Metodologia Jurídica*, cit., pp. 149 ff. This distinction concerns two aspects and two possibilities for experimenting with legal statutes, one of them *(ratio legis)* considering *commands* (as an expression of *voluntas*) and the corresponding *programmes* in their specific immanent teleological rationality (or, in the words of Dworkin, their indispensable *arguments of policy*), and the other (*ratio juris*) testing the *juridicalness* of the corresponding *criteria*, i.e. confronting their immediate teleological intelligibility

warrants and, as such, not merely encountered as an *inference* from constitutional particular traditions). Critically reconstructed... but also *practically consonantly* performed (and in accordance with this same *ratio juris*), I would add, not only to emphasize that addressing plurality in this context depends on a constitutive circle and its *dialectics* (which we identify by invoking the perspectives of *system* and *problem*), but also to recognize that it is the *methodological priority* of *controversy* that gives this re-composition its practical-cultural specific meaning, distinguishing (analogically comparable) *concreteness* from pure *singularity*[65] and restoring *interpretatio* to its fully normative (*not* hermeneutical) «integral sense» of «law's realization»[66].

All these thematic elements (and the perspectives they productively cross) are, in fact, indispensable when enquiring about the kind of critical and reflective relations European societies can establish with their practical and cultural legacy — at a time when recalling the past (and the reconstruction of identitarian *continuities*), creating disturbing *labels*, so often produces ideological division! — and, in particular, which autonomous role we can expect from law as a key element of such a legacy and as a plausible answer to the issue of *inclusion*. The experience will perhaps not confirm Europe as a *constitutional project* (as it will perhaps not contribute directly towards reducing the democratic deficit in forming public opinion), but will instead confirm that the reinvention of law's legacy in terms of its cultural *continuity* (including the *constitutional legal culture*) is certainly one of the inescapable aspects of a plausible response...

---

as rules with the normative claims and demands of principles (considering *arguments of policy* from the predominant perspective of *arguments of principle*).

65 See the arguments I have developed in «Phronêsis und Tertialität: Die Behandlung des Neuenals Kern des "geworfenenEntwurfs" des Rechts», cit., pp.46–48, 51 ff.

66 See Castanheira Neves, *Metodologia Jurídica*, cit., pp.74–77, 83 ff., and, in particular, *O actual problema metodológico da interpretação jurídica,* Coimbra, Coimbra Editora, 2003, pp.45ff.

Anna Kalisz[1]
Humanitas University of Sosnowiec, Poland

Mediation and the European Legal Culture

Abstract: The paper begins with a brief introduction to the topic of conflict, norms used for its resolution and mediation as a way to deal with it. Its purpose then is to point out and argue the thesis, that mediation and its development in legal area corresponds with such features that are said to be distinctive for "European constitutional culture". Hence, the institution of mediation and its extending within contemporary legal systems – in legislation as well as in decision-making process – may be viewed as a form of expression of the changes outgoing in European legal culture as well as in a role of the state in conflict resolving.

Key Words: (social) norms; conflict; dispute resolving; mediation; agreement; legal culture; Law as a project of Communications

I. Social norms versus regulative function of law

The **mechanisms of social control**[2] can be either formal or informal.[3] Such control is mainly done through socialization in which people come to identify with a social system and its values and norms that seem to be natural and evident for the **particular culture** (also – the culture in its legal aspect).

It is worth to begin with the quite evident statement that the relations among various individuals and groups (or other bodies) as well as their behaviors are determined by different kinds of **norms** (of legal, moral, religious or customary nature), composing so-called "**social control system**"[4]. Such norms allow to

---

1 *PhD in Law, Assistant Professor.*

2 The notion of social control was introduced to social sciences by L. F. Ward and E. A. Ross in the be – see: J. J. Chriss (ed.), Social Control, Informal, Legal and Medical, Sociology of Crime, Law and Deviance, vol. 15 /2010, p.2.

3 Lindzey, Gardner (ed.),. Handbook of Social Psychology. I. Theory and method. II. Special fields and applications. (2 vols), Oxford, 1954, pp. II, 655–692.

4 Further reading on social and legal norms, their acceptance and co-relation between them: R. Pound, Social Control through Law, New Haven 1942, passim ; H.L.A. Hart, The Concept of Law, Oxford 1994, p.255.

predict the consequences - sanctions or gratifications - of actions or non-actions undertaken, and thereby motivate or demotivate to them.[5]

It is also worth to emphasize - especially in case of the mediation issue, which is a central point of the paper - that apart from the "external" and **imperative norms**, for instance: legal or religious ones - there is a category of **dispositive** norms created on the basis of needs, wants and interests of parties to the conflict. They are also a **product of culture**, since such individual norms also arise from the social control system and their scope and contents are limited by binding law.[6]

Although, the law is not the only system to regulate the social interactions, it is still worthy to look closer in the context of its various functions, in particular the **regulative function**.[7] Its nature is to keep in order (regulate) behaviors of individuals or groups. They are regulated either *a priori* (in order to prevent conflicts) or *a posteriori* (in order to solve the conflicts that have already appeared in social reality).[8] Thus, the legislator provides the parties with the arranged outlines and schemes. What is important, the ADR methods of dealing with conflicts (including mediation in particular) allow the parties to the dispute - as has been mentioned -to modify such rules within the limits of binding law.

II. Conflict versus (legal) dispute. Adjudication and resolution

Conflict is a notion[9] mostly defined as a **disagreement** through which the parties involved perceive a threat to their needs, interests, values or concerns. It is also a multilevel phenomena of social and individual dimension - what makes it interdisciplinary issue (and so does mediation as a way to deal with it). However, this quite particular type of interaction it is neither possible nor worth of being eliminated from social life and it is rather to be effectively dealt with. What is more,

5 See: A. Korybski, Norma - instytucja: gotowe rozwiązania dylematów decyzyjnych [w:] P. Chmielnicki (ed.) Pochodzenie, tworzenie i efektywność prawa, LexisNexis, Warszawa 2014, p. 30 i 35.

6 Further Reading on legality, justice and acceptance of norms in mediation: A. Kalisz, A. Zienkiewicz, Wymiar sprawiedliwości a mediacja [w:] Rozdroża sprawiedliwości we współczesnej myśli filozoficznoprawnej, B. Wojciechowski, M. Golecki (red.), wyd. Marszałek 2008, p. 263–274.

7 *Vide*: I. Bogucka, Funkcje prawa. Analiza pojęcia, Zakamycze 2000, passim; M. Borucka-Arctowa, Społeczne poglądy na funkcje prawa, Ossolineum, 1981, passim.

8 More: A. Kalisz, A. Zienkiewicz, Mediacja sądowa i pozasądowa. Zarys wykładu, Wolters Kluwer, Warszawa 2014, s. 17.

9 There are several definition of conflict - further Reading, e.g.: T. K. Sibanda, Conflict Issues Across Disciplines, Xlibris Corporation, 2010, chapters I i II (pp. 11 - 52).

the constructive solution may result with alteration of interpersonal interactions or even the social norms – so may be viewed not solely as a display, but also as a **base of cultural change and progress.**

The conflict definition consist of a few elements: the interest (needs/values) and **goals differential; the parties** to the conflict and – last but not least – **the interdependence** outgoing between them. The process of proper recognition of these elements is called "**conflict diagnosis**"[10] and is a starting point to identify and apply a proper solution (also throughout the mediation).

The conflict causes natural and various **reactions** of its parties as well as of the state (as a body imposing the law upon society and individuals). The most common reaction of the parties is usually (not always though) entering **the dispute.** The latter term can be, however, defined as a "conflict revealed" – which means that "objective" state of conflict turns into an intentional and "subjective" sequence of activities aimed to improve or retain the parties' situation.

Thus, conflict and dispute are not identical, but synonymous notions.[11] "A conflict" is a term of a wider sense, containing and consuming the more limited notion of "a dispute" – as one of a few possible reactions to the conflict. *Ergo*: the conflicts may, but not necessarily must lead to entering the dispute.

With a good reason the conflicts regulated by law are termed **the legal disputes** – since law provides rules solely for the external behaviors and not for internal states of mind. Moreover the state strives for an effective "**conflict management**" – throughout the regulation, reduction, adjudicating or solving. In any of these, is more or less active and imperious.

As mentioned before, conflicts are typical for any society, but the state varies in dealing with them (and so do the parties involved). Contemporary modern democratic state of law tends to handle the issue of conflicts and disputes slightly differently from the longtime tradition of suppression or traditional paradigm of court-solving problems.[12]

The court-solving (**judicial**) **paradigm** of decisional process involves *imperium* of the state and results with external and binding decision passed by the court as

10 More: L. S. Coltri, Conflict Diagnosis and Alternative Dispute Resolution, Prentice Hall 2004, passim; L. S .Coltri, Alternative Dispute Resolution: A Conflict Diagnosis Approach , Prentice Hall 2009, passim.

11 Ibidem, s. 20.

12 Such paper deal with interpersonal conflicts or group conflicts. For international conflict and mediation see: J. Bercovitch, R. D. W. Jackson, Conflict Resolution in the Twenty-first Century: Principles, Methods, and Approaches, The Michigan University Press, 2009, passim.

a state authority. It consists of several stages, such as: recognition of facts, recognition of law (namely: the sources of law that shall be applied to these facts); legal interpretation; legal subsumption, decision on legal consequence and – at the end – the justification (the grounds).[13]

Dispute resolution, by contrast, is a far less formal and structured process, where the impartial and neutral "third body" is involved to assist the parties to the dispute in reaching the accepted agreement. It means that the process itself as well as the result (decision) is controlled or created by the parties themselves and by their dispositive norms.[14]

Hence, the aforementioned paradigm of decisional process do not apply to ADR procedures, including the mediation. Firstly – the facts (in other words: past affecting present) are less relevant than expectations (present reflect upon the future). The parties are re-oriented form "rights" to "interests". Secondly – the legal regulations determine the limits of the settlement rather than its contents – for the reason that the individual and dispositive norms cannot stay in contrary to law. Thirdly – the final agreement (settlement) does not need the statement of reasons or the legal grounds, since the parties are not to "deliver justice", but to find an acceptable and satisfying solution for particular situation. The "**justice**" in such cases is replaced by "**acceptance**" than.

III. Mediation versus other ADR methods. Mediation in legal area

The acronym ADR (Alternative Dispute Resolution) stands for the procedures and methods of resolving disputes other than by litigation. Putting another way – "**alternative**" means genuinely "alternative to the traditional judicial paradigm". This leads to lowering the degree of state authority being involved as well as to increasing the role of the parties in creating the agreement draws on social norms other than legal ones and focused rather on "meeting the expectations" than "proving facts and rights".

ADR traditions have a long history[15] and vary somewhat by times, country and culture, but there are significant common factors that make them popular and

---

13 Szerzej na temat modelu stosowania prawa przez organy państwowe zob.: L. Leszczyński, Zagadnienia teorii stosowania prawa: doktryna i tezy orzecznictwa, Zakamycze 2004, passim.

14 A. Korybski, Alternatywne rozwiązywanie sporów w USA, Lublin 1993, s. 31–37.

15 Further reading: J. Barrett, J. Barrett, A History of Alternative Dispute Resolution: The Story of a Political, Social, and Cultural Movement, Jossey-Bass 2004, passim.

attractive. What is more, contemporary version of ADR has gained widespread acceptance in recent years, and there are obviously more reasons for it, than – the most frequent mentioned one – the increasing caseload of courts.

Such **benefits** may be lined as: flexibility of procedure (the entire process – as has been pointed out – is determined and controlled by the parties to the dispute); less complexity; lower costs, likelihood and speed of settlements; confidentiality and – at the end – the chance to preserve the relationships or reputations.[16]

In jurisprudence ADR is generally classified into a few types[17] (at least three basic ones): negotiation, mediation and **arbitration**. The latter one is the closest to the judicial paradigm of making decisions, since the decision is imposed to the parties by the arbitrator (though the decisional body is designated by the parties themselves). The first one, **negotiation**, is a dialogue between two or more parties intended to resolve points of difference and to reach an understanding and settle the dispute. There is though no third party who facilitates the resolution process or imposes a resolution.

Mediation, by contrast, employs the third party – the mediator – who facilitates the resolution process, but does not impose a resolution on the parties. The mediator's role is – *inter alia* – to: listen actively, reframe issues, help to communicate, help to develop and evaluate new options for the issues, offer "shuttle diplomacy", balance the power between the parties, do the reality testing for the agreement. In other words: to assist and guide the parties toward their own resolution. Nevertheless, it is worth to stress out that the mediator may play more or less active role, depending on one of three strategies adopted: the facilitative strategy of mediation (soft mediation); the evaluative strategy of mediation (hard mediation); the empowerment and recognition strategy of mediation (transformative mediation)[18].

---

16 Further reading – e. g.: M. Freeman, Alternative Dispute Resolution, New York University Press, passim or A. J. Pirie, Alternative Dispute Resolution: Skills, Science, and the Law, Irwin Law, 2000, passim. Also: A. Rau, E. Sherman, S. Peppet, Processes of Dispute Resolution. The Role of Lawyers. Third edition, New York 2002, passim.

17 There also a classification for primary and secondary (mixed) forms of ADR – further reading: A. L. Greenspan, Handbook of Alternative Dispute Resolution, Austin 1990, passim.

18 More: L. Riskin, *Understanding Mediator's Orientations* Strategies, and Techniques, Alternative to the High Costs of Litigation,..., s. 7 i n.; S. Imperati, *Mediator Practice Models: the Intersection of Ethics and Stylistic Practices in Mediation*, Willamette Law Review 1997, nr 33, s. 707–714; R. Moberly, *Mediator Gag Rules: Is it Ethical for Mediators to Evaluative or Advise?*, South Texas Law Review 1997, nr 38, s. 670–678; M. Levin, *The Propriety of Evaluative Mediation: Concerns About the Nature and*

In any case the mediator provides the assistance to the communication (discourse, debate, dialog) between the parties, which leads to a **trialog** type of interaction.

Since mediation – like all the ADR methods – is **based on „negotiation-approach"**, there are three fundamental factors of complete and successful mediation: voluntarism; relative balance of power and interdependence.

Moving to the issue of mediation in legal system, its mechanism can be used and applied to – practically – any type of state authority operations (of legislative, executive and judicial nature), as well as in any areas and branches of law.

As a method of dispute solving, mediation is applicable in **numerous areas**: public disputes (e.g. land-use); civil and commercial ones (for instance: contracts, medical malpractice, personal injury, partnerships); consumer disputes; labor disputes (wrongful termination, discrimination, harrasement, labor management), criminal disputes (especially minor and juvenile crimes); family disputes (premarital agreements, financial or budget disagreements, separation and divorce, alimony, parenting plans, estates), *et cetera*.

In short – it does exist in any – private or public branches of law, but the agreement itself concerns rather "private" or even "extra-legal" elements – connected with human and social relationships and factors as emotions or interests of the parties that may be freely created, changed, modified or shaped by them.

As it has been mentioned before – a **paradigm of mediation** varies significantly from the judicial one. It includes:

1. recognition of interests, needs and values of the parties involved (instead of the facts) – which stands for "conflict diagnosis";
2. recognition of so-called "common ground" for finding the best option of the solution for dispute diagnosed;
3. "subsumption" – that is to say – applying the accepted option to solve particular dispute in order to meet the parties' expectations;
4. final agrement (settlement).

And as has been also pointed out – the sufficient grounds for it is an acceptance of the parties, and the "just decision" turns into "acceptable" one.

Quality of Evaluative Opinion, Ohio State Journal on Dispute Resolution 2001, nr 16, s. 267 i n.; J. Stulberg, *Facilitative versus Evaluative Mediator Orientations: Piercing the "Grid" Lock*, Florida State University Law Review 1997, nr 24, s. 985 i nast. See also: R. Baruch Bush, J. Folger, *The Promise of Mediation: Responding to Conflict Through Empowerment and Recognition*, San Francisco 1994.

IV. Mediation and its development in European legal culture – the conclusions

Conflict, disagreement, dispute, pluralism, dialog and consensus – are notions that seem to be basic and fundamental for the idea and practice of modern democracy. The constructive solution may become a beginning for bringing the modifications to the culture – also in its legal aspect. Contemporary European legal culture[19] (at the level of European democratic states as well as at the supranational level – the European Council law and European Union law) shows a tendency to deal with the issue of conflicts and disputes in a **conciliatory way**.

Though one of the state's functions remains providing resolving-procedures for the disputes, there is more and more "negotiations" and "dialogue" approach in it. In other words – there is "**less state**" imposing the decisions (judgments) and **more "private will"** – where parties to the conflict may choose the norms and decide themselves on the contents of the final agreement.

The norms according to which the agreement is made and the rules for making decisions are no more imposed by state only – they may be also create or modified by parties to the conflict within the limits of binding law. The new paradigm of dispute-solving process has been established and the new type of relationship between the parties in this process is becoming more and more popular.

"European identity" arise from – *inter alia* – the concept of the **"social contract"** between state and society – what may also mean that dispute can be solved not just by the state authority, but also by other social bodies or even individuals, on the grounds of **"minor social contracts"** – as a result of negotiation or mediation.

It may then confirm the thesis, that Europe is currently facing a shift from a rather formal and positivistic to a more substance-oriented approach to law. The emerging new elements of European legal culture are definitely less formalist and law – especially the private one, not solely though – is regarded more as instrumental to political, economic, social, cultural and other aims, than solely to a tool of state *imperium*. There is also is less belief in right answers.[20]

In this context mediation serves as an example of ADR – with its philosophy, elements and benefits as well as an example of changes in European culture. Apart from being a tool of solving disputes it also a kind of "response" for economic,

---

19 In the context of the European Union see also: G. Helleringer, K. Purnhagen, Twards European Legal Culture, Hart Publishing Limited, 2014, passim.

20 M. W. Hesselink, The New European Legal Culture, Kluwer 2001, http://papers.ssrn.com/sol3/papers.cfm?abstract_id=1029573.

social, cultural and other individual needs. The creative solution – within the limits of binding law – may be also viewed as an expression of **evolution of social norms** upon which the agreement is based.

Mediation and its development in legal area – in legislation as well as in decision-making process – refers also to such features and notion that are said to be distinctive for "European legal culture" in its constitutional aspect: pluralism of values and convictions; **deliberative democracy**, open society and democratic state of law.[21] The development of mediation meets the idea that the state is a significant, but one a few others actors of social dialog. It may be viewed simultaneously as an expression of the "liberal" approach to individual interest as well as the "collective" value of social peace.

Its development – either on legislative or on decision-making level – also leads to a "privatization" of social services – here particularly: the "dispute resolution service".

And its extending within contemporary legal systems may be viewed as a form of expression of changes outgoing in European legal culture. Mediation based on dialogue also corresponds with the concept of **"Law as a project of Communication"**, since the "constitutional" ideas of post-national Europe are the **"will of discourse"** and reaching the **"common grounds"**.

21 Different aspects *vide*: J. Elster (ed.), Delibarative democracy, Cambridge 1998.

Part II
The Human Rights Culture and the Power of Judgment

Leszek Leszczyński
Maria Curie-Skłodowska Univeristy of Lublin, Poland

On Human Rights Protection in the European Union Legal Order: Between Pragmatism and the Axiology of Integration

Abstract: The article indicates and analyses processes of Europeanisation which led to the specific situation of the human rights within the European legal order. On the one hand the normative and judicial aspects of human rights protection are an element of the constitutionalization of *acquis communautaire* (understood as establishing a coherent system of principal norms, which encompass traditional constitutional matter). On the other hand the processes of Europeanisation proceed in-between the pragmatic and axiological view of European integration. The articles unmasks and discusses processes which has led to forming this postmodern and multicentric junction-structure of the European Union.

Key Words: human rights (fundamental rights), European integration, the European Treaties, the CJEU (ECJ) case law

1. Introduction

There are several factors defining the current methods and scope of human rights protection in the European Union legal order, and it is not only during the last few years that this system has been made really multidimensional and complex. Considering, on the one hand, the legislative and jurisdictional sources, divided in turn into the Council of Europe and strictly European Union standards, and, on the other hand, the state and supra-state levels, the multicentric image of this protection has been present and visible from the early stages of the integration of the European Communities, even if its scope and complexity is limited.

Human rights, broadly understood, is the subject matter of this elaboration. Such a broad approach is usually free from any doubts in the area of the theory of law, and this approach is becoming increasingly important in the context of the features of the laws of the European Communities and of the European Union. It acquires an even broader perspective when looked upon within the framework of the notion of a legal order which, unlike the notion of a system of laws, comprises not only Treaty of Europe regulations or the EU statutory law but also the jurisdiction of European courts, including the Court of Justice, courts of EU Member States and to some extent, the decisions of the European Court of Human Rights.

Such a wide array of courts is conducive to perceiving 'the judicial dialogue' which shapes this order. And the less elaborate the normative regulations are, the bigger the order formative power of this dialogue. Being aware of this debate and its role is particularly topical in the area of human rights, where the deficit of normative acts was for years a characteristic feature of the European Community and European Union laws.

The nouns used in the subtitle of this elaboration, which stress either the pragmatism or axiology of the European integration, can actually deepen the outlook on the integration process if put in the context of human rights. After all, they appear in the context of some 'competitiveness' and, at the same time, of 'combined action', complementing each other across the entire legal order of the European Union.

Neither of the relations, in turn, negates a thesis that normative and judicial aspects of human rights protection are an element of the constitutionalization of acquis communautaire (understood as establishing a coherent system of principal norms, which encompass traditional constitutional matter). This is so not only because the protection of human rights is part and parcel of the constitutional order but also because, increasingly, human rights regulations become principles of law, and they are treated as such in normative acts of treaty law and in judicial decisions of the ECJ.

2. Human Rights and Evolution of European integration

Generally speaking, until 1992, European integration focused predominantly on economic matters, and specifically on establishing institutions and fundamentals. It focused later on consolidating and deepening the single market for the exchange of goods, people, services, and capital—with due consideration for the principles of competition. Protection of human rights was never at the forefront of normative acts or the jurisprudence of the Tribunal of Justice. These rights did not become a normative legal category in the draft on economic issues, and the term 'human rights' was absent from the community legal order. If it did appear, it was replaced with such notions as the rights of individuals or basic or fundamental rights.

Looking at the matter from the pragmatic and axiological viewpoints—as indicated in the title of this elaboration—it can safely be said that the pragmatic aspect was predominant. Oriented towards economic efficiency, it linked the axiology of integration with the defining of relations among Member States and structures of the European Communities rather than with the determining of the legal status of individuals and their rights. This legal status largely referred to the rights of natural persons, since legal persons enjoyed their rights and entitlements insofar as their activity was connected with business.

It was only the Single European Act of 1986 that changed somewhat the perception of the political aspects of integration and, by extension, the human rights protection that falls within its framework. The next steps consisted in making an open reference to the construction of human rights and to the rights' various sources in Article 6 of the Treaty on European Union, made at Maastricht in 1992, and in setting out a catalogue of rights in the Charter of Fundamental Rights of the European Union of 2000, a type of 'soft law' at the time. Although the provisions of Article 6 of the TEU opened up the issue of human rights protection in the EU in normative terms, the formal stance of the EU towards the matter, and of the Council of Europe specifically, remained unchanged. Such an attitude was reinforced by a negative opinion from the Tribunal of Justice of 1995 concerning the legal capacity of the European Communities to join the European Convention on Human Rights and Fundamental Freedoms.

Fundamental changes on the normative level were not made until the new provisions of the treaty law of 2007, primarily through the revision of Article 6 of the TEU and the entry into force of the Charter of Fundamental Rights along with the coming into force of the Treaty on the Functioning of the European Union (Treaty of Lisbon). Equally important was the opening of the process of accession of the EU to the European Convention.

Thus, a question arises as to what extent the ideology of the European integration set forth at its initial stage, largely through economic pragmatism, has evolved since 1992 towards a more tangible inclusion of the axiology of integration. Does the area of EU law related to the protection of human rights play a particular role in this evolution? Assuming that the answer to this question is affirmative, it should be further determined to what extent this has been brought about by the normative changes in the EU legislation and by the evolution of court practice, i.e. by the jurisprudence of the CJ and by the judicial debate held among national and international courts (including the ECHR), respectively. This determination could, a rebours, have an effect on a new measure of relations between pragmatism and axiology, i.e. removing the aspect of competitiveness and replacing it with some 'axiological pragmatism' which determines the aims of integration, with due consideration for the interests of Member States with respect to human rights protection.

The aforementioned considerations led to a somewhat natural, albeit significant, periodization regarding this aspect of development of EU laws, linked with the role of human rights protection, notably in the context of establishing relations between pragmatic and axiological aspects of this protection. And so, the first period would comprise the functioning of the legal order of the European Communities until 1992; the second would span the years 1992–2009 and cover the shaping of the legal order of the EU; and the third, which continues to this day, would refer to the functioning of this order following the entry into force of the Treaty of Lisbon. This elaboration offers a fairly limited analysis of the latter period, since the jurisprudence of the CJ continues to evolve on the basis of new fundamentals, and some aims stipulated in the Treaty have not yet been achieved (e.g. accession of the EU to the Convention).

3. Before Maastricht

1. The rights which by construction and category are linked with human rights already appear, albeit limited in scope, in normative acts of the treaty laws of the European Communities in the context of provisions which shape the process of economic integration and in connection with the execution of fundamental liberties of the Communities and principles of competition. They include, for example, anti-discriminatory regulations (Articles 12, 13, 17, 34, 39, 43, 49, 50, 137, and Article 141 of the Treaty Establishing the European Communities (TEC), which are also included in the statutory laws of the Communities (e.g. Council Directive 2000/78/OC or Council Decision of 20 December 2000). The link between the rights of the individual and the goals and process of economic integration translates into a greater interest in community economic and social rights than personal and political ones, in terms of drafting legal acts.

The rights of the individual, which are not expressed in a binding manner in the form of normative acts, acquire the form of a declaration, in the perspective of a political discourse. Such declared rights can be seen in the Joint Declaration of the Council, Commission and Parliament of 5 April 1977, in the Declaration of the European Parliament of 12 April 1989, or in the Declaration on Human Rights signed in Luxembourg in 1991. While the Community institutions do not treat these sets of declarations as binding law, they do, however, indicate the integration-related significance of human rights, something that can be linked with future stages and dimensions of integration.

The appearance of human rights protection in the treaty law as a separate normative category dates back to 1986 when the Single European Act was published. By using such terms as 'fundamental rights' and 'human rights', the drafters referred to more universal axiological and normative standards in the document, or, to be more precise, in its Preamble. Being the first act of the Community legislation of such import, and going beyond economic pragmatism, the document specifies the aim of the Communities, i.e. 'to continue the work undertaken on the basis of the Treaties establishing the European Communities and to transform relations as a whole among their States into a European Union' alongside the respect of human rights. The document indicates a need to work together to promote democracy on the basis of the fundamental rights recognized in the constitutions and laws of the Member States, in the Convention for the Protection of Human Rights and Fundamental Freedoms, and in the European Social Charter, notably freedom, equality, and social justice.

The Single European Act paved the way for the European Convention to enter the normative juridical discourse on the protection of human rights in the European Community. Nevertheless, the basic classification remained unchanged, since the said Convention did not become part and parcel of the legal order of the Communities (acquis communautaire). Thus, political attempts to make the Communities part of the Convention system did not result in normative legal solutions.

2. Until 1992, the jurisprudence relating to the protection of human rights in the European Community was shaped largely by the decisions of the European Court of Justice, supplemented by some acts of national courts, mainly constitutional tribunals, in reaction to the theses that appeared in the decisions of the ECJ.

The ECJ developed during that period, on the basis of the treaty norms (as regards fundamental rights which these regulations referred to) and, in a sense, independent of these norms, in the form of judicial decisions that originated from a variety of sources.

Similar to the normative acts of acquis communautaire, the CJ does not use the term 'human rights', shaped in international law, as a category in itself. Nevertheless, it uses the term whenever references are made to the sources where human rights are mentioned. This usage largely refers to the European Convention, where human rights are used in the title, and which does not use other notions to describe this normative construct.

In terms of the need to protect fundamental rights in the European Community, the judicial decisions can be divided into a few stages of a gradually increased scope of such protection.

During the initial stage, the key relation was that between Community and national standards of protection of human rights. The essential boundary was clearly set in the headnotes to the decisions from the 1960s (Flaminio Costa and Walt Wilhelm). Based on these headnotes, there can be no doubt as to the establishment of the principle of precedence or primacy of Community law over all norms of national laws. Following the decision in the Internationale Handelsgesellschaft case, this principle extended also to fundamental rights, which were previously recognized in the form of general laws of Community law in the judgment in the Stauder case.

At the beginning of the 1970s, the protection of human rights was expressed in a statement issued by the ECJ on the need to guarantee the protection of fundamental rights, which constituted an integral part of the general principles of Community law. This protection was actually inspired by the constitutional traditions common to all Member States. Interestingly enough, the perception of fundamental rights as general principles of Community law, inspired by constitutional traditions, did not have any direct normative basis at that time. It took several years for this basis to materialize.

The principle of supremacy was, however, correlated with the headnotes, resulting for the first time with such force from the increasingly heard debate with the participation of national courts. In 1974, the German Constitutional Tribunal questioned the principle of the direct supremacy of Community law over national constitutional laws concerning human rights (Solange-Beschluss). While these rights were protected by the national legislation, there was no such protection afforded on the normative level by Community law.

Taking the matter up with other constitutional tribunals and participating in this constitutional debate on the Community level will in time change the approach of the acquis to human rights protection as such. However, before that happens, there will be sporadic and ad hoc corrections effected by way of judicial decisions of the Court of Justice of the EU.

Inspiration that stemmed from common constitutional traditions was already reinforced in the headnotes of the J. Nold case, which extend the connection with the basic rights established and guaranteed in the constitutions of the Member States through the ban on measures which stand in contradiction to said rights. In the aforementioned judicial decision, the CJEU clearly refers to international law, the agreements of which, provided that the Member States are parties thereto, can act as points of reference within the framework of Community law and the jurisprudence of the ECJ. In this light, although not expressis verbis, the European Convention is treated as an act which may be used by the ECJ as a validation tool in determining the wording of the standard protection of human rights.

Irrespective of highlighting the assumption of the role of international law agreements as patterns for the Community protection of human rights, the decision in the Hauer case seems to be pointing to a will to maintain a certain balance. On the one hand, the court held that any breaches of fundamental rights by an act of Community bodies of authority are subject to assessment exclusively on the ground of Community law and that any inclusion of national law in this context would violate the material unity and efficacy of Community law. On the other hand, however, the court repeated the premise of the ECJ concerning the obligation to seek inspiration in constitutional traditions of the Member States, under which the measures that contradict fundamental rights expressed in their respective constitutions cannot be accepted in the Community.

Another dimension of this balance, which, in a sense, returns to the idea of 'economic pragmatism', is applied in a later case, i.e. Wachauf, under which the scope of protection of fundamental rights recognized by the CJEU is determined by their social function and, specifically, by the aims of economic objectives and the organization of the common market.

The next group of judgments, in chronological order, addresses yet another question. Expanding jurisdiction also to cover, in addition to constitutional traditions, generally worded international agreements concerning human rights that the Member States of the European Communities are parties to has inevitably increased the role of the Convention regarding the matter of protection. Interestingly enough, from the uniformity of objectives and the actual execution of the process of integration, this process has been underway alongside the development of the SEA, in which the Convention is mentioned as a source of human rights. The judgment in the Cinetheque case is the first sign of the new trend. The headnotes to this case indicate no jurisdiction of the ECJ regarding national regulations on human rights. In other judgments, the Convention appears in a totally different role—as a strong validation argument taken into account while passing judgments by the ECJ. There is also a clear reference to the specific provision contained in the Convention. In the judgment in the Kent Kirk case, the principle of no retroactivity of law expressed in Article 7 of the Convention is treated not only as a fundamental right but also as a general principle of law duly protected by the ECJ. In the judgment of the Hoechst case, the provisions of Article 8 of the Convention become a reference point with respect to the standard of protecting the right of privacy. These provisions acquire the role of principles which introduce uniformity of the scope of protection where differences in the scope of protection occur with respect to the seat of the entrepreneur. In the Elliniki case, the court judgment refers to the Community's freedom to render services as justification for the freedom of expression laid down in Article 10 of the Convention. The Court underlines that said freedom of expression is a principle of law whose observance is overseen by the ECJ.

In short, during the period preceding the Treaty of 1992, the structure of individual rights protection in the EU was based primarily on judicial decisions of European courts with their particular jurisdictional powers. Naturally, the decisions of the Court of Justice of the European Communities played a very special role in this respect. However, equally important were the decisions of national courts (and of Constitutional Tribunals) as well as of the ECHR. These decisions clarified the model of protection (also by defying the practice of the ECJ by Constitutional Tribunals in a more or less straightforward manner) or provided a point of reference and an additional source on which the reconstruction of the protection model was effected. As regards the latter, the standards set by the ECHR were used for this purpose.

4. Between Maastricht and Lisbon

1. During the second stage of European integration, protection of human rights, as expressed in statutory provisions as well as judicial decisions relating thereto, underwent some changes.

Human rights (fundamental rights) became part and parcel of the Treaty law. Article 6 of the Treaty of Maastricht on European Union of 1992 (TEU) regulates in a highly specific manner the place of human rights in the European Union and the protection thereof, referring, in terms of the subject matter, to the SEA, but locating the provisions exclusively in the Preamble. With such a solution in place, the regulation acquires the status of an immediately binding norm.

The legislators use the term 'human rights and fundamental freedoms', making a clear reference to the same term used in the European Convention, even where there are no references made thereto (Para 1 of Article 6 of the TEU). Moreover, these rights acquire a high status, since respecting these rights becomes one of the principles on which the European Union is founded (Para 1).

Respecting these rights, referred to interchangeably as fundamental rights in Para 2, is regarded again as an obligation of the European Union. Making a reference to the traditional Community terminology (fundamental rights) is not hindered by the fact that this reference points to the guarantees of such rights in the European Convention on Human Rights, where such terminology is not used.

The category of fundamental rights is also referenced further on, in Para 2 of this provision, stating that the constitutional traditions common to Member States are deemed to be the source of these fundamental rights. Such wording reflects the classic construction of human rights rather than the Community category of fundamental rights (which, of course, does not indicate an auxiliary function of the term itself).

The above-mentioned principle of respecting human rights and fundamental freedoms, listed in Para 1 jointly with the principle of liberty, democracy, and the rule of law, becomes further reinforced in Para 2, which provides that these rights (as fundamental ones) establish general principles of Community law.

The provisions of Article 6 of the Treaty on European Union did not, however, change the formal position of the EU towards the system of protection of human rights within the framework of the European Council. This was best reflected in the opinion issued by the European Court of Justice of 28 March 1995. The Court held that the European Community does not have the power under the treaties to accede to the European Convention on Human Rights. This opinion closed the matter for several years to come. The Court held that no provision of the Treaty authorized the European Community to lay down provisions or to conclude agreements concerning human rights protection, and accession to the Convention would entail a major change of the present Community system of human rights protection and, as such, would require amendments to the Treaty law.

Irrespective of the provisions of Article 6 of the TEU, the rights of individuals became the object of separate regulations within the framework of revising the Treaty on European Union. Part II of this Treaty regulates citizenship of the Union. Thus, the rights included in the Treaty are supplemented with the rights resulting from citizenship in the Union, e.g. the right to move and reside freely within the territory of the Member State, the right to vote, and the right to petition the European Parliament.

The rights of individuals, listed under the category of 'fundamental rights', became the object of a separate statutory act concluded in 2000, i.e. the Charter of Fundamental Rights of the European Union.

Despite the declarative nature of the Charter, the rights acquired a somewhat different status, since the Charter is a fairly comprehensive catalogue of these rights which, with respect to personal and public rights, refers to the European Convention and which actually expands the list of rights to include economic, cultural, and social ones.

The Charter also contains important interpretation declarations, combined with references to axiology and defining relations to constitutional traditions of EU Member States and the European Convention. As regards axiological declarations, Paragraphs 2 and 3 of the Preamble define values. Paragraph 5 of the Preamble to the Charter, in turn, reaffirms the role of constitutional traditions common to the Member States as well as the rights resulting from the European Convention for the Protection of Human Rights and Fundamental Freedoms and the case law of the European Court of Human Rights. Article 52 provides a clear rule of interpretation under which the meaning and scope of rights contained in the Charter shall be the same as those laid down by the Convention (Para 3) and by the common constitutional traditions (Para 4). These sources are classified under the provisions of Article 53 into the catalogue of sources which specify the minimal level of protection of fundamental rights in the EU.

The Charter, as worded originally in 2000, was then incorporated into the Constitution for Europe as Part Two, an act perceived to grant the same binding force across the European Union. Thus, it did not follow the path of the key project, which put on hold the process of expressing human rights in terms of basic norms for a few years. The breakthrough in this respect came with the coming into force of the Treaty on the Functioning of the European Union.

2. The case law of the ECJ in the years 1992–2009 was, in principle, a continuation of the stand expressed in the decisions taken in the matter of the protection of the rights of individuals and the experience in exchanging views on jurisdictional matters with national constitutional tribunals. In this context, pragmatism, which developed from this experience and from establishing a certain iunctim between the aims of integration and the expectations of the Member States, proved durable enough not to implement any major changes, despite a fairly clear regulation of human rights in Article 6 of the Treaty on European Union (references to common constitutional traditions and to the European Convention), let alone the appearance of the catalogue of rights laid down in the Charter of Fundamental Rights in 2000. Nor was there any bigger effect of axiology on the matter of fundamental rights, although the legislators used in Article 6 of the Treaty a normative construction of general principles of law (which, after all, cannot have axiological content).

The opinion No. 2/94 issued by the ECJ did not bring major effects either. As a result of this opinion, the Convention could not become the only validation available to the court, which was the case before. Nevertheless, the provisions of Article 6 of the TEU reinforced the interpretative role of the Convention, since its regulations, which acquired the status of principles, could now constitute an important component of principles in terms of axiology and purpose as well as serving as the grounds for legal inferences. They could also serve in determining the so called axiological margin with respect to extralegal axiology (general clauses) as well as constituting the basis and the object of weighing values (principles). The potential role of the Convention as a source of reconstruction rose significantly, although, in their essence as described before, the examples indicate that even without such normative regulations de facto, such roles can be attributed to some extent to the provisions of the Convention.

The incorporation of the European Convention into the catalogue of sources under the provisions of Article 6 of the TUE brought about one more important effect. As a result of this measure, decisions of the ECHR became, albeit optionally, a validation argument for case law of the ECJ. Naturally, such a situation was not impossible prior to this incorporation, since the Convention was referred to without any normative grounds. Nevertheless, the provisions contained in Article 6 put this practice in a different dimension, i.e. that of a recognized standard. It operates indirectly, since the decisions of the ECHR are not mentioned indirectly. However, given that the jurisprudence of this Court acquires de facto the role of a validation argument for the use of human rights protection in the system of the Council of Europe (and, by extension, in national legal orders of the Member States that are parties to this Convention), the indirectness mentioned loses its functional significance. In addition to that, the fourth paragraph of the Preamble to the Charter of Fundamental Rights of the EU refers to the case law of the ECHR as a source of rights reaffirmed thereby.

Constitutional traditions common to the Member States acquire the same properties as the Convention. Similar to the Charter, they are also listed as a source of law under the provisions of Article 6 of the TEU. However, contrary to the case law of the ECHR, the decisions of national courts pertaining to human rights do not acquire the status of a source of law. Nevertheless, this does not exclude using such decisions by the ECJ, given the significant role that the decisions of such courts, notably supreme courts and constitutional tribunals, play in building the catalogue of sources for the reconstruction of norms relating to human rights protection.

The examples of the case law from the period described refer to all the general jurisdictions listed above.

And so, in the Kremzow case, which corresponds to opinion No. 2/94 in terms of timing, the ECJ stresses caution in making references to the Convention, although it does so within the terms of reference to its non-competence regarding its interference in the process of the construction of national laws by national courts in the context of the regulations laid down in the Convention. At the same time, however, sometimes the ECJ treats the case law of the ECHR as an element of legal grounds on which to make a judgement. The Roquette Freres case is a good illustration of this approach.

The judgment in the Schmidberger case, whose subject matter is, in its essence, similar to that of Elliniki, is by far the best example of a certain evolution in the case law of the ECJ concerning the scope of fundamental rights protection in the EU, in the context of their relations with the rights listed in the Convention. Here, one of the Community freedoms, i.e. movement of goods, is confronted with one of the rights laid down by the Convention, i.e. freedom of assembly and association. Besides indicating common constitutional traditions and the Convention as a source of fundamental rights of the Community, the ECJ refers to the judgment of the ECHR in the Demirel case. The Court indicates the provisions of Articles 10 and 11 of the Convention, weighing their significance with respect to the free movement of goods as one of the key principles of Community treaty laws. This is further linked with the clause concerning public interest, on the grounds of the case law of the ECJ (Cassis de Dijon). This weighing process takes into account the provisions of the so-called restrictive clauses contained in Para 2 of the two

Articles of the Convention, which by themselves create freedoms of expression, and of assembly and association. These Articles also make the latter freedoms be perceived in the context of social aims which justify some interference in these rights. Hence the need to weigh the two principles. While this may give some 'pragmatic advantage' to Community regulations, especially in the matter of responsibility of the state for the activity of protesters, it nevertheless highlights the construction of the Treaty in line with human rights.

Although the Charter of Fundamental Rights of the European Union does not enjoy the status of a binding norm, it does become a validation argument in the case law of the ECJ. While the Charter does not constitute the exclusive grounds for judgments, it is among the validation arguments used most frequently with the treaty laws of the EU and the case law of the ECHR, as regards carious rights regulated in the Charter.

The jurisprudence-related dialogue continues, with the Federal Constitutional Court of Germany being particularly active. This court has already made several attempts at defining precisely the relations between the rights of the individual, stemming from the German laws and EU legal provisions. The Constitutional Tribunal in Poland has also made its contribution to this debate by issuing, during the first period following Poland's membership in the EU, its judgments concerning voting rights to the European Parliament and the European Arrest Warrant as well as concerning more general relations between EU and Polish laws.

5. After Lisbon

1. With the amendment of the provisions of Article 6 of the TEU, human rights acquire a new, deeper perspective in the legal order of the EU.

First, Para 3 of the previous Article 6 is retained. Under this provision, reference is made to fundamental rights as guaranteed by the European Convention for the Protection of Human Rights and Fundamental Freedoms and as they result from the constitutional traditions common to the Member States, and such fundamental rights constitute general principles of the Union's law. However, this provision is expressed in a separate paragraph with a stronger stylistic appeal. The Union's old axiological construct of respecting such rights is replaced with a new clause whose nature is that of a basic norm and which indicates that these rights shall constitute general principles of the Union's law.

Second, the Charter of Fundamental Rights of the EU appears as a formal source, and of the same legal value as the TUE, of rights under protection. Third, there appears a proviso whereby the provisions of the Charter shall not extend the competencies of the Union as defined in the Treaties. Fourth, the object regulated by the Charter, i.e. protected rights, is defined here as the rights, freedoms, and principles—a set of three nouns which is quite a novelty. Fifth, Article 6 provides that the rules of interpretation of these rights, freedoms, and principles are in Title VII of the Charter and in the explanations referred to therein. Sixth, Para 2 of this provision provides that the Union shall accede to the European Convention for the Protection of Human Rights.

The provisions of Article 6 of the TEU should be correlated with the revised provisions of Article 2 of the same Treaty, in which the Union's values on which human rights protection is based are listed. These include human dignity, freedom, democracy, equality, the rule of law, nondiscrimination, tolerance, justice, and solidarity. Thus, axiological aspects of this protection have been reinforced.

2. The rules of interpretation indicated in the Charter remain unchanged with respect to the original wording of 2000. However, given a somewhat different status of the Charter on the grounds of the revised version of the TEU, they grant a new dimension to the provisions of the Convention as well as to the case law of the ECHR. This does not necessarily have to lead to collision-free relations as regards the implementation of both legal acts in the case law of the ECJ and the ECHR in cases of breaches of specific human rights (fundamental rights) as well as in formulating more general standards of protection.

Interestingly enough in the context of the legal role of the Charter and with respect to the Polish legal order, the provisions of Protocol No. 30 to the Charter do not coincide with the presence of the Charter in the judicial decisions of Polish courts, although this presence is marked with a negative observation as to its binding force in the Polish legal order. The Charter is referred to where the provisions used as grounds for the judicial decision make references to the Charter but also where there is no such direct connection, and relevant references to the Charter are made in view of the international context of such a decision. This largely refers to the case law of the Supreme Court as well as the Supreme Administrative Court and voivodeship (district) administrative courts.

3. The general dialogue concerning the case law also continues in the last period of integration evolution under analysis here. This largely pertains to the Federal Constitutional Court of Germany (FCC). One can safely say that this dialogue has brought about some new elements such as the first-in-history request of this court for a preliminary ruling of the CJEU. The actual matter was not directly connected to the protection of rights of the individual, but the object of the request concerned the scope of participation of Germany in integration and, by extension, also fundamental rights, which are also regulated by law. The Constitutional Tribunal of Poland has also marked its presence in this debate.

6. Between Pragmatism and Axiology

1. Characteristic features of the three periods of integration described above are superimposed on separate relations between pragmatic and axiological aspects of human rights protection as a component of the integrated legal order.

The biggest diversity of relations occurred in the period that ended in the Maastricht Treaty. During its first part, which spanned the 1960s and the first half of the 1970s, the idea of establishing a common market gave rise to a strong pragmatic orientation focused on greater convergence of market-related legislation (economic integration). Somewhat weak elements of human rights protection could manifest themselves mainly in the form of the case law of the ECJ, which 'reconciled' the scope of protection of these rights by way of a jurisprudential dialogue. Hence, in the second part of the period, which covers the second part of the 1970s and the 1980s, the system of protection in judicial decisions, while retaining the pragmatic caution in determining its standards, could refer to the idea of human rights as principles of law in the context of constitutional principles of law of Member States and law of the European Council as well as the principles of the Community legal order. Such a solution reinforced the axiological aspect of protection of human rights and, in consequence, this was manifested, albeit cautiously, in Treaty law in 1986.

Commencing from the 1990s, the axiological aspect of human rights protection became more visible, which stemmed from the essence of the Union as an integration institution combining economic and political goals. In terms of normative acts, this increasing visibility was connected with the regulations incorporated in the TEU and with the declaration that the Charter contained a set of protected rights. Equally important was the idea of constitutionalization, which reached beyond treating Treaty laws as the Union's constitutional law. This idea manifested itself clearly in the publication of a Constitution for Europe, and while this proved to be a failure in 2005, the trend was set for good. In this case, the axiological aspect was somewhat corrected by the pragmatic approach, which was sensitive to various degrees to which the scope of European integration was perceived. The case law of the ECJ in the period exemplifies the weighing of axiological and pragmatic aspects and an ever-increasing recourse to the regulations of the European Convention. This weighing of arguments on the grounds of the Convention, the Treaty law, and national standards in order to determine the scope of protection is perhaps best seen in the judgment concerning the Schmidberger case.

The last period brings a double weighing of arguments, in the sphere of decision-making and in the sphere of application. However, the highlights of the time include, undoubtedly, the granting of the status of binding law to the Charter and the effects when the Union accedes to the Convention at a future date as well as the case law of the ECHR. While the changes made to the Treaty law in Lisbon reinforce the axiology of human rights protection, the case law of the ECJ and of national courts seem to determine the scope of protection along the lines and proportions delineated before.

2. The analysis presented above leads to a conclusion that the first period proved to be fundamental in shaping the human rights protection system in the EU. Lack of normative regulations was not a hindrance; on the contrary, it fostered the activity of the ECJ in developing case law standards which reflected the spirit behind the Treaty law and Community positive law as well as the court's own jurisdiction, established independently but in the context of the jurisdiction of the ECHR and of national courts. These standards corresponded to the model of deepened integration, which entailed a more pragmatic approach to protection on the level of acquis communautaire and some 'axiological collisions' with the systems in place in the Member States (most visibly in the case of Germany). All this came to the fore on the level of case law, which was gradually corrected by the decisions passed by the ECJ under the influence of national constitutional tribunals. Thus, a strong interference on the part of legislators was somehow avoided, contributing to the reinforcement of the pragmatic aspect of human rights protection. Where adjustments were made, they referred to specific factual states which always allowed for making a given standard more particular, and to the context of an actual state of affairs (objectives, tasks, practice, and circumstances) of integration. The participation of national courts (passing judgments within the terms of reference of constitutional traditions of the Member States) in the 'juridical dialogue' underline the axiological aspect on the grounds of national standards. Nevertheless, they do so only in the context of corrections with respect to the case law of the ECJ.

These adjustments to the ECJ case law result increasingly from the fact that the ECJ takes into account the standards of the European Convention (including the judgments of the ECHR), which, although not deprived of the pragmatic component on the grounds of the integration within the framework of the Council of Europe, contain a bigger axiological load which, in turn, enters EU standards. A more sweeping change in this area is likely to occur when the Union accedes to the Convention. Having said that, this accession is also likely to cause 'reverse pragmatism' of human rights protection, since this will give rise to the disclosure of tensions between the ECHR and the ECJ. These two courts have somewhat different experience in passing judgments, and their respective judgments are differently grounded. Never mind the fact that following the Union's accession to the Convention, the role of the ECHR with respect to the case law of the ECJ will be largely controlling in nature.

The advantage of the pragmatic approach over the axiological is also seen in the current state of the EU legal order, despite the reinforcement of the axiological aspect in the form of granting the Charter a binding force and adopting new provisions of Article 6 in the TEU. EU law must always consider the pragmatic aspect more clearly than national regulations do. The only way to change the status quo is to 'constitutionalize' EU law. Consequently, human rights would be determined by a normative act (as already is the case in the United Europe), and relevant regulations would be incorporated into the constitutional principles of law (as already is the case), but, more importantly, these regulations would be incorporated into a lasting constitutional axiological system based on accepted and recognized values.

While the pragmatic approach to human rights protection increases the presence of its axiological component, a new tendency comes to the fore which treats human rights as principles of EU law. This is so where the status of principles results directly from the case law of the ECJ (such a state of affairs continued until 1992) and also where the status stems from Treaty law (the provisions of the TEC listed above) or, indirectly, through references made to the Convention or constitutional traditions common to the Member States (Article 6 of the TEU) or where such a status is granted by way of a special act addressing human rights protection (the CFR). The granting of binding force to such an act is also an element of the constitutionalization of EU law.

Each link between the system of protection of human rights in the EU and political aspects of integration on the one hand, and normative and case-law-related decisions of the Member States and of the Council of Europe on the other hand, will invariably increase the axiological component of this protection. A stronger axiological component of human rights on the EU level, which was brought about with the publication of the CFR in 2000, acquired after 2009 a normative dimension on a constitutional level. Thus, it became an element of the 'constitutionalization' of EU law in terms of its 'principalization'.

For the time being, the EU is a structure with a postmodernist and multicentric junction where various segments of human rights protection meet. This junction serves as a meeting point between economic and political stages of European integration, between the Union and its Member States, and between the EU and the Council of Europe as various types of integration, between principles and rules, between normative regulations and ECJ jurisdiction, and between the Luxemburg Court and national court jurisdictions. Finally, it is a junction between pragmatism and axiology of human rights protection.

Paweł Mazur, Ewa Nowak[*]
Adam Mickiewicz University, Poznań, Poland

How Moral Judgment Competence Fosters Discretionary Powers: A Dilemmatic Approach

Abstract: When applying law, and seeking for a just sentence, judges reason, judge and make decisions in an institutionally determined and limited discourse space. However, their personal moral judgment competences are strongly challenged in these proceedings. Each new case demands fresh non-routine situation- and context-related decisions, judgments, and sentences. In particular, establishing a just sentence in the face of complex issues such as dilemmatic situations, – so called "hard cases", or countertypes – can be specifically demanding for judges. Our chapter examines the condition of moral judgment competence in such challenging contexts, whilst referring to both the limits and the potential of discretionary power.

Key Words: discretionary power, moral judgment competence, dilemmatic situations, hard cases, countertypes

1. Moral judgment competence in law

Let us recall Lawrence Kohlberg's moral judgment competence, defined as the "capacity to make judgments and decisions which are moral, i.e., which are based on inner principles, and to act accordingly" (Kohlberg, 1964). And let us recall Immanuel Kant's "faculty of judgment", which subsumes a way of action (articulated in the so-called practical maxim) of the perpetrator under an appropriate general norm. The subsumption shows if the perpetrator acted in a legal or illegal way, and at the same time, the subsumption indicates whether the perpetrator should be sentenced or is innocent. However, the jury must not simply establish a sentence, but *a just sentence.* It is therefore not enough for a judge to be law-conforming in his reasoning whilst elaborating a sentence. He must know as much as possible about the opportunities of the examined action; he must adequately interpret general legal rules by following recommended interpretative schemes and rules; he must strive for a just sentence, and provide normative legitimation for it. This is why Gustav Radbruch once highlighted that laws have to aspire to justice. As Hans Kelsen in his book *The Pure Theory of Law* (1934) emphasized, laws are already

* ewanowak@bluewin.ch; pawelmn@amu.edu.pl.

done, but justice is still a task. This task challenges moral judgment competence in all professional judges. This competence and judicial ethics belong together[1].

Following Jabłoński and Kaczmarek, personal moral cognition and competence remain the ultimate protectors of justice when institutional guidelines for a judge's course of action fail. On the one hand, legal rules, courts of law, procedures and proceedings must be provided in order to eliminate the lack of normativity in a society (status iustitia vacuum, so to speak with Immanuel Kant). Courts must resolve conflicts to ensure citizens′ security, social peace, and justice. On the other hand, courts and judges take responsibility for protection of such values like security, peace, and justice (as well as responsibility for judgments resp. sentences including unjust and unhumanitarian ones; "Verantwortlichkeit für unmenschliche Richtersprüche"[2] in Radbruch). This requires a space for judges′ personal moral judgment, because imposing just solutions does not mean simply following rules and applying them to the performed action in an unreflected way. Thus judges' education focus on the "specific judicial skills"[3], as Leonidas Ralph Mecham underlines. Legal, ethical, and philosophical research belongs to their self-education. "Judges carefully supervise and review the work of their chambers staff. By using their staff to conduct legal research and other tasks that do not involve exercising discretionary powers of a judge, each judge is better able to perform the task of judging"[4].

The protective function of moral judgment competence manifests itself in looking and being responsible for the right answers in the face of everyday questions that judges confront. But moral judgment competence is also crucial "in exceptional circumstances (e.g. the Nuremberg Trials), where personal moral competencies allow judges to sentence and punish individuals of lawbreaking behaviour even though, in the light of the same legal code, the sentence would

---

1 In the Continental legal traditions, the judge's role "as part of the lawmaking process through interpreting or refining the law, setting new precedents etc.", is quite limited when comparing it with Anglo-Saxon traditions. A. Colby, L. Kohlberg et al., Eds., *The Measurement of Moral Judgment*, Vol. II, Standard Issue Scoring Manual. Cambridge Univ. Press, Cambridge 1987, p. 138.

2 G. Radbruch, *Gesetzliches Unrecht und übergesetzliches Recht*, in „Rechtsphilosophie", ed. by R. Dreier and S.L. Paulson, 2nd updated edition. C.F. Müller, Heidelberg 2002, p. 214.

3 L. R. Mecham, *The Federal Court System in the United States. An Introduction for Judges and Judicial Administrators in Other Countries*. Administrative Office of the U.S. Courts, Washington 2001, p. 21.

4 Ibidem.

be hard to justify"[5]. Allies´ legislation and Nuremberg Code after 1945, however, allowed to create a normative framework for such sentences, and punish several Nazi-offenders.

Moral judgment competencies were desperately lacking in Germany between 1933–1945, when many judges and juries imposed sentences and punishments by simply following the positive laws and orders. This was a total moral fiasco of judges´ moral competence and a debasement of their profession. Following Radbruch, in the light of intolerable degrees of injustice and *statutory lawlessness* ("des gesetzlichen Unrechts"[6]), laws "lose their legal character or legal validity (…) even if they are socially effective and legally enacted", as Fiałkowski, a Radbruch-expert, assumes. To Radbruch, in this context, "the law is not only wrong but possesses no legal quality"[7]. A "meta-justice", as Fijałkowski formulates it, is to expect from judges. Following Radbruch,

> „Kein Richter kann sich auf ein Gesetz berufen und die Rechtsprechung danach handhaben, auf ein Gesetz, das nicht nur ungerecht, das *verbrecherisch* ist. Wir berufen uns auf die *Menschenrechte* (…) Von diesen Erwägungen ausgehend, glaube ich, dass Richter angeklagt werden müssen, die mit den Geboten der Humanität unvereinbare Urteile gesprochen (…) haben"[8].

It was Fritz Bauer, a public prosecutor from Frankfurt/Main who accomplished Radbruch's formula outlined above. Bauer, a Radbruch-follower, initiated and conducted the most efficient NS-trials of the 20th century (the so-called Auschwitz Trials) in 1964–7. For him, judges and prosecutors must be aware of the following principle:

„Über jedem Gesetz und über jedem Befehl gibt es noch etwas, was unverwüstlich und unzerstörbar ist, die klare Erkenntnis, dass es gewisse Dinge gibt, die man auf Erden nicht tun kann. Einmal, weil sie in den zehn Geboten verboten sind, und dann natürlich, weil sie wider alle Religionen und Moral sind (…) Und

---

5 P. Jabłoński, P. Kaczmarek, *O trzech granicach władzy prawniczej* (English *On Three Limitations of Legal Power*), Archiwum Filozofii Prawa i Filozofii Społecznej, no 1/2013, Wolters Kluwer, Warsaw 2013, p. 107. First Gustav Radbruch, and later Fritz Bauer who initiated the Frankfurt trials in 1960s, explicitely appealed to public prosecutors and judges for seeking for normative criteria beyond the narrow framework of the existing law, see R. Steinke, *Fritz Bauer oder Auschwitz vor Gericht. Mit einem Vorwort von Andreas Voßkuhle.* Piper, München 2013.

6 G. Radbruch, *Gesetzliches Unrecht….*, pp. 211–219.

7 A. Fijałkowski, *Retroactive Laws and Notions of Retrospective Justice. Key Aspects of the German and Polish Experiences*, http;//sccanada.net.index

8 G. Radbruch, *Gesetzliches Unrecht…*, p. 214.

das … bedeutet ganz einfach das Gebot des passiven Widerstandes. Es war im ganzen deutschen Reich, im ganzen Mittelalter, in der Frühzeit und noch in der neueren Zeit ganz selbstverständlich (…) es gab Mut und Courage in jeder Richtung gegenüber dem äusseren Feind. Man hat aber völlig übersehen, dass die Zivilcourage – der Mut vor dem Feind im eigenen Volk – genauso groß, wahrscheinlich größer ist und nicht weniger verlangt wird. Man hat völlig übersehen, dass es ehrenhaft ist, dass es Pflicht ist, auch in seinem eigenen Staat für das Recht zu sorgen“[9] and to use own moral judgment competence – primarily if one is a representative of law.

Moral judgment competences that protect judges (and citizens) from a blind norm-conformism have a powerful tradition in legal philosophy. Two centuries ago Immanuel Kant wrote something revolutionary in his *Conflict of Faculties*, in which he proclaimed if political authorities are unable to judge what is right or wrong, all citizens are free to judge so. Hegel followed him in this line of reasoning in his *Philosophy of Law*. "We do not need the services of a shoemaker to find out if the shoe fits“[10], he said. To examine laws in such a *postconventional* (Kohlberg) way and to conclude "that the obedience to the law (or to conventional moral rules) is not always morally right,"[11] judges make use of their discretionary power.

2. Discretionary powers′ domain

"Discretionary power of the judge is seen as an essential part of a just legal system,“[12] Colby and Kohlberg assume. They defined discretionary power as a personal ability and, to anticipate Nussbaum and Sen's *capability approach*, as an objectively (constitutionally and politically) institutionalised space for practicising that ability. Here we clearly differentiate between personal-cognitive abilities on the one hand and the institutional capabilities on the other. A legal positivist, however, may say *stop*, *objection:* Being a representative of law, a judge should obey existing laws.

9 R. Steinke, *Fritz Bauer oder Auschwitz vor Gericht*, pp. 175–177.

10 In his book *Intuicja prawnicza. W stronę zewnętrznej integracji teorii prawa* (Engl. *Juridical Intuition. Integrating Legal Theory From Outside*), Difin, Warszawa 2012, T, Pietrzykowski emphasizes that contemporary jurists themselves admit that on the level of legal reasoning the "juridical reason" performs operations very similar to those performed by ethicists, engineers, or bakers.

11 Colby, Kohlberg et al., op. cit., Vol. I, p. 100.

12 Idem, p. 138.

But judges are sometimes confronted with "hard choices", "hard cases"[13], legal-moral dilemmas, and so-called "countertypes,"[14] as Ronald Dworkin, Jerzy Zajadło, and Władysław Wolter put it. Kohlberg's famous *Heinz's dilemma* concerns stealing an extremely expensive drug for Heinz's tumour-striken wife. On what should the judge reflect prior to determining whether Heinz is innocent or guilty of lawbreaking: should the judge protect laws and so protect the whole society by sending Heinz to jail, or should he "be able to put human life before the law"[15], and treat Heinz's behaviour as a highly moral act or an act of civil disobedience, which is justified by post-conventional and more universal principles than private property[16].

In fact, citizens may practice their morality or civil disobedience in the name of higher principles. Workers, for example, can strike against injust employment legislation; medical professionals may resort to the conscience clause to avoid a conflict between their personal principles and legal rules (but their principles and patients′ rights may fall in a radical conflict). By contrast, judges and juries cannot stop or avoid judgment making and sentence imposing. They must follow the state principle of legalism and legal safety, and their general, inalienable duty of proceeding in a reasonable period of time.[17] They work regardless of deficient evidence, of how difficult the case is, and of how many controversies or dilemmas it contains. They work within practical discourse[18] which enables the possiblity of solving them. Thus we note a difference between judicial and scientific knowledge[19]. Following Bartosz Wojciechowski,

> "Discretionary power appears wherever a judge [...] does not use the law in a strictly formalized, binding manner. In such a case the judge does not face the task of [...] simple, rational subsumption but is authorized to weigh a larger number of alternatives [...]. The

---

13 J. Zajadło, ed., *Fascynujące ścieżki filozofii prawa (*English *Fascinating paths of legal philosophy)*, Lexis Nexis, Warsaw 2008.

14 Reference to Montesquieu; the judge is the mouth-of-law, in *The Spirit of the Laws*, "which makes the King to be a speaking law, and the law a dumb king".

15 Colby and Kohlberg, op. cit., Vol. I, P, p. 253.

16 One may study all the pros and cons, reasonings and hesitations in Colby and Kohlberg's book *The Measurement of Moral Judgment.*

17 Time restrictions are involved here and society is quick to accuse juries of sluggishness.

18 "Insofar as the dogmatics is not limited to empiricism and logic but is utilized in the quite considerable normative dimension it concerns practical questions. As dogmatic discourse relates to practical questions it is a practical discourse. Being characterized by certain specificity, it remains a specific case of practical discourse", as Alexy puts it in his *Theorien der juristischen Argumentation*, p. 428.

19 M. Zieliński shows it further in his book *Poznanie sądowe a poznanie naukowe* (English *Judicial vs. academic knowing*), Wydawnictwo Naukowe UAM, Poznań 1979.

> judge may, in such a case, make the choice between two contradictory decisions, e.g. giving or withholding authorization [...]. The freedom of the subject who applies the law concerns the process of thinking, factual evaluation, the interpretation of legal norms, the determination of their relationships, and, sometimes, lawmaking"[20].

Hence, individual or collegial[21] application of law contributes to the sentence but the sentence is not derived directly from the laws. Even though judges are dependent on the law, they cannot be "passive cogs in the law machine" (German *Maschinen desselben*) but ought to be "organs of the law" (German *Organe des Gesetzes*). Their freedom does not mean 'arbitrariness'. It should be, at the same time, independent of economic and ideological interests, and other political powers. Looking for instances that would protect the Constitution and the discretionary power from such outside influences, Hans Kelsen proposed the constitutional tribunal. However, each such instance would require supervision by a higher instance and so ad infinitum. As external protection fails, the only guarantee of autonomous discretionary power seems to be strengthening internal moral judgment competence in judges.

A strong ability of moral judgment making is highly welcomed when facing *hard choices in light of laws whose letter requires intepretation and correction.* Zajadło is right when stating, it "does not [...] make sense when applied to simple, well-defined, undisputable cases"[22]. "That becomes apparent especially when some unreasonable law is to be applied"[23], Alexy adds. So the letter of the law cannot be followed blindly. It engages both a judge's normative cognition and his moral judgment competence. As the German researcher clarifies:

> "the only task of a judge who imposes a sentence on the basis of his independent discretionary power... is to aim at a just and right sentence [...]. In certain situations a judge is free in the process of choosing from among the legal means at his disposal [...] but it must be remembered that the rules of a democratic state... as well as the rules of legal discourse

20 B. Wojciechowski, *Model zakresu swobody interpretacyjnej prawa administracyjnego,* in R. Hauser, Z. Niewiadomski, & A. Wróbel, eds., "Wykładnia w prawie administracyjnym", CH Beck, Warsaw 2012, pp. 469–470.

21 Thorsten Berndt speaks about "self-importance" as a judicial type contrasting with the "collegial" one and associates that distinction with the scope of not only competence but also responsibility, see his *Richterbilder. Dimensionen richterlicher Selbsttypisierungen*, VS Research, Dissertationen der Universität Konstanz, Konstanz 2009, p. 89.

22 J. Zajadło, 2008, p. 10.

23 R. Alexy, op. cit., p. 430.

> which ought to be respected by a judge preparing a sentence constitute an effective limitation of the judge's actions. The realm of justice [...] demands correct use of law".[24]

But the realm of justice says nothing about solving dilemmatic issues. We only know that a judge cannot become a "moralist." That is what happened to *Judge Steinberg,* as we will examine in the next chapter. In Zajadło's words:

> "if legal discourse was not created in a direct relationship with the existing law (that is possible, after all), then it would simply become moral discourse. Therefore, to be valid and effective, legal discourse must be of dogmatic character".[25]

However, a judge can make a mistake if she uses her independent discretionary power only to follow existing laws. "Legal sentences do not aspire to the absolute rightness but only to rightness limited by the conditions of the current legal order. They are right when they can be rationally justified within the framework of law, prejudication, and dogmatics"[26], as Robert Alexy assumes. Discretionary power is thus not sufficient but only a necessary condition for making just sentences. Following Gustav Radbruch, making justice requires personal awareness of "how problematic law and justice can be"[27] and the "sense of rightness" that begins with intuition and empathy, and finishes with cognitive, conscious, rational, discoursive and proceduralized operations. "Of all of the virtues, justice can least rely on intuition, feeling, and the naïve, unlearned consciuousness (...) Justice needs abstraction of two kinds: it has to empathize with the situation of others and to generalize it. The generalization requires not only the sense of fairness but also the capacity to make judgments. That capacity is difficult to develop without exercise"[28], i.e., without learning-by-doing as James Dewey expresses it.

3. Discretionary power confronted with legal-moral dilemmas

"The most complex *hard cases* encountered by a lawyer in his practice usually concern the conflict of law with morality", Zajadło assumes. This researcher proposed

---

24 B. Wojciechowski, op. cit., pp. 470–472.

25 J. Zajadło, 2008, pp. 10–11.

26 R. Alexy, op. cit., p. 430.

27 G. Radbruch, *Politische Schriften aus der Weimarer Zeit*, vol. II, C.F. Müller, Heidelberg 1993, p. 191.

28 Ibidem, p. 264. See also E. Nowak and G. Lind, *Mis-Educative Martial Law – The Fate of Free Discourse and the Moral Judgment Competence of Polish University Students from 1977 to 1983.* In B. Wojciechowski, M. Zirk-Sadowski, and M.J. Golecki, Eds., *between Complexity of Law and Lack of Order.* Adam Marszałek, Toruń-Beijing 2009, pp. 145–165.

three main types of such dilemmas. The first type adresses new and yet unsolved dilemmas generated by the scientific-technical boom, social changes, etc. The second type adresses the classical, well-known dilemmas in which the pros and cons have been virtually exhausted but people still argue about: abortion, euthanasia, death penalty, etc. The third type adresses the dilemmas which have been solved, in the realms of law and morality, a long time ago and which, as it seems, need not be re-assessed, e.g., the bans on slavery, torture and inhuman, degrading treatment.[29]

Sometimes, the old dilemmas return in a new and drastic scenery. They are faced by somewhat confused juries that dispose of laws which they are not ready to solve. Those dilemmas appear in the courts of both young democracies with their transitive justice and in states with long democratic traditions, human rights declarations, basic rights etc. The latter are clever insofar that they subcontract the operation of prisons for terrorists to the former. As regards the torture interrogation of ticking-bomb terrorists and kidnappers, the issues are some of the "most complex, hard cases encountered by lawyers in their practice", as noted by Zajadło. The author examines that complexity in four points;

> "1) in the legal science, and especially in the philosophy of law, the matter is the subject of the most widespread and heated discussions;
> 2) it focalizes virtually all [...] dimensions of law: its creation, application, interpretation, validation, and observation;
> 3) it concerns a principle which was deemed self-evident as late as yesterday;
> 4) if the function of law is, first and foremost, to serve humanity then the highest value, the inborn dignity of a human being, is put on the scales of the debate"[30].

Furthermore, Zajadło identifies the origins of the most actual and dramatic legal-moral dilemmas worldwide. They are as follows:

1. the responsibility to protect and rebuild[31] through "the use of force by a state or a group of states beyond the borders of that state, in order to halt mass and serious violations of human rights (...) without the state consent of the state"[32] in the face of a "supreme humanitarian emergency"[33];
2. preventive war as a phenomenon morally distinguished from the so-called *justa causa*, i.e. a just war which does not entail a sense of a dilemma. Nowadays,

29 Zajadło, *Po co prawnikom filozofia prawa* (English *For What Reasons Need Lawyers Legal Philosophy*), Oficyna wydawnicza Wolters Kluwer, Warsaw 2008, p.16.

30 Ibidem.

31 Ibidem, p.65.

32 Ibidem, p.69.

33 Ibidem, p.70.

preventive wars are ruled by supranational laws. Such wars had evoked moral controversies of past moral thinkers (Hugo Griotius, Emer de Vattel) long before categories such as human rights, genocide and homicide were defined.
3. the institution of *cultural defense* with respect to "killings, the treatment of children, drug use, the attitude toward animals, the institution of marriage, specific clothes, the treatment of the deceased"[34], suicide, honor killings, etc.
4. the institution of *respondeat superior*, i.e. the relationship of superiority and subjectedness from which the authoritatively justified duty to abide by an order or a rule is derived[35] (e.g., killing under order from a commander in the military[36]; in Catholic church the example of Polish priest Wojciech Lemański who practices a kind of "priestly disobedience"; and, finally, the problem the authors of this paper are interested in, i.e.,
5. the torture interrogation of ticking-bomb terrorists[37], a method included in the arsenal of "war on terror"[38].

4. The New Actuality of Judge Steinberg's Dilemma

The torture interrogation is illustrated by *Judge Steinberg's dilemma*, and proves to be highly stimulating material during KMDD sessions. It contains a legal-moral dilemma although quite different in nature from *Heinz' dilemma*. Judge Steinberg is the representative of a legal system. He chose a solution which was, in his view, morally right enough to violate the law which forbids torture and, at the same time, to violate the human right concerning freedom from suffering. Steinberg passed his decision "without legal grounds"[39] as well as against the existing law,

34 Ibidem, p.87.

35 Ibidem, p.92.

36 "In the words of the renown British constitutional judge Albert V. Dicey, in such a situation a soldier faces a weird choice: either to be shot for the refusal of following an order, on the basis of a verdict of a military court, or to be hanged for following the order, on the basis of a verdict of a common court", Zajadło, ibidem, p.93.

37 See W. Brugger, *Darf der Staat ausnahmsweise foltern?* In *Liberalismus, Pluralismus, Kommunitarismus. Studien zur Legitimation des Grundgesetzes*, ed. W. Brugger, Nomos Verlag, Baden-Baden 1999, pp.411–439; B. Wojciechowski, *Rozstrzyganie tzw. trudnych przypadków poprzez odwołanie się do odpowiedzialności moralnej* (English *Sentence Issuing in the So-Called Hard Cases by Referring to the Moral Responsibility*), Studia Prawno-Ekonomiczne 2004, Vol. LXX; R. Dworkin, *Taking Rights Seriously; Law's Empire.*

38 It ought to be remembered, though, that contemporary terrorism is not well defined, including its legal definitions

39 J. Zajadło, *Po co prawnikom filozofia prawa*, op. cit., p.105.

even though he carried it out in good faith, *bona fide*[40]. For a moment, Steinberg suspended the principle of legalism in the prediction that the testimonies forced from the ticking-bomb terrorist will save many innocent people's lives. He weighed that argument, and possibly several other reasons, against law-intrinsic reasons, such as the value of a single life and the dignity of all.

Steinberg's decision was passed hurriedly, on the basis of deficient evidence; security services only had proof that the captured woman was a member of a terrorist network. He made his decision probably alone, whereas comprehensive, collegial discourse might have led to a different conclusion[41]. Judges who transgress the law also go beyond the boundaries of their discretionary power. Meanwhile, an enhanced moral judgment competence could enhance both discretionary power and autonomy without perverting the law that, in this case, seems to be a *just law.*

Utilitarians would say that decision making in the face of dilemmas means an impersonal, neutral choice between greater and lesser evil, and immediately transpose the scale of the evil onto its amount. From the deontological viewpoint, however, the moral quality of an action cannot be expressed in quantitative terms. As Thomas Nagel shows,

> "On a deontological view, the five people I could save by killing the one cannot appeal to me for their lives, against my refusal to save them/they may appeal against *their* killers… but not against me…/ Such a constraint expresses the direct appeal to the point of view of the agent from the point of view of the person on whom he is acting. It operates through that relation. The victim feels outrage when he or she is deliberately harmed even for the greater good of others, not simply because of the quantity of the harm but because of the assault on his value of having my actions guided by his evil. What I do is immediately directed against his good; it doesn't just in fact harm him"[42].

Not everyone would agree with Nagel's deontological argument. Dilemmatic issues as such are not equally evident to each individual. As emphasized by Georg Lind, a dilemma is in the eyes of the beholder. However, efficient moral judgment competence does not consist in reducing or simplifying a complex dilemmatic issue to one option. Rather it consists in translating it into dilemmatic thinking and making the most justified decisions based on principles and norms. Neither does moral judgment competence involve interpreting legal understatement – or producing a 'precedence' – so as to allow an action which may no longer be

40 Ibidem, p. 67.

41 Cf. ibidem, when the author talks about a jury which gives up *prima facie* decision-making on behalf of "deeper philosophical and legal reflection," p. 104.

42 T. Nagel, *Agent-Relativity and Deontology*, in S. Darwall, ed., "Deontology", Blackwell 2003, p. 110.

called "torture interrogation" but "coercive interrogation"[43], as it increasingly turns into "outsourcing torture,"[44] ordering it to be done abroad for interested states[45]. Zajadło explains that one of the reasons for the representative situation in Guantanamo was an overinterpretation of the American federal *Torture Statute*, including the McCain Amendment, and, further, a semantic manipulation.

We assume that a judge can only be protected against the temptation of such an overinterpretation and manipulation by his personal moral judgment competence. When senator MacCain, an adamant opponent of torture and cruel, degrading treatment, was asked

> "what would you do if you caught a prisoner who probably knows where an atom bomb was placed in New York? The health and life of one terrorist against the life and health of a few million Americans? Are no holds barred in a case like that? McCain admits that in such a case, under the pressure of time, torturing the prisoner might be the only choice. However, that does not mean it should be legal" (Zajadło 2008).

Senator McCain's personal moral judgment competence is voiced here. It indicates that only justifiable rules can be make public because public reason i.e. the reasonable citizens are able to recognize if they are justified or not. Politicians and rulers cannot delude citizens; but they can disguise exceptions to every rule. Individuals, although they are conscious of moral or legal principles, may occasionally deviate from them. Being aware of a morally problematic status, they try to cover up or gloss over this fact[46]. In sum, McCain seems to be aware that torture and coercive interrogation are immoral, so they are illegal too (or, following Kant, they are unfit as laws – German: *sie sind untauglich als Gesetze*)[47].

The contemporary legal practice in courts differs significantly from the well-known Montesquieu's model of a judge as the "mouth of law." The role of juries is not to apply a legal norm to a given state of affairs automatically. Nowadays, juries are independent in imposing sentences. The lawmakers have allowed them free space for decision making. That independence, known as discretionary power,

---

43 J. Zajadło, *Po co prawnikom filozofia prawa*, Chapter 3.

44 Ibidem.

45 The so-called *torture by proxy*, as Zajadło characterises it. The reality is just "cruel, inhuman, and degrading treatment", he continues, ibidem.

46 I. Kant, *Religion within the Limits of Bare Reason*, trans. by J. Bennett, 2010–2015, http://www.earlymoderntexts.com/pdfs/kant1793part1.pdf

47 "But even the most limited man is capable of being struck by respect for an action conforming to duty—a respect that is greater the more he isolates it in thought from self-interested incentives that might influence the maxim of conduct", ibidem, p. 25.

is related to power over the addressing of legal rules[48]. It appears to be necessary and has its source in the semantic openness of normative acts, in the dogmatic advancement of many legal institutions, and in the complexity of social reality. Moreover, it is ineluctable: we cannot return to the relatively simple world based on common law and casuistic lawmaking aimed at describing each possible situation and prescribing each possible behavior.

A significant element of the independent discretionary power is moral evaluation, moral judgment and moral decision competence. Importantly, moral judgments, as will be demonstrated below, *determine criminal responsibility.* The criminal code represents an example of the importance of judges' moral judgments in the practice of law. Its functions are to protect the most precious social goods and do justice when damage is done[49]. Thus, the criminal code is strongly interrelated with morality. Still, that interrelation is not of a validating kind. A rational lawmaker and, consequently, also a jury which abides by the law, only include in their operational field a certain group of behaviours, i.e., those which violate the norms regulating certain legal goods.

A comprehensive evaluation of a crime involves the authorization of a jury to make value judgments. The lawmaker's intention, then, is to allow the jury to be a sentence-making organ of independent judgment which is based on the set of legal and, at the same time, just principles, so that a just sentence might be elaborated.

5. Discretionary power confronted with *countertypes*

An interesting example of the challenges which face judges' independence are the so-called "countertypes". The term was introduced into the Polish legal language by Władysław Wolter in 1965. It refers to a circumstance which excludes the illegality of an action[50]. Such a case happens when the perpetrator's action has the characteristics of a crime but the action is not deemed to be a crime on account of special circumstances. A countertype, then, involves a conflict of legal goods. The conflict cannot be solved by a lawmaker. It must be identified and solved by a jury.

We speak of a countertype when all the following conditions are fulfilled:

---

48 A. Kozak, *O pojęciu władzy dyskrecjonalnej* (English: *On the Notion of Discretionary Power*), in L. Leszczyński, ed., "Zmiany społeczne a zmiany w prawie. Aksjologia, konstytucja, integracja europejska", Wydawnictwo UMCS, Lublin 1999, p. 249.

49 Ł. Pohl, *Prawo karne. Część ogólna* (English *Penal law. General Chapter*). Lexis Nexis, Warsaw 2013, pp. 30–31.

50 W. Wolter, *Funkcja błędu w prawie karnym* (English *Mistake's Role Within Penal Law*), PWN, Warsaw 1965, p. 6.

1. there is a conflict of at least two goods protected by law,
2. the perpetrator is conscious of an objective need to sacrifice one of the conflicting, legally protected goods, for the benefit of the other one,
3. the sacrifice of a legally protected good in the conditions of objective necessity is socially profitable[51].

Such situations show that there are no legal goods subject to absolute protection. The jury must deliberate, rank, decide, and indicate to which of the conflicting goods it ascribes primacy. That seems to be a very demanding task, among others, because in a countertype situation a given legal good has the same value as in a non-contrariantype situation. The judges must, then, decide themselves if sacrificing one legal good for the other is beneficial to the society. Importantly, not all solutions beneficial for the society are accepted by it[52]. Solving a countertype situation is more complex than simply stating that a perpetrator has violated a prohibition resulting from a sanctioned norm and punishing the perpetrator for that violation.

An interesting case of a countertype is a *necessity situation*. It involves sacrificing one legal good for the benefit of another that is more valuable, so as to deflect an immediate threat to the perpetrator, when the danger could not be avoided (art. 26, section 1, criminal code of Republic Poland). In the German legal system *necessity* is rarely applied, i.e., only when 1. No guilt can be ascribed to the perpetrator, and 2. The perpetrator acts in order to deflect a danger to him- or herself, his or her life, health, or freedom, or a danger to his closest fellows.

A countertype both results from moral dilemmas and implies them. *Heinz' dilemma* developed by Lawrence Kohlberg should on such accounts match the countertype. On the contrary, *Judge Steinberg's dilemma* developed by Georg Lind[53] does not. Let us illustrate this with another example from the literature. A mountain guide led a group of climbers from a dangerous situation to a safe place. During the rescue operation, one of the climbers got stuck on the ladder and refused to go further. The guide's persuasion skills were futile. The guide then ordered the climber to be thrown off the ladder so that the remaining climbers could reach safety.

---

51 Ł. Pohl, ibidem, p. 239.

52 Ł. Pohl, *Prawo karne* (English *Penal law*), in A. Zoll, ed., *Okoliczności wyłączające bezprawność czynu*, Wydawnictwo Prawnicze, Warsaw 1982, p. 103.

53 See G. Lind, *Moral ist lehrbar* (English *Morality can be taught*), Oldenbourg, Munich 2009.

In the case described above, the jury declared the guide innocent[54]. Solving such serious, non-trivial problems demands rational, critical thinking along the lines of Popper's criticism. In such situations critical moral reflection allows, most importantly, to recognize a conflict of legal goods, solve it, and justify the solution. But moral judgment competence is necessary here because in the face of the moral conflict a choice must be made.Moral judgment, though, ought not to be exhausted by intuitions and moral emotions alone. Still, it would be naïve to ignore their role in the process of cognitive construction, understanding, and decision making when faced with dilemmatic and sometimes dramatic issues. Solving such difficult conflicts requires mature moral reasoning and judgment competence. A sentence is a product of many cognitive operations, of a certain mental effort. It is an ideal proof for the fact that combining reasoning and activities addressed by Tadeusz Kotarbiński is possible:

> "The antithesis of 'action' and 'reflection' seems to be clichéd. Some people exalt the thinker type over the activist, seeing the former as essentially superior, and holding vita contemplativa in the highest regard. Others believe that a man of actions towers over the throughly impractical, useless theoretician. Be that as it may, in both cases reflection and action are considered as somehow opposite. In reality, though, the relationship is similar as in the case of action and word. It is true that to think about an action is not exactly the same as to do what one is thinking about. At best, it is a kind of preparation for the activity. If someone stops at only thinking about projects and does not realize them, it is hard to call him a perpetrator of any part of the projects. Still, thinking itself is a kind of activity. Is it not, sometimes, work? Often it is very hard work… Does it not require effort? Does it not involve, constantly and necessarily, the tension of muscles, caused by the deliberate focusing of the mind? Do we not achieve, by way of deliberation, certain effects, results, works in the form of solutions to problems?"[55]

It is highly problematic for the jury which does not have at its disposal clear criteria of choice or any axiological basement. A judge who solves *dilemmas* and *countertypes* might refer to the lawmaker's system of values. Still, that requires dealing with a rational and morally conscious lawmaker, with an axiologically perfect subject who created the laws guided by the best system of values. The constitution allows the reading of axiological preferences declared by a lawmaker but it can only play an auxiliary role in the choice of the criteria which could aid a judge in his judgment- and choice making. However, even if we assume the

54 J. Lachowski, *Stan wyższej konieczności* (English *Higher necessity state*), C.H. Beck, Warsaw 2006, p.74.

55 T. Kotarbiński, *Czyn. Wybór pism* (English *Action. Selected Writings*). Vol. I, "Myśli o działaniu", PWN, Warsaw 1957, pp.424–425.

existence of an axiologically perfect (or at least defined and consequent) lawmaker, judges will also take into account their own axiological preferences. After all, key cognitive operations, especially evaluations and judgments, occur in their minds.

This raises the question of which limitations this kind of power encounters. Firstly, it should be noted that moral thinking is included in the formal and routine practice of jurisprudence. The essence of moral thinking is the internal dialogue in my "I"[56], in my Self. Hannah Arendt described the condition of a thinker as solitary. This means, there is an inner personal "inclination (…) to think (…), to do more with his intellectual abilities, his brain power"[57] regardless of striving for cognition and decision making. The one thinking is a kind of two-in-one (along with this "I"). Thinking interrupts any other activity. As Arendt noted, "For it is true that the moment we start thinking on no matter what issue we stop everything else, and this everything else, again whatever it may happen to be, interrupts the thinking process; it is as though we moved into a different world"[58]. The analytically oriented theory of law stresses, moreover, that thinking is a process, and therefore it takes place in some period of time[59]. Moral judgements may be of different validity[60], but some of them indicate that there are reasons and reasonings that are sufficient to convince any rational person[61].

Certain institutional requirements may constrict (or collide against) judges' moral thinking and judgment making in their professional practice. Basic and increasingly enforced standards of hearing the case within a reasonable time are to be mentioned here. These are formulated against the courts, regardless of their duties schedule. Moral reflection is thus taken under the pressure of time, resulting from arbitrarily established time limits. What is more, the court, being bound to settle the case, may not avoid the explicit formulation of moral judgment, even if the thinking process was full of dilemmas and doubts. Therefore, moral thinking and judgment making take place in environments that reward efficiency and haste. This implies transformation of many jurisprudence activities into routined and automatic ones. In all practical activities, automatism seems to be necessary because it economises

56 H. Arendt, *Responsibility and judgment*. Schocken Books, NY 2003, p. 165.

57 Ibidem, p. 163.

58 Ibidem, p. 195.

59 W. Patryas, *Uznawanie zdań*,(English *Recognizing Assessments*), PWN, Warsaw – Poznań 1987, p. 15.

60 For example, they may have or not have a justifying power. One of the authors analysed this problem in E. Nowak, *Experimental* Ethics, Chapter Normative *Dissonance vs. the Order of Argumentation*. LIT, Berlin – Münster 2013, pp. 35–56.

61 R. M. Hare, *Freedom and Reason*. Oxford Univ. Press, Oxford 1965, p. 86.

psychological and operational energy, in particular when judges are confronted with numerous hard cases; which they in fact are. However, it also brings negative consequences, particularly for autonomous thinking. These may include, for instance, intuitively guided, inadequately reflected, and justified decision making[62].

Judges, like other legal professionals, operate in inside-institution space, which imposes certain limitations. Artur Kozak drew attention to the problem of practitioners' embarrassment because of various professional customs. It manifests itself in unconciously developed habits, i.d., cognitive operations which repeat routinely[63]. Kozak expressed a fairly radical position, namely

"Regularities of lawyers' behaviour in the process of applying the law can be reconstructed from the outside as those subject to the rules of conduct, and therefore covered by the sphere of freedom and hence of the imperative nature. However, from the internal perspective, a lawyer often does not 'make alternative course(s) of action present'. The nature of the world in which he lives gives him only one possible action. A lawyer deciding has the same choice as the falling man; nature of the world gives him only one possible direction of movement."[64]

It seems that the author assessed legal practice too harshly. However, this is evident in the practice of the most independent judicial levels, such as apellate courts. A legal practitioner, duplicating patterns of behaviour, may tend to avoid individual moral reflection, judgment making, and personal responsibility which follows such an engagement. Finally they will strive for a solution (sentence, justification of sentence etc.) in a more superficial way.

The autonomy of moral thinking is also limited by one of the core values of law: legal certainty. In Radbruch's triad of legal values, security is rated top but it strongly relates to justice. Legal security, in this case, means the uniformity of decisions of the courts. However, this has consequences for judges' judgmental freedom. Law unification and the uniformity of decisions imposes, and sometimes shapes, routine or conformist attitudes among judges[65].

---

62 T. Szczurkiewicz, *Znaczenie teorii dla praktyki*, (English *The Meaning of Theory in the Practice*). In "Studia Socjologiczne", PWN, Warsaw 1968, p.23. An exemplification is the so-calles *bench trial* as a "trial by a judge without a jury in which a judge decides which party prevails", in Mecham, *The Federal Court System*, p.50.

63 A. Kozak, *Granice prawniczej władzy dyskrecjonalnej* (English *Legal Limits of Discretionary Authority*), Kolonia Limited, Wrocław 2002, p.157.

64 Ibidem, p.5.

65 J. Leszczyński, *Legitymizacja instytucji ujednolicających orzecznictwo sądowe* (English *Legitimizing institutions of the unification of judicial decisions*), in S. Waltoś, ed.,

Another factor that actually restricts selection from a variety of solutions of moral problems is the level of difficulty in the proper use of certain institutions of criminal law that require moral judgments. Their use requires an appropriate theoretical base. For example, a state of greater necessity is based on a quite intellectually sophisticated theoretical foundations. The criteria to be taken into account when balancing rights are disputed and, what is more, they have diverse philosophical justifications, such as Kant's autonomy of the individual, or Bentham's utilitarianism[66]. Determining whether there is a higher state of necessity in a given case cannot therefore be based only on intuition, hidden behind categorical statements. It should be based on solid theoretical foundations, which in practice, are underestimated or even ignored. This impacts the narrow choice of possible solutions to the problem, and thus it effectively reduces the freedom granted to the courts[67].

6. The erosion of judge's independent discretionary power in Poland

Judges' discretionary power may, however, clash with certain legal values, such as legal certainty, consisting in the predictability of proceeding and sentence making. The independent judgments made by judges may raise fears because the boundaries of independence are, after all, set by legal rules and not moral principles or judges' personal judgments. Do we have reason to be worried?

The Polish Ministry of Justice has announced a reform of criminal courts that ought to free judges from the supplementation and verification of evidence, i.e., the knowledge about the evaluated actions. Until now, Polish judges were obliged not only to impose sentences but also to supplement the evidence by, for example, interviewing witnesses. They often obtained minumum information and circumstantial evidence from the public prosecutor's office and expert witnesses. From 2015 they shall no longer be obliged to do that – their only task should be to arbitrarily evaluate the evidence presented by the parties of the court process. The public prosecutor and the attorney will advocate or, rather, fight for a guilty or innocent verdict, according to the principle of contradiction. In the new, reformed system a judge

"Uniformity of decisions in criminal matters". Zakamycze Publishing, Warsaw 1998, pp. 37–39.

66 See Z. Jędrzejewski, *Okoliczności wyłączające bezprawność czynu w prawie karnym* (English *Opportunities that exclude illegality in criminal law*). In "The science of a crime Exclusion and limitation of liability". C.H. Beck Publishing, Warsaw 2013, pp. 94–129.

67 R. Legutko, *Traktat o wolności* (English *The Treaty on Freedom*). Słowo, Obraz, Terytoria, Gdańsk 2007, p. 86.

> "could not, as a matter of fact, do anything on his own initiative. Nor could he get involved in determining the truth if there were a risk of stark injustice due to the evident awkwardness of one of the parties. In the end, a few days ago an official amendment by the Ministry was submitted to the Parliament. According to the amendment, a judge only can, ex officio, request the opinions of expert witnesses and the criminal records, nothing more"[68].

Judges´ reduced institutional competences cannot support their personal competences such as a competence for making judgments. Comparing the former with magistrate judges´ duties in the U.S. courts system[69], one may understand controversies growing among judges in Poland because of that new, radical attempt at limiting discretionary power and judicial independence – and that is, perhaps, what Polish society and the international community ought to fear.

---

68 V. Krasnowska, *Sąd ostateczny* (English *The Day of Judgment*), Polityka no 28 (2966), 9.07.2014.

69 Following Mecham, magistrate judges´ duties "fall into four general categories: (1) conducting most of the initial proceedings in criminal cases (including search and arrest warrants, detention hearings, probable cause hearings, and appointment of attorneys); (2) trial of most criminal misdemeanor cases; (3) conductinga wide variety of other proceedings referred to them by district judges (including deciding motions, reviewing petitions filed by prisoners, and conducting pretrial and settlement conferences); and (4) trial of civil cases, if the parties consent", in Mecham, *The Federal Court System*, p.47.

Gülriz Uygur[**]
Ankara University, Turkey

The Job of the Judge in the Context of Silenced People: The Opuz Case[*]

Abstract: In this article, silence is regarded as one of the requirements of attention. In this respect, silence is considered as a way of communication. Here, rhetorical listening is important and is used many ways. When connected with attention, rhetorical listening is regarded as openness or open-mindedness. The article discusses this form of listening in the context of the job of the judge. The Opuz case reflects how the epistemic injustice as silencing forms can cause gross human rights violations.

Key Words: the oppressed groups, silence and listening, seeing the injustice, the role of the judge, Miranda Fricker

I. Introduction

What is the meaning of silence? In fact there are multiple meanings of silence, since, as Miranda Fricker rightly stated, there are different kinds of silence. Fricker says that the concept of silence "*has two aspects—a positive and a negative. In the negative aspect, there is the imposed silence of those who are in some way prevented from making their voices heard. This kind of silence is normally affected by way of an injustice. In the positive aspect, there is the active, attentive silence of those who are listening, perhaps trying to make out a voice that is seldom heard. This kind of silence belongs with a moral attitude of attention to others—an openness to who they are and what they have to say*"[1]. Following Fricker, I will discuss these two aspects of silence, namely positive and negative, in this paper. The negative aspect is connected with the oppressed groups or people which I mention here as silenced people. The positive aspect is connected with the job of the judge.

---

* The author is thankful to Grace M. Frank for constructive comments and for the English editing.

** School of Law.

1 Miranda Fricker," Silence and Institutional Prejudice", *Out From the Shadows: Analytical Feminist Contributions to Traditional Philosophy*, eds. Sharon Crasnow and Anita Superson (OUP 2013) http://www.shef.ac.uk/polopoly_fs/1.152331!/file/SilenceInstPrej.pdf (01.09.2014) p.1.

Connected with the job of the judge, it is possible to regard silence with listening. In this meaning, far from the traditional meaning, silence is not equated with the absent. In fact, Ancient Egyptian and Phythagorean ideas reflect the positive effects of silence and the value of silence and listening. These ideas regard silence and listening as a way of learning[2]. In this meaning, silence and listening are also regarded as a way for the preparation of speaking. In this article, silence is regarded as one of the requirements of attention. In this respect, silence is considered as a way of communication. Here, rhetorical listening is important and is used many ways. Krista Ratcliffe regards it "*as a trope for interpretive invention and as a code of cross-cultural conduct. Defined generally as a trope for interpretive invention, rhetorical listening signifies a stance of openness that a person may choose to assume in relation to any person, text, or culture. Defined more particularly as a code of cross-cultural conduct, rhetorical listening signifies a stance of openness that a person may choose to assume in cross-cultural exchanges.*"[3]. In this article, connected with attention, rhetorical listening is regarded as openness or open-mindedness, and I try to explain this form of listening in the context of the job of the judge.

Conversely, the negative effects of silence reflect the power of speaking. Silence, in this sense, is used as a means of oppression or domination of a people[4] and is equated with powerlessness. In order to gain power, an individual or a group who is silenced "*must activate voice in order to resist and transform the conditions of their oppression*"[5]. But this meaning does not exclude silence as a way of communication. Namely, to have a voice does not necessarily require speech. It requires that one "*possess both the opportunity to speak and the respect to be heard*"[6]. In this respect, to hear the voices of silenced persons does not only require for them to have the opportunity to speak, but also other ways of communication which include silence.

In this article, when I talk about silenced groups, I use silence as a means of oppression. This meaning of silence is generally understood from an ideological

---

2 Cherly Glenn-Krista Ratcliffe, "Introduction", *Silence and Listening as Rhetorical Arts*, Eds.C.Glenn-K.Ratciffe, Southern Illinois University Press, Carbondale 2011, p.1.

3 Krista Ratcliffe, *Rhetorical Listening:Identification, Gender, Whiteness*, Southern Illinois University Press Carbondale 2006, p.1.

4 Glenn-Ratciffe, p.2.

5 Sheena Malhotra-Aimee Carillo Rowe, "Reflections on Silence", *Silence, Feminism, Power: Reflections at the Edges of Sound*, Eds. S. Malhotra-A.C.Rowe, Macmillan Publisher, Hampshire 2013, p.1.

6 Lana F.Rakow-Laura A. Wackwitz, *Feminist Communication Theory: Selections in Context*, Sage Publication, London 2004, p.9.

perspective[7]. I will, however, try to discuss this meaning of silence as an epistemological problem. Since epistemologists need general conditions of knowledge which are universal and have a certainty, silence is not generally an effective condition. Rather, a person who does not have the power of speech is regarded a suspect person[8]. However, silenced people are not regarded as having the capacity to inform, to be a knower. But they have that capacity, if they are heard. For example, the sex of the knower is epistemologically important in the legal practices and, as I state below, it causes epistemic injustice. In fact, Lorraine Code asked "*is the sex of the knower epistemologically significant?*" in 1981[9]. **In this article, moving from Fricker**, I claim that the sex of the knower, if s/he belongs to silenced groups, is epistemologically significant, at least in legal practices.

Silenced people or groups may be defined as traditionally oppressed groups, such as women. And in these groups, silence causes human rights violations. In fact, people who have been silenced face gross human rights violations. Human rights law should protect silenced groups. This law should give voice to human suffering and make it visible[10]. *The problem is that* "the voices that should be empowered by human rights law are often disregarded by human rights law and frequently even further silenced by it"[11]. *It is possible even to say that critical legal theorists and other scholars embrace theories which give place to silenced groups, like feminism*[12]. *Furthermore, there is some progressive development in the meaning of human rights, like women's human rights, and we can see some special treaties and conventions about women, like CEDAW and the Convention on Preventing and Combating Violence against Women and Domestic Violence (Istanbul Convention).*

For example, the Istanbul Convention is important regarding women's human rights. This convention takes a strong stand against state agencies and jurists who encourage, or do nothing to prevent, violence against women and against harmful traditional practices which block – or act as an obstacle to – seeing the women's position. But jurists generally do not recognize this aspect of the Convention and

---

7 On the other hand from this perspective, silence is also regarded as a means of resistance.

8 Lorraine Code, Feminist Epistemology and the Politics of Knowledge: Questions of Marginality, p. 1 http://www.uk.sagepub.com/upm-data/63480_Evans__The_SAGE_HB_of_Feminist_Theory.pdf, 25.08.2014.

9 Code, p. 1.

10 William Paul Simmons, *Human Rights Law and the Marginalized Other*, Cambridge University Press, Cambridge 2011, p. 2.

11 Simmons, p. 3.

12 Simmons, p. xv.

it is possible to see gendered interpretations of treaties[13]. The problem, then, is connected with the jurists. As Paul Simmons rightly stated, if the judges, lawyers and others learn to hear the voices of the silenced groups, these groups can realize their human rights[14].

In this paper, I present a basic question. This is, what is the role of judges regarding these groups, or how can judges learn to hear their voices, since the voices of these groups, or persons, are not known or are ignored and oppressed. I will claim that the job of the judge is to see injustice and for this s/he should pay attention. Namely, if the judge hears the voices of silenced groups, s/he has some virtues, like attention. I will claim that the main obstacle to hearing these voices is epistemic injustice which causes them to be silenced. For this, I claim that jurists should know how to see injustice in a particular case. I also claim that it is the job of the judge to see injustice in a particular case. To support this claim, it is necessary to explain the job of the judge in the ethical context. This explanation, I later will try to make clear by examining the job of the judge in the case of Nahide Opuz.

II. The Job Of The Judge: Seeing Injustice

As persons, judges do their jobs according to their characteristics[15]. A part of their actions as persons consists of judicial decisions, and those decisions make up their personhood.[16] S/he reflects her/his personality in her/his job.

For this reason, the judge must have an ethical core to be ethically responsible to the parties to the case before her/him. Ethical responsibility "*begins with the very concrete exposure to the face of the Other*"[17]. He/she cannot give up this responsibility, or hide behind unethical laws in skirting it For example, as Zenon Bankowski makes clear, we claim that if the judge sentences a person to death but do not believe in the death penalty as an ethical institution, this does not mean that "*the judge is not killing the defender but the Law is.*"[18]. S/he is responsible for this decision.

In this way, we can say that the meaning of the job of the judge is determined in an ethical context and the judge should behave according to ethical requirements.

---

13 Simmons, p.6.

14 Simmons, p.3.

15 Kuçuradi, Ioanna Kuçuradi, *Etik*, Türkiye Felsefe Kurumu, Ankara 2011, p.153.

16 Kuçuradi, p.155.

17 Simmons, p.14.

18 Zenon Bankowski, "In the Judgement Space: The Judge and the Anxiety of the Encounter", *The Universal and the Particular in Legal Reasoning,* Eds. Z. Bankowski-J.Maclean, Ashgate, Burlington 2006, p.29.

According to Ioanna Kuçuradi, in the evaluation process of a case, the judge should take all the necessary steps to rendering justice. These are acquiring knowledge of the case, trying to give context to that knowledge, and rendering a verdict[19]. In the first step, the judge should understand the reasons behind the action: "*By 'acquiring knowledge' I mean that the judge receives, and inquires into the truth of, the information given to him on a case, and while doing this learns the reasons of the action of the individual who has performed it*"[20].

For this, we should go back to the question and ask again "what is the meaning of the job of the judge?" If we claim that it is connected with correct understanding, correct adjudication, and not arriving at an arbitrary decision, we should say that this question is an ethical question and should be answered from an ethical perspective. From this perspective, we may claim that to understand correctly, the judge should see the injustice connected with the case. In this respect, we should ask how is it possible to see injustice? Martha Nussbaum rightly states that *humanity does not automatically reveal itself to strangers*[21]. If so, the judge who wants to see injustice should be aware of reasons which cause injustice.

Seeing injustice requires paying attention[22]. To pay attention, the judge must see parties as persons. To see them as persons, the judge should know to see herself/himself as a person. In this regard, to see injustice requires certain virtues. S/he who wants to realize justice should pay attention to the particular case for seeing.

Iris Murdoch says that it is a duty to see the world as it is.[23] For this, it is necessary to pay attention to a particular case seen as it is being presented. Simone Weil regards paying attention as a means for understanding things. She says that it is a method for the exercise of intelligence and it requires looking into things until they can be seen clearly[24]. To grasp things clearly, the judge should have the experience of paying attention. To explain this point, Aristotle's concept of the phronesis is useful.

Phronesis is connected with the particulars and it provides a means of making judgements according to the concrete circumstances in the light of the knowledge of value and values. Since phronesis requires seeing particular situations, it

---

19 Kuçuradi, p. 133.

20 Kuçuradi, p. 133.

21 Martha Nussbaum, *From Disgust to Humanity*, Oxford University Press, Oxford 2010, p. xvii.

22 The detailed knowledge about seeing injustice : Gülriz Uygur "Seeing Injustice" *Philosophy of Justice*, Ed. G. Floistad, Springer, Netherlands 2014.

23 Iris Murdoch, *The Soverignty of Good*, Routledge, New York 1970, p. 91.

24 Simone Weil, *Simone Weil: An Anthology*, Ed. Sian Miles, Virago Press, New York 1986, p. 215.

is necessary to have an awareness of the obstacles which block being able to see into those situations. Returning to the judge, being able to see past obstacles and into the truth or reality of a situation means that s/he should be open-minded.

Generally, open-mindedness is understood as being ready to acknowledge one's fallibility as a thinker or believer, and to change one's ideas[25]. This meaning of open-mindedness is important regarding biases and prejudices. But open-mindedness in another context, that of being attentive to the other, is important in relation to the judge. In order to see particularities of a case, the judge must be open to others and to the complexities of their situations[26]. This meaning of openness refers to the necessity of listening to others patiently. Namely, to be open-minded it is necessary to pay attention, since to listen to the other we have to be open to that other.

But listening is so hard, and obstacles like human frailty, stand in its way. For this reason, the judge should be aware of the obstacles which block being able to listen to one another, to the seeing of injustice. Judges should have this virtue of seeing beyond such obstacles. Moving from Weil and Fricker, it is possible to say that to understand peculiarities of a case or to see injustice, the judge must take the perspective of silenced persons. Otherwise, s/he will seldom deliver a just decision. Weil says that:

Human beings are so made that the ones who do the crushing feel nothing; it is the person crushed who feels what is happening. Unless one has placed oneself on the side of the oppressed, to feel with them, one cannot understand.[27]

In this regard, Weil says, a person's standpoint is itself an obstacle.

A standpoint is a point of view afforded (though never guaranteed) by a given social identity positioning and the range of social experience that typically attends it—social positionings that we might begin to capture with categories such as "elderly," "woman," "gay," "straight," "disabled," "able-bodied," "man," and various complexes of such simple identity categories. In the macro-economic frame, the thought is if you are at the top of the heap, you are not in a position to grasp fully the situation of those at the bottom.[28]

How then can someone put herself/himself on the side of the oppressed? As we stated earlier in our discussion of Murdoch and Weil, attention requires listening to others patiently. In this regard, if we claim that judges should learn to read the

25 Wayne Riggs, "Open-mindedness", *Metaphilosophy*, 2010, p. 172.

26 Gülriz Uygur, *Hukukta Adaletsizliği Görmek*, Türkiye Felsefe Kurumu Yayını, Ankara 2013, p. 73.

27 I took this paragraph from Miranda Fricker. See Fricker, 2013, p. 1.

28 Fricker, 2013, p. 2

circumstances that demonstrate an injustice and to overcome obstacles[29], then we are saying that they should listen the voices of silenced persons. For this, they should be aware of the obstacles or oppressions which block seeing, because these obstacles block openness and their ability to put themselves in another's place, or, namely, to pay attention.

Obstacles, then, block a full understanding of the case at hand. It is possible to regard some of these obstacles as silencing mechanisms. On this point, as Cherly Green rightly stated, we should ask: "what are the silencing mechanisms?"[30]. Regarding women, it is possible to say that one of these mechanisms is "an enclosed life" (domestic confinement). Another mechanism is legal practices. These mechanisms are powerful examples of the structural oppression which I will examine in the Opuz case.

Moving from Fricker, it is a possible to say that these obstacles – and the silencing mechanism they put into play – cause epistemic injustice. To understand the relationship between obstacles and epistemic injustice, I now turn to the case of Nahide Opuz.

III. Opuz Case

Nahide Opuz, who is the applicant in the case, "*alleged that the state authorities had failed to protect her and her mother from an insidious and ongoing pattern of domestic violence. The result was the murder of the applicant's mother and her own continued abuse by her ex-husband H.O., despite the fact that the authorities had been repeatedly alerted of his consistently threatening and violent behaviour. The undisputed facts in the case showed that between April 1995 and February 2002, the authorities had learned of at least eight incidents where H.O. had committed violent acts against Nahide Opuz and her mother, including stabbings, beatings, and the running over of the two women with his car. The applicant and her mother had filed a number of criminal complaints against H.O. with the authorities, but had later withdrawn them due to H.O.'s persistent death threats*"[31].

We can easily see that in this case, the state fails to discourage domestic violence. It should be stated that Turkey signed and approved international legal texts which define state responsibility in instances of violence against women. The problem

29 Richard H. Bell, *Simone Weil: The Way of Justice as Compassion*, Rowman & Littlefield Publishers, Boston 1998, p.39.

30 Glenn-Ratcliffe, p.3.

31 Rosa M. Celorio, "Introductory Note to the European Court of Human Rights: Opuz V. Turkey", *International Legal Materials*, 2009, p.907.

in the Opuz case is not the legal instruments, but the police officers and judiciary. Despite the legal improvements regarding domestic violence, the institutions and officers have not yet changed. In the example of the Opuz case, the problem does not only concern the application of the law, but also seeing the differences and peculiarities of a domestic violence case. The judge should be aware of them. In other words, in order for the judge to makes the law a positive force, s/he should pay attention.

In the Opuz case, one can easily see that officers did not believe Nahide and her mother. Their words are not regarded as credible owing to prejudice and oppression. In fact, in the Opuz case, one can easily see structural oppression. According to Iris M. Young, "*some groups suffer as a consequence of often unconscious assumptions and reactions of well-meaning people in ordinary interactions, media and cultural stereotypes, and structural features of bureaucratic hierarchies and market mechanisms-in short, the normal processes of the everyday life. We cannot eliminate this structural oppression by getting rid of the rulers or making some new laws, because oppressions are systematically reproduced in major economic, political, and cultural institutions*"[32]. In the Opuz case, police officers contributed to maintaining and reproducing oppression in the conduct of their daily lives without being unaware of it. They regarded their dismissal of the violence complaints as normal human behaviour, and did not think of themselves as agents of oppression.

Here, we can see epistemic injustice in the Opuz case – even the two types of epistemic injustice that Fricker defines: testimonial injustice and hermeneutical injustice.

> Testimonial injustice would become evident to a later court, as its ruling shows:
>
> "*The domestic authorities had remained totally passive in the face of death threats issued by H.O. and had left her and her mother to the mercy of their aggressor*"[33]. In Fricker's words, ,we can say that "*they suffer a distinctive form of injustice-they are undermined as a knower*"[34].

---

32 Iris M. Young, *Justice and the Politics of Difference*, Princeton University Press, Princeton 2013, p. 41.; I used same paragraph in my another article. See Uygur, 2014.

33 Opuz v. Case, European Court of Human Rights, Case of Opuz v.Turkey-Application no 33401/02 (http://docs.google.com/viewer?a=v&q=cache:1fXv64qZLmIJ:www.legislationline.org/download/action/download/id/2946/file/OPUZ%2520v%2520Trukey%2520June%25202009.pdf+%22Opuz+V.Turkey%22&hl=tr&gl=tr&pid=bl&srcid=ADGEESiFFOotetPxVHXcaQWA5YibLNZAuTn2LYeEz60IkcukiX8ZdNw4Lzbg0zaqXJnQ1ObFCdxw9HcpU79_xm9FRqBSPuTaqHggt5dUOSZL8v7SVSxRgTUrELr8WbE2ZJGpmV3LIpOr&sig=AHIEtbSaqFXtAT8QCXhq43w17LU1yxM3WA) (5 February 2010) 119.

34 Fricker, 2013, p. 1.

According to Fricker, the epistemology of testimony is connected with the human practise about hearing and accepting what people are told.

> *"Practices of testimony involve attempts at conveying knowledge to others, but what if those others do not, cannot, or will not, hear? At this point perhaps the speaker is silenced."*[35]

In the Opuz case, we can say that Nahide and her mother are silenced. In this example, the officers did communicate with Nahide and her mother. But they heard the women's circumstances without accepting them, and by doing so deflated the credibility of their words. As Fricker rightly stated, *the deflation of credibility is owing to prejudice. The proper mechanism by which we receive the word of others, and gauge their credibility, is being corrupted by a prejudice in how the hearer perceives the speaker*[36].

To be aware of oppression, the judge should listen to the parties patiently. S/he should be open-minded to understanding them and place her/himself on the side of the oppressed. Namely, to understand a social phenomenon, s/he "*had better look at it from the perspective of those whose voices are hard to hear*"[37]. In this regard, as Fricker rightly stated, it is important to listen to the silences. In the Opuz case, Nahide and her mother's voices were not heard by anyone, since there was a prejudice which caused them to be disregarded. This case is a powerful example of testimonial injustice "*whereby prejudice distorts a hearer's perception of a speaker so as to deflate the credibility given*"[38]. Following Fricker, we may claim that there is the intrinsic epistemic injustice done to Opuz, who was wronged in her capacity as a knower specifically, as a giver of knowledge. She was blocked by prejudice from passing on knowledge she had to give[39]. In fact, there is institutional genderism in the Opuz case. The members of the police and judiciary committed genderist conduct.

Nahide and her mother were unjustly silenced. The authorities ignored their capacities as knowers. Moving from Fricker, it is possible to say that they were silenced in two ways. First they were, as Fricker calls it, pre-emptively silenced[40]. In this silenced form, people are excluded from communication. For example, in the Opuz case, the police did not move according to Nahide and her mother complaints. In the second kind silencing, people are accepted to participate in communication, but their

35 Fricker, 2013, p. 4.
36 Fricker, 2013, p. 5.
37 Fricker, 2013, p. 3.
38 Fricker, 2013, p. 4.
39 Fricker, 2013, p. 7.
40 Fricker, 2013, p. 7.

contribution is not given the same regard as others[41]. In the Opuz case, the officers accepted their complaints and they communicated with the women, but they did not properly hear them. The officers did not recognize them as the source of the knower.

It is also possible to see hermeneutical injustice in the Opuz case. According to Fricker, hermeneutical injustice is connected with social understanding which causes epistemic injustice. This injustice occurs when a certain group does not participate in social process of meaning-making and does not share their experiences.[42] Fricker states that there is a hermeneutical inequality which arises from social inequality. This inequality is connected with silenced groups and, as she explains, it is possible to refer to these groups as hermeneutically marginalized groups.

> "*...when there is unequal hermeneutical participation with respect to some significant area(s) of social experience, members of the disadvantaged group are hermeneutically marginalized. The notion of marginalization is a moral-political one indicating subordination and exclusion from some practice that would have value for the participant. Obviously there can be more and less persistent and/or wide-ranging cases of hermeneutical marginalization. Although the term will be most at home in cases where the subject is persistently denied full hermeneutical participation in respect of a wide range of social experiences, nonetheless we can apply the term in slighter cases. Thus someone might be hermeneutically marginalized only fleetingly, and/or only in respect of a highly localized patch of their social experience. But hermeneutical marginalization is always socially coerced. If you simply opt out of full participation in hermeneutical practices as a matter of choice (perhaps, fed up with it all, you become a modern hermit) then you do not count as hermeneutically marginalized—you've opted out but you could have opted in. Hermeneutical marginalization is always a form of powerlessness, whether structural or one-off.*"[43]

The Opuz case is an example of systematic hermeneutical injustice[44]. This injustice is another silencing form and connected with systematic oppression. Since oppressed groups cannot share their experience and cannot participate in the interpretative processes of the social world, they face gross human rights violations. In the Opuz case, since police officers, prosecutors and the judge regarded the events as a family matter, they did not understand Nahide's and her mother

41 Jose Medina, Hermeneutical Injustice and Polyphonic Contextualism: Social Sciences and Shared Hermeneutical Responsibilities", *Social Epistemology: A Journal of Knowledge, Culture and Policy*, 2012, p.4.

42 Miranda Fricker, "An Interview with Miranda Fricker," Susan Dieleman, *Social Epistemology*, 2012, p.256.

43 Miranda Fricker, "Powerlessness and Social Interpretation", *Episteme: A Journal of Social Epistemology*, 2006, http://www.shef.ac.uk/polopoly_fs/1.152343!/file/3.1fricker.pdf (01.09.2014) p.5.

44 Fricker states that there are two sorts of hermeneutical injustice : systematic and incidental. (Fricker, 2006, p.8)

suffering. Structural biases or prejudices caused a wrong understanding of domestic violence. In the absense of the concept of domestic violence from the gender perspective, people like Nahide are silenced.

Nahide and her mother spoke and cried "we are suffering", but could not make their voices heard by the police and judiciary. According to NGOs' reports, "*when victims report domestic violence to police stations, police officers do not investigate their complaints but seek to assume the role of mediator by trying to convince the victims to return home and drop their complaint. In this connection, police officers consider the problem as a family matter with which they cannot interfere*".[45] In the other words, wrongful interpretative obstacles cause authorities to not hear the voices of Nahide and her mother. In this point, it is possible to regard hermeneutical injustice within structural oppression and as a silencing mechanism, since it affects silenced people and their expression of themselves.

The judgment of the European Court of Human Rights (hereinafter "the Court") of 9 June 2009 in the Opuz case clearly reflects the inadequacies of the state's obligations in respect to law enforcement officers, prosecutors and judges[46]. In this case, the Court decided that the state did not act with due diligence to protect women against domestic violence and to prevent other crimes. In this case, the Court stated that the Turkish Government violated articles 2, 3 and 14 of the European Convention on Human Rights. These articles include provisions about right to life and prohibition of torture and inhuman treatment and prohibition of discrimination.

Did the judges in the Court pay attention to Nahide and her mother?

The Court, unlike the Turkish court, treated her as an individual who has abstract rights. But, differently from the traditional rights approach, the Court based its decision on gender discrimination. Firstly, it regarded the violence against Nahide and her mother as gender-based violence. Secondly, it considered the gender-based violence as a form of discrimination against women. In this regard, we may say that the Court is aware of the prejudices concerning gender. If so, can we say that there is no epistemic injustice in the Court's decision?

In some respects, yes, we can, since the Court was open to the content of what was said. It seemed open to the applicant. The Court's position may seem unconventional in the context of human rights law, because, as we stated earlier, human rights law is criticized for silencing the others. For example, through the abstract nature of rights language, it causes the invisibility of the other[47]. But, in other ways, the Court

---

45 Opuz v. Turkey.
46 Opuz v. Turkey.
47 Simmons, p. 133.

too is guilty of epistemic injustice. Its just decision did not overcome the obstacles to injustice in the wider community. To fully hear the voice of the silenced person, the judges of the Court should pay close attention. On this point, the positive kind of silence is important. For this, as we said earlier, the judge should patiently listen to the silenced person.[48] In this meaning, silence does not mean passivity or unproductivity. It is not the same as absence. It is connected with understanding and as Fricker rightly stated, it goes together with attention. To listen to her/his voice firstly, the judge should be open-minded and aware of oppressions and prejudices in all their forms. Secondly, imagination is necessary and it is based on patient listening[49].

In the Opuz case, the Court tried to hear Nahide's voice through CEDAW, the NGOs' reports and the CEDAW Committee's decisions. In this way, the Court listened to their voices and heard gender biases. Thus the Court tried to regard abstract rights language from the gender perspective. For example, the Court determined the meaning of discrimination in the context of violence against women by applying CEDAW. The Court assessed the position of women living in Diyarbakir according to the NGOs' reports. The Court stated that discrimination in the Opuz case "was not based on legislation, but rather resulted from the general attitude of the local authorities, such as the manner in which the women were treated at police stations when they reported domestic violence and judicial passivity in providing effective protection to victims"[50]. The Court also applied the due diligence principle connected with the state's responsibility. For this, the Court used, inter alia, decisions of the CEDAW Committee. The Court tried to understand the nature of domestic violence. For example, the Turkish national authorities said that Nahide and her mother withdrew their complaints and had prevented authorities from pursuing criminal proceedings against H.O. But the Court stated that:

125. *Referring to international practice, Interights submitted that where the national authorities failed to act with due diligence to prevent violence against women, including violence by private actors, or to investigate, prosecute and punish such violence, the State might be responsible for such acts. The jus cogens nature of the right to freedom from torture and the right to life required exemplary diligence on the part of the State with respect to investigation and prosecution of these acts.*

126. *In the context of domestic violence, victims were often intimidated or threatened into either not reporting the crime or withdrawing complaints. However, the responsibility to ensure accountability and guard against impunity lay with the State, not with the victim. International practice recognised that a broad range of interested persons, not*

48 Fricker, 2013, p.17.

49 Simmons, p.142.

50 Opuz v. Turkey, 192.

just the victim, should be able to report and initiate an investigation into domestic violence. Further, international practice increasingly suggested that where there was sufficient evidence and it was considered in the public interest, prosecution of perpetrators of domestic violence should continue even when a victim withdrew her complaint. These developments indicated a trend away from requiring victim participation towards placing the responsibility for effective prosecution squarely on the State.

127. *While a decision not to prosecute in a particular case would not necessarily be in breach of due diligence obligations, a law or practice which automatically paralysed a domestic violence investigation or prosecution where a victim withdrew her complaint would be. In respect of these obligations and with reference to the Fatma Yıldırım v. Austria decision of the CEDAW Committee (cited in the relevant international material section), it was submitted that the State had not only to ensure an appropriate legislative framework, but ensure effective implementation and enforcement practice.*[51]

Thus, the Court tried to see human rights law from the perspective of the silenced groups. Furthermore, differently from the traditional human rights law, the Court decided that the Turkish Government violated the article 3 of Convention which contains prohibition of torture and inhuman treatment. In this respect, the Court's decision in the Opuz case may seem a just decision. However, all this was not sufficient to overcome the obstacles of injustice. For example, the Court accepted the state's responsibility to prevent domestic violence. But it did not refer to the state's responsibility in creating the necessary conditions for the fulfilment of the potentialities of Nahide. Furthermore, the Court did not consider domestic violence as a systemic oppression.

Conclusion

In the Opuz case, Nahide and her mother were faced with the silencing forms of the Turkish authorities. These forms are central forms of testimonial injustice and hermeneutical injustice. In this example, epistemic injustice and human rights violations were together. Namely, epistemic injustice caused gross human rights violations. If the officers had seen the conditions of injustice and heard the voices of Nahide and her mother, Nahide's mother would have not died and Nahide would not have suffered. But they did not. Nahide and her mother's voices were constrained and minimized. Their capacities as knowers were ignored. The officers could not see conditions of injustice because they were relying on gender stereotypes. Nahide and her mother were silenced.

When the Court states that violence against women is a form of discrimination, did the judges decide from the perspective of the silenced persons or did they

51 Opuz v. Turkey 125–126–127.

regard it only within the abstract rights approach? To do the job of the judge well, it is important to hear the voices of Nahide and her mother with their intersecting identifications with gender, and this rhetorical listening should precede conscious identifications. "*Such conscious identifications are important because they may provide grounds for revising identifications troubled by history, uneven power dynamics, and ignorance; as such, they may foster cross-cultural communication on any topic.*"[52].

The judges of the Court, while they did their job, they did not do their job as well, or as fully, as they could have – and should have – done it. Why did the Court only partly succeed at its job? Firstly, it is possible to say that the Court did not rule relying on gender biases. The Court did try to listen to the women through biases. For example, the domestic violence was regarded by the Turkish court as a private matter. But the Court stated that national authorities are obligated to interfere in family life for the protection of individual rights. Secondly, the Court tried to hear the voices of Nahide, not only from her text but also through the CEDAW Committee's decisions and NGOs' reports which concern domestic violence and the situation of women in Turkey. This wider context is necessary for hearing troubled identifications. The Court, however, did not see the case in the larger genderist situation. The Court regarded the position of the women in Turkey, but it did not see domestic violence as a public matter or see the genderist institutional behaviours that are at the root of this case. For this reason, the Court did not determine sufficiently to overcome obstacles of injustice. The decision of the Court did not sufficiently reflect gender visibility. In this regard, the Court decision may be regarded as an example of testimonial justice. But it has some problems connected with the hermeneutical injustice.

The Opuz case reflects how the epistemic injustice as silencing forms can cause gross human rights violations. As we see in the Opuz case, Turkish authorities silenced Nahide and her mother and they did not hear their voices. As Fricker says, "*when a speaker should be heard, but is not heard, he is silenced*".[53] But even though the Court's decision is not sufficient, it is a step forward. The Opuz Case reflects it is indeed possible, through law well applied by judges open to listening and hearing the silenced, to overcome such injustice. For this to happen, expanding on Weil, I claim that the judges and jurists who want to realize justice, must learn to hear fully the conditions of injustice.

52 Ratcliffe, p. 19.

53 Fricker, 2013, p. 4.

Marek Zirk-Sadowski
University of Łódź, Poland

The Emergence of the Identity of the Administrative Law in the Process of Building the Relation of the Administrative Courts vis-à-vis the Case Law of the Constitutional Tribunal[1]

Abstract: The presented article is devoted to the problem of constructing a new identity of the Polish administrative law. This is a phenomenon that is difficult to separate from the search for the European legal identity. The European cultural identity is under construction process, though the conviction of its existence is already deeply rooted. In Poland, however, like in Germany, a new identity of the administrative law develops mainly in line with the results of the pro-constitutional interpretation. The articles argues that the Polish constitutional practice still lacks the principle of the radiation of the Constitution, known in the German law. It is postulated to introduce this principle into the Polish conceptions of the relations between the private law and the Constitution. On the basis of the public law in Poland this concept refers to the postulate of applying the constitutional principles to the interpretation of evaluative and vague phrases as well as general clauses.

Key Words: cultural heritage of the member states, constitutional rights, pro-European interpretation & pro-constitutional interpretation, constitutional identity of the state, interpretative autonomy

1. The presented article is devoted to the problem of constructing a new identity of the Polish administrative law. This is a phenomenon that is difficult to separate from the search for the European legal identity. The creation of the European cultural identity is a relatively new process. The starting point was the then encountered cultural autonomy of the respective Member States, which became even stronger after the last enlargement of the EU in 2004. The European cultural identity is therefore under construction process, though the conviction of its existence is already deeply rooted. We are today confident that the development of this phenomenon will not result in subordinating these Member States which have recently joined the EU to stronger legal cultures.

1 The following text was prepared as a part of a research grant financed by National Science Center (Poland), No. DEC-2012/05/B/HS5/01111.

There constantly exists a certain "space" for the discourse that creates the cultural identity and enriches it with the experiences of one's own country and culture[2]. The source of this potentiality is primarily the autonomy of the Constitution in relation to the EU law. For the constitutional courts of Germany, France and Poland sovereignty turns out to be an inalienable feature in favour to the international organizations. Despite the desire to cooperate in constructing the European Union, they seek to preserve the cultural heritage of their peoples. The case is similar with the fundamental rights, for which one is looking for a specific meaning resulting not only from the judgements of the ECtHR, but also from the historical and cultural conditions of respective countries. Since neither on the basis of the EU law nor under the Convention we deal with the "prescriptive" system, based on imposing specific institutional arrangements, it is always possible to agree on the conceptions of the European integration with the constitutions of the respective Member States by a specific self-regulatory system existing in the EU. In the field of the administrative law, an essential component of this mechanism is the attempt to delimitate the limits of this law by its so-called pro-European interpretation and, on the other hand, through so-called pro-constitutional interpretation.

However, in Poland, like in Germany, a new identity of the administrative law develops mainly in line with the results of the pro-constitutional interpretation.

2. Contemporarily there is no need to prove the thesis of the close interrelations between the administrative law and the Constitution. Being the fields of the public law, both these branches of law are closely related, yet it does not mean that the administrative law is a mere derivative of the constitutional law. The Constitution merely sets the insurmountable framework of the administrative law in terms of the content and the procedure.

This thought has been vividly expressed in the Polish literature by E. Ochendowski, when he stated that **the administrative law is the instantiated constitutional law**, at least in the sense of the political system[3].

Its superior position in the legal system has been expressed by the Constitution itself, since article 8 paragraph 1 states that "the Constitution is the supreme law of the Republic of Poland". The supremacy of the Constitution is also derived from the words of the preamble and from the principle of the sovereignty of the

2 This problem has been extensively discussed by me in: Flexible normative space between the European law and the Member State Law as a Source of Constitutional Identity, in: Towards recognition of Minority Groups. Legal and Communication Strategies, eds. M. Zirk-Sadowski, B. Wojciechowski, K. Cern, Ashgate 2014, pp. 237–261.

3 E. Ochendowski, Prawo administracyjne: część ogólna [Administrative Law: General Part], Toruń 1997, pp. 17ff.

nation contained in article 4 paragraph 1 as well as from article 79, article 89, article 188 and article 193[4]. As stated by M. Safjan, the hierarchical **supremacy of the Constitution** vis-à-vis all norms of the legal system is an expression of the constitutional identity of the state[5].

It is also confirmed by the case law of the Supreme Administrative Court in very different contexts. The power and the supremacy of the Constitution has been emphasized in the resolution of the Supreme Administrative Court of 7 December 2009, case reference number I OPS 9/09. In the thesis of this resolution the Supreme Administrative Court stated that in a situation where the party has filed the cassation appeal and, subsequently, the Constitutional Tribunal rules that the normative act on the basis of which the contested court decision was rendered, if this unconstitutional legal provision was not indicated in the merits of the cassation appeal, the Supreme Administrative Court shall apply directly article 190 paragraph 1 and paragraph 4 of the Polish Constitution and take into account the judgement of the Constitutional Tribunal, while not being bound by the contents of article 183 § 1 of the Act on the proceedings before the administrative courts of 30 August 2002 (Journal of Laws No. 153, item 1270, as amended).

The Supreme Administrative Court therefore held that the supremacy of the Constitution overcomes even the basic principles which provide the foundations of the Supreme Administrative Court's regulations and the construction of the cassation appeal.

As noted by the Supreme Administrative Court, the wording of article 183 § 1 of the Act on the proceedings before the administrative courts would suggest that in the proceedings before the administrative courts the legislator adopted, as a general rule, that the appellate court is bound by the limits of the appeal[6]. This rule, however, does not have an absolute character, because when the Supreme Administrative Court adjudicates the case, it shall *ex officio* take into consideration the invalidity of the proceedings. Consequently, it entails that the power of the Supreme Administrative Court does not cover, in principle, the control over the defectiveness of the decision of the court of first instance from the perspective

4 A. Chmielarz, Funkcja prawna konstytucji na przykładzie Konstytucji Rzeczypospolitej Polskiej z 2 kwietnia 1997 r. [Legal Function of the Constitution on the Example of the Constitution of the Republic of Poland as of 2 April 1997], Warszawa 2011, p.89.

5 Cf. M. Safjan, Konstytucja a członkostwo Polski w Unii Europejskiej [The Constitution and the Polish Membership in the EU], PiP, 3/2001, p. 19.

6 The Act on the proceedings before the administrative courts as of 30 August 2002 (Journal of Laws of 2012, item 270, as amended).

of the arguments which were not indicated in the cassation appeal. The Supreme Administrative Court explained, however, that the latter fact could not block the supremacy of the Constitution and the obligation of the administrative court to restore the legal relations to their compliance with the Constitution in a particular case. Therefore, the reasoning explained: "The acceptance of the ruling, isolated in a group of the Supreme Administrative Court's decisions referred to in this resolution, that refuses, due to the Court being bound by the limits of the cassation appeal within the meaning of the first sentence of article 183 § 1 of the Act on the proceedings before the administrative courts, to take into account the judgement of the Court that declares the unconstitutionality of the provisions applicable in the case, which were not included in the merits of the cassation appeal, would make it impossible to undertake the operationalization of article 8 paragraph 2 of the Constitution in relation to the courts being a part of the public authority; they would impede the restoration of the state of constitutionality and the application of the interpretation of the legal provisions in accordance with the Constitution; they would also impede the implementation of democratic rule of law principle that realizes the principle of social justice; this principle being the basis of the individual's right to assume and expect that in the situation when it has successfully appealed against the court's judgement, its appeal will be taken into consideration, the more that the contradiction of the underlying norms with the objective constitutional order has been ruled in the judgement of the Constitutional Tribunal.

Due to the above-mentioned constitutional values, relevant to the implementation of the protection of rights and freedoms and the right to court, it is necessary to approve of the case law being in favour of excluding the occurrence of the exceptional situation of the court of cassation being bound by the limits of the cassation appeal due to the position of the party to the proceedings which it had no influence on."

According to the Supreme Administrative Court, one cannot, even indirectly, limit the supremacy of the Constitution in any adjudicated case at any stage of the proceedings.

In the Supreme Administrative Court's view, the supremacy of the Constitution, or the supremacy of the specific rights contained in it must be of a real character, rather than merely formal one. This is expressed, among others, in the statement of reason of the Supreme Administrative Court of 25 May 2011, case reference number I OSK 1221/10, in which the Court held that the proper implementation of the party's right to a fair trial (article 45 paragraph 1 of the Constitution) takes place when the judicial protection is real, i.e. substantive rather than merely formal.

3. The abovementioned fragments of the statements of reason of the Supreme Administrative Court also show that the principle of the supremacy of the Constitution has a decisive influence on the position of the Constitution in the process of interpreting the administrative law when determining the individual's legal position. According to P. Tuleja, **the content of the fundamental rights of the individual stems directly from the provisions of the Constitution**; these rights are binding for all public authorities, and the individual may seek to protect them relying directly on the Constitution[7].

However, the mere act of providing the guarantee of the protection of these rights by the state does not always mean that each public authority may take decisions only on the basis of the provisions of the Constitution[8]. This can be done through the content of the act of law.

When setting the position of the individual by reference to the Constitution and in the manner that takes into account both subjecting the Polish constitutional order to the European Convention on Human Rights and to the Charter of Fundamental Rights, it must be kept in mind that an important factor in determining the rights of the individual is the existence in the Polish Constitution of so-called **limitation clause**, which was introduced to the Constitution in article 31 paragraph 3. In accordance with this clause, the restrictions on the exercise of the constitutional freedoms and rights may be imposed only by statute, and only when they are necessary in a democratic state for its protection or for public order, or in order to protect the environment, public health or morals, or the freedoms and rights of others. These restrictions cannot limit the essence of freedoms and rights of others[9].

Limitation clauses are accompanied by regulations that are considered to be barriers to the application of the former. They must be clearly established and, therefore, there are so-called objective prohibitions of limitation[10]. An absolute prohibition of limitation is contained in article 30 of the Constitution. The latter sets forth that dignity "is inviolable". Objective prohibitions include also the prohibition of corporal punishment (article 40, second sentence), the prohibition

---

7 P. Tuleja: Stosowanie Konstytucji RP w świetle zasady jej nadrzędności – wybrane problemy [The Application of the Constitution of the Republic of Poland from the Perspective of its Supremacy – Selected Issues], Kraków 2003, pp.61–62.

8 Ibidem, p.62.

9 On the issue of the said clauses, cf. in the Polish literature the work of M. Piechowiak, Klauzula limitacyjna a nienaruszalność praw i godności [Limitation Clause and the Inviolability of Rights and Dignity], Przegląd Sejmowy 2(91)/2009, pp.56–57.

10 Ibidem, p.58.

of preventive censorship of mass media and licensing of the press (article 54, paragraph 2), the prohibition of forcing someone to attend or participate in religious practices (article 53, paragraph 6), and the prohibition, relating to public authorities, of being forced to disclose one's religious beliefs or religion (article 53, paragraph 7).

The Constitution sets out a general limitation clause for the whole catalogue of rights contained in it; thus not only for the rights contained in Chapter II, but in the entire Constitution. The fact of implementing a general limitation clause to the Polish Constitution results in increasing the role of the judge in determining the limits of law which this clause is applied to. Even in cases where laws do not raise serious doubts, from the point of view of the nature of the limitation clause, in some cases there indeed arises uncertainty. The fear of legal uncertainty and of an excessive judicial activism can be reduced by assuming that the international law constitutes a certain complement to the Constitution when applying the limitation clause and this is a peculiar way to reduce discretionary creation of the constitutional standards[11].

Defining the limits of the rights and freedoms of the individual poses a problem often analysed in the jurisprudence of the Supreme Administrative Court. What is disadvantageous is the fact that some judgements make use of this possibility only through the jurisprudence of the Constitutional Tribunal. There rarely takes place a direct application of the Constitution and of the limitation clause. In the administrative courts there prevails the tendency to indirectly interpret rights and freedoms of the individual through specific rulings of the Constitutional Tribunal. We can therefore speak of the tendency to issue indirect imitative judgements[12].

Nevertheless, there are indeed some exceptions in the form of making direct references to the constitutional limitation clause. A well-known example is the judgement as of 1 September 2011 (OSK 1075–1011). In the said case, the court relied on the list of conditions that must be met in order to be able to apply the limitation clause: "Limiting the right of access to public information, in accordance with article 61 paragraph 3 of the Constitution, can take place only due to a specific statutory protection of the rights and freedoms of other people and

---

11 Cf. M. Wyrzykowski, Granice praw i wolności — granice władzy, [Limits of Rights and Freedoms – Limits of Authority] [in:] Obywatel — jego wolności i prawa. Zbiór studiów przygotowanych z okazji 10-lecia urzędu Rzecznika Praw Obywatelskich [A Citizen – his Freedoms and Rights. The Collection of Studies Prepared on the 10th Anniversary of the Ombudsman Office], prepared by B. Oliwa-Radzikowska, Warszawa 1998, p. 58.

12 Cf. the judgement of the Supreme Administrative Court as of 5 March 2009, case reference number I OSK 1256/08.

economic subjects as well as the protection of the public order, public security or important economic interests of the state. This requirement is not met by the provision which governs only the mode of access to certain public information (its aim is to identify the specific mode of access, rather than to restrict the access to other information). Denying the access to public information, due to the importance given to this issue in the Constitution, must therefore be direct and justified by the abovementioned premises."

4. The influence of the case law of the Constitutional Tribunal is also reflected in the acceptance of **the presumption of constitutionality of the statutes** on the basis of the interpretation undertaken by the administrative courts. This principle of interpretation is referred to as a presumption, because it results, as any legal presumption, in shifting the burden of proving the unconstitutionality of the statute on the party who claims that the statute or its provision are unconstitutional. Without such evidence the individual fragments of the statute cannot be deemed unconstitutional[13].

The presumption of constitutionality is rebutted only when it turns out that it is impossible to undertake such an interpretation of the provisions of the statute which would lead to its constitutionality. This view has been presented by the Constitutional Tribunal in several of its rulings. One of the examples in this respect can be found in a recently published decision of the Constitutional Tribunal of 26 February 2008, case reference number SK 89/06. In its statement of reasons the Tribunal held there (points 4.2. and 4.3.) that if, due to the flexibility of the legal provision, it is possible to arrive at the interpretation being in compliance with the Constitution, the wording of the provision cannot be considered unconstitutional. The Tribunal stressed here, at the same time, that it is not in itself unconstitutional that the adjudicating courts have a duty to clarify vague terms, not precisely defined by the legislator.

An important issue, which turned out to be essential for the administrative courts, was the question of the moment when the presumption of constitutionality of the statute stops operating. In its judgement of 13 March 2007, case reference number K 8/07, (OTK-A 2007, No. 3, item 26), the Constitutional Tribunal formulated a guideline for the courts to take into account the Tribunal's judgements in pending cases. The Constitutional Tribunal held that the very fact of the judgement being delivered by the Constitutional Tribunal, following control proceedings, even if it does not produce an immediate derogation, is not devoid of legal

13 Cf. L. Morawski, Zasady wykładni prawa [The Principles of the Legal Interpretation], Toruń 2006, pp.158–159.

significance for the proceedings pending before the administrative authorities. It is already upon the moment of publicly delivering a judgement (which is always earlier than the date of the derogation of the unconstitutional provision by the promulgation of the judgement) that there takes place the rebuttal of the presumption of the constitutionality of the provision under control. This causes that the bodies which apply the provisions declared unconstitutional either in the period of a postponed entry into force of the Tribunal's judgement (postponement of a derogation of a given provision in the judgement of the Tribunal), or because of the intertemporal principles, or, for example, due to the application of *tempus regit actum* principle (which is characteristic of the administrative courts), should take into account the fact that these are provisions in respect of which the presumption of constitutionality has been rebutted. According to the Tribunal, this kind of interpretative autonomy vested in courts is the expression of the direct application of the Constitution by way of being guided by the interpretation consistent with the Constitution.

5. In the Polish literature devoted to the interpretation of the Constitution, the phenomenon of the dominance of the Constitution in the judicial practice is sometimes called **radiation of the Constitution**. It should be noted that in the Polish literature the category of "the radiation of the constitution" can be encountered as a metaphor, which is to present the idea of the constitutionalization of the law[14]. In contrast to the Polish doctrine and case law, this category has a strong and definite position on the basis of German doctrine.

Radiation of the Constitution through the entire legal system was for the first time expressed in the judgement of the Federal Constitutional Court in the case of E. Lüth (BVerfGE 7, 198, Lueth). The judgement was given on the basis of private law. The president of the press association in Hamburg called for a boycott of the film directed by V. Harlan, the director of anti-Semitic films produced in the Third Reich. Film distributor filed the petition to court for an injunction to prevent E. Lüth from such statements. The court in Hamburg issued an order which was appealed by E. Lüth to the Federal Constitutional Court. In the appeal he argued that the judgement of the court in Hamburg was in breach of the freedom of speech. The Constitutional Court held that the purpose of the constitutional rights is not to merely protect the individual against the state, but they also embody the objective order of values, thus providing guidance and impetus for the legislator, the administration and the judiciary. Since the constitutionality creates an

14 Cf. M. Safjan, Wyzwania dla państwa prawa [Challenges to the Rule of Law], Warszawa 2007–2008, p.65.

objective order of values, it "radiates" on all areas of law, and thus it has implications for the relationships between individuals, including the contracts concluded by them. Constitutional freedom cannot be treated only as an individual right, but rather as a principle which is important in all areas of law. When weighing divergent interests (in the case at issue it was the freedom of speech versus the protection of economic interests), the courts should take into account this radiation of the Constitution on the private law and they should in this spirit interpret the general clauses applied in the private law. Due to the fact that in the analysed case the main problem was the issue of whether the constitutional rights simply provide the individuals with the proper tools to defend against the state, or whether they have a horizontal effect in the form of an impact on the relationships between the individuals, German literature referred to this problem as the so-called horizontal effects of the constitutional rights (*die Drittwirkung*).

A vertical perspective on the Constitution would mean that it protects only the relationship between the individual and the state, but not its relation to third parties. A horizontal approach to the constitutional law provides the obligation of the state to guarantee also a particular freedom of the individual (e.g. the protection of personal data) against their infringement by third parties[15]. For the administrative courts the horizontal doctrine would stand for declaring unconstitutional those statutes that omit in their content the measures that aim to ensure the protection of individual rights.

Poland is dominated by a vertical understanding of the impact of the Constitution[16]. Nevertheless, the very idea of the radiation of the Constitution in the sense of the German "*die Drittwirkung*" indeed has its reference there[17].

On the basis of the public law the concept of the radiation of the Constitution often changes its meaning in relation to the equivalent concept that operates in the relation of the Constitution to the private law. In the public law this phrase is used in order to provide some interpretative guideline. It is suggested that wherever the legislator used vague and ambiguous concepts as well as general clauses, the law-applying body should always take into account the constitutional norms and

15 Cf. M. Jagielski, Prawo do ochrony danych osobowych. Standardy europejskie. [The Right to Personal Data Protection. European Standards], Warszawa 2010, p. 61.

16 Cf. B. Banaszek, Prawo konstytucyjne [The Constitutional Law], Warszawa 2001, p. 389.

17 Cf. P. Czarny, Trybunał Konstytucyjny a wykładnia ustaw w zgodzie z konstytucją [The Constitutional Tribunal and the Interpretation of Statutes in Accordance with the Constitution] in: Polska kultura prawna a proces integracji europejskiej [The Polish Legal Culture and the European Integration Process], ed. S. Wronkowska, Zakamycze 2005, pp. 82–83 and the literature quoted there.

principles when undertaking the interpretation[18]. In such case the provisions of the Constitution act as interpretative guidelines for a pro-constitutional use of the margin of decision contained in the law, while not being direct means of control of the conformity of statutes with the Constitution.

6. To summarise the above considerations, it can be noted that the basic assumptions made by the administrative courts when using the Constitution in the process of interpreting the administrative law include: the assumption of the supremacy of the Constitution, the assumption of the possibility of deriving the individual rights directly from the Constitution, the assumption of the possibility of limiting the constitutional rights and freedoms while complying with the requirements set out in the limitation clause.

In turn, what is absent in the Polish constitutional practice is the principle of the radiation of the Constitution, known in the German law. It is postulated to implement this principle into the Polish conceptions of the relations between the private law and the Constitution. On the basis of the public law this term defines the postulate of applying the constitutional principles to interpret vague phrases and terms of evaluative nature as well as general clauses.

7. **The obligation of a direct application of the provisions of the Constitution** was imposed on courts and other public authorities in the article 8 paragraph 2 of the Constitution.

As indicated in the doctrine, the current Constitution of the Republic of Poland of 2 April 1997 was given "(…) such form and content, which made it a normative act that allows the authorities to apply it, primarily in a direct way, due to which (…) in case of applying the Constitution by courts, there is the possibility of applying its provisions to provide the outcome of the court case when there is no opportunity to apply the relevant statute (…) if the court declared it as contrary to the Constitution."[19]

The said constitutional provision on the direct application of the Constitution was preceded by the judicial practice. It was noted in the literature that the Supreme Administrative Court played a fundamental role in this respect, since from

18 P. Czarny, Trybunał Konstytucyjny a wykładnia ustaw…, *op. cit.*, p.83.

19 R. Hauser, J. Trzciński „Prawotwórcze znaczenie orzeczeń Trybunału Konstytucyjnego w orzecznictwie Naczelnego Sądu Administracyjnego" [Lawmaking Importance of the Decisions of the Constitutional Tribunal in the Case Law of the Supreme Administrative Court], Warszawa 2010, pp.24–25 and the literature quoted there.

the beginning of its judiciary activity it adjudicated on the basis of the provisions of the Constitution, most often applying them together with statutory provisions[20].

As is clear from the case law of the Constitutional Tribunal, a direct application of the Constitution by the courts can take two forms, namely, it can rely on adopting the relevant provision of the Constitution as the sole basis for the adjudication (**inherent application of the Constitution**) or on a **concurrent application of the Constitution and the statutes**[21].

The case law of the Constitutional Tribunal shows that the constitutional provision may become the sole basis of a court decision when a given matter is not regulated by a statute, while at the same time the relevant provision of the Constitution is sufficiently specific and precise. Concurrent application of the Constitution and the statutes relies either in that the constitutional provision, having a sufficiently specific and precise content, becomes the building block, along with the statutory provision, for constructing a legal norm as the basis of the adjudication, or in determining the meaning of the statute in accordance with the Constitution (not excluding the general constitutional principles).

In its judgement of 28 November 2001, case reference number K 36/01, the Constitutional Tribunal pointed out, however, the inadmissibility of a direct application of the Constitution in the situation when the statute of a contrary content is binding and applicable. This judgement confirms the inadmissibility of an incidental review of the constitutionality of statutes by the courts. The Constitutional Tribunal in its case law has consistently held that in such cases only the Tribunal has the power to declare the unconstitutionality of the statute.

The Tribunal has repeatedly emphasized that despite the obligation to directly apply the Constitution, which was imposed on the courts and other public authorities, the Constitution does not vest any public authority, except the Constitutional

---

20 Cf. P. Sarnecki, Stosowanie konstytucji PRL w orzecznictwie Naczelnego Sądu Administracyjnego, Studia Prawnicze [The Application of the Constitution of the Polish People's Republic in the Case Law of the Supreme Administrative Court, The Legal Studies], vol. 3/1988, p.53ff; this thesis was also confirmed by the studies undertaken by A. Kabat and presented in A. Kabat, Bezpośrednie stosowanie Konstytucji RP w orzecznictwie Naczelnego Sądu Administracyjnego [Direct Application of the Polish Constitution in the Case Law of the Supreme Administrative Court], in: Bezpośrednie stosowanie Konstytucji RP [Direct Application of the Polish Constitution], ed. K. Działocha, Warszawa 2005, p.88ff.

21 A. Kabat, Bezpośrednie stosowanie Konstytucji RP w orzecznictwie Naczelnego Sądu Administracyjnego [Direct Application of the Polish Constitution in the Case Law of the Supreme Administrative Court], *op. cit.*, p.85; More diversified forms of a direct application of the Constitution have been presented by A. Chmielarz, *op. cit.*, pp.198–203.

Tribunal, with the power to declare the unconstitutionality of the statute and to refuse the application of the statutory provisions that were declared unconstitutional. In order for the court to refrain from the application of the unconstitutional statutory provision, it needs to address the Constitutional Tribunal with a question of law (article 193 of the Constitution).

In the abovementioned judgement of 28 November 2001, the Constitutional Tribunal pointed at two irregularities. The first one can be observed in a peculiar constitutional deficit, when the court fails to perceive the doubts as to the compatibility of an applied statute with the Constitution even in situations where the need for a referral of a question of law to the Tribunal is manifest. The second, in turn, takes place, in the form of a peculiar constitutional hyperactivity of the court manifested in taking independent decisions by the court in respect of the unconstitutionality of a given statute, without using the procedure of addressing the Tribunal with the question of law, which assumes the form of a direct application of the Constitution.

The cases of a direct application of the Constitution by the administrative courts are generally associated with the provisions of the Constitution, which are referred to as self-executing (e.g. article 46 or article 217) or whose applicability has been determined by the case law of the Constitutional Tribunal (e.g. article 2 of the Constitution, and the resulting principles of justice, the protection of the rights acquired, or the prohibition of retroactivity)[22].

The scale of using these provisions by the administrative courts is enormous. The phrase "article 217 of the Constitution" (including tax structure), is contained in more than 13.000 judgements in the Central Database of the Administrative Courts Judgements, and the phrase "article 2 of the Constitution" (including the concept of the rule of law) occurs in more than 50.000 judgements. Even if only a part of these judgements contains inherent application of the Constitution, the problem is worth in-depth research. With regard to the concurrent application of the Constitution, their goal could be to provide the answer to the question of what type of concurrent application prevails in the case law of the administrative courts. According to L. Garlicki, there are three types of dependencies involved here. He mentions, firstly, the ornamental concurrent application, when the court relies on a provision of the Constitution, although the statute provides him with a sufficient basis for the adjudication of the case, secondly, the interpretative concurrent application, when the court – while applying the statute – determines its norm, taking into account both the norm of the statute, as well as the relevant

---

22 Cf. R. Hauser, J. Trzciński, *op. cit*, p. 25.

constitutional norm and, thirdly, modified concurrent application which will be manifested in the situation where the application of this technique is to "save the constitutionality of the statute"[23].

It should be added that there can be recently encountered an opinion expressed in the literature that the fact of the courts using clearly indicated judgements of the Constitutional Tribunal when adjudicating cases is the manifestation of a direct application of the Constitution[24].

Accordingly, the Constitutional Tribunal held in the already quoted resolution of 7 December 2009, case reference number I OPS 9/09 NSA, that there was no doubt that the decisions of the Tribunal bind the administrative courts and these decisions are often of law making character for their jurisprudence.

8. From the constitutional perspective, the main interpretative task of the administrative courts, however, is to undertake such an interpretation of the text of the statute, which is referred to in the literature as **the interpretation consistent with the Constitution**. The experience of judicial decisions and the abovementioned literature show that the compliance with the Constitution must be interpreted widely, namely to include not only the very text of the Constitution itself, but also its content indicated in the jurisprudence of the Constitutional Tribunal.

The Supreme Administrative Court has widely discussed the concept of the interpretation consistent with the Constitution. It has done so in the resolution of the Commercial Chamber of the Supreme Administrative Court of 22 June 2011, case reference number I GPS 1/11, indicating in its statement of reason that the method of interpretation in conformity with the Constitution of the Republic of Poland envisages, among others, that in the absence of the relevant regulation of a certain issue by the legislator, there may arise the necessity to restore the norm that regulates this issue directly on the basis of other regulations being in force in the legal system, including the constitutional regulations. This procedure involves the inference of the legal norm not only on the basis of a statutory provision but also with the application of the provisions of the Constitution of the Republic of Poland.

In the present case, when stating that the Tax Code does not contain the full definition of "overpayment", as well as that the tax law does not comment on the premise of the "impoverishment" of the taxpayer, the court found it necessary to

23 Cf. L. Garlicki. Bezpośrednie stosowanie konstytucji [Direct Application of the Constitution] in: Konstytucja RP w praktyce. Konferencja naukowa [The Constitution of the Republic of Poland in Practice. Academic Conference], Warszawa 1999, pp.24–26 – a reference to this work is made after A. Kabat, Bezpośrednie..., *op. cit.*, footnote 4.

24 R. Hauser, J. Trzciński, *op. cit.*, pp.145–148; cf. also A. Chmielarz, *op. cit.*, p.202.

attempt to find the norms that regulate this issue in the provisions of the Polish Constitution, though it is not governed by the ordinary legislator. At the same time, the Supreme Administrative Court has refrained from a literal interpretation of the provisions of the overpayment institution, recognizing that the literal interpretation cannot result in a blatant infringement of the norms of the Constitution of the Republic of Poland, as well as to lead to a distortion of the rationale of the interpreted legal institution. In this case, what proved to be the interpretation consistent with the Constitution was the systemic interpretation in which the rationale of the provision was searched by making a reference to the provisions of the Constitution.

It is therefore considered that the Supreme Administrative Court in this resolution did not apply the Constitution directly; it did not either refrain from applying the statute, since another solution would be contrary to the view expressed, among others, in the judgement of the Constitutional Tribunal of 4 October 2000, case reference number P 8/00. The Constitutional Tribunal stated in the said judgement that in the current constitutional state it was unfounded when the adjudicating court refuses to apply the statutory norm due to its conflict with the constitutional norm (in this case it was the norm expressed in article 178 paragraph 2 of the Constitution), and rules directly on the basis of the constitutional regulation.

If the court applies the interpretation consistent with the Constitution, it cannot as a result refuse the application of the existing statutory provision, but it modifies its meaning so as to bring it into line with the Constitution. Otherwise, it would have to address the Constitutional Tribunal with a question of law.

9. Pursuant to article 193 of the Constitution of the Republic of Poland, any court may address the Constitutional Tribunal with **a question of law** as to the conformity of a normative act with the Constitution, ratified international agreement or statute, if the answer to the question of law will determine an issue currently pending before the court[25].

---

25 A detailed analysis of the institution of the questions of law addressed to the Constitutional Tribunal, undertaken on the basis of the case law of the Supreme Administrative Court, is contained in the work of R. Hauser and J. Trzciński, Prawotwórcze znaczenie orzeczeń Trybunału Konstytucyjnego w orzecznictwie Naczelnego Sądu Administracyjnego [Law Making Character of the Judgements of the Constitutional Tribunal in the Case Law of the Supreme Administrative Court], Warszawa 2010, pp. 37–45; cf. also M. Wiącek, Orzeczenia Trybunału Konstytucyjnego wydane w następstwie pytań prawnych sądów administracyjnych 1997–2007, Materiały Szkoleniowe NSA, 6/2009 [The Judgements of the Constitutional Tribunal Issued as a Consequence of

The administrative court suspends the proceedings *ex officio* if there has been addressed the question of law to the Constitutional Tribunal (article 124 § 1 point 5 of the Act on the proceedings before the administrative courts). The purpose of the question of law is to initiate before the Constitutional Tribunal the procedure of the control of legal norms, the aim of which is to eliminate the legal norms that are in conflict with the constitutional norms. Article 193 of the Constitution sets forth a functional premise of addressing a question of law by the court, namely, the court may use this remedy if the answer provided by the Constitutional Tribunal to the addressed question of law will influence the adjudication of a specific case pending before that court.

The fact of relating the procedure with a specific case allows also to draw the conclusion that the question of law may only concern such a legal issue which can be settled only by means of the judgement of the Constitutional Tribunal, declaring a given provision, relevant in a specific case, as being consistent with the regulation of a higher legal order, or declaring it to be inconsistent, thus resulting in repealing the erroneous provision.

The subject of the question of law addressed by the court may be a legislative act which constitutes the source of universally binding law. As stated by the Constitutional Tribunal in its ruling of 7 July 2002, case reference number P 22/02, Z.U. 2004/7A/76, the judgement of the Constitutional Tribunal, in addition to its effects at the general level (*erga omnes*), should at the same time allow the adjudication of an individual case, in connection with which the question of law was formulated.

In the proceedings before the Constitutional Tribunal the procedural position of the court addressing the questions of law differs from that in the abstract proceedings and in the proceedings initiated by the constitutional appeal. Since the ruling that formulates the question of law is issued by the bench, it is regarded as the procedural document available to the parties. The bench, in particular, defines the scope and the content of the question of law and draws up the statement of reasons and, therefore, the representative of the bench who possibly participates in the hearing before the Constitutional Tribunal cannot withdraw the question of law, or even change its content. At the hearing, the representative of the bench may only discuss the addressed question of law and exercise his right to argue.

Since the control in the form of addressing the Constitutional Tribunal with the question of law has an incidental character (it is connected with a specific case), it

---

the Questions of Law Addressed by the Administrative Courts 1997–2007, Training Materials of the Supreme Administrative Court, 6/2009], Warszawa 2009.

is considered, as a rule, that if the adjudication of a specific case is possible without initiating the question of law procedure, there are no grounds for assuming that the premise for addressing such question has arisen. According to A. Kabat, this situation occurs in particular when it is possible to clarify the arising legal uncertainty by means of a relevant interpretation of the provision of an ambiguous legal act or by treating the provisions of another act as the basis of adjudication[26].

It should be noted, however, that despite its specificity and thereby the protection of the interests of the individual parties to the dispute, the basic aim of this legal institution is to protect the Constitution, therefore this task is implemented to the extent required by the conditions of providing adequate protection[27].

10. The mere answer to the question of law contains the conclusive validation issues that in fact do not constitute the subject of these considerations. On the other hand, what raises doubt is **the interpretative aspect of the judgements of the Constitutional Tribunal**. The latter is the case because, despite the fact that since 1997 this interpretation cannot be regarded as universally binding, it is indeed manifested in different forms in a number of the judgements issued by the Constitutional Tribunal.

It should be emphasized that this form of active co-operation of the administrative courts and the Constitutional Tribunal is very developed. Between 1997 and 2010 there were addressed about 60 questions of law. They covered all the main areas of the administrative law[28].

The answers to the questions of law provided by the Constitutional Tribunal assume various forms and they differently determine the validation issues. From the point of view of the interpretation of the Constitution, the so-called interpretative judgements have the most fundamental role.

The interpretative judgement is generally understood as such, in the operative part of which the Constitutional Tribunal decides not only on the constitutionality of the analysed provision, but it also sets out its specific interpretation. In such case, the following phrases contained in the judgement of the Constitutional Tribunal are characteristic: "provision *x* understood in the way that" or "provision *x* understood as" – are consistent with the Constitution (positive interpretative

---

26 A. Kabat, Pytania prawne do Trybunału Konstytucyjnego [Questions of Law Addressed to the Constitutional Tribunal], Białystok 1995, p.77.

27 Cf. R. Hauser, A. Kabat, Pytanie prawne jako procedura kontroli konstytucyjności prawa [Questions of Law as a Procedure for Controlling the Constitutionality of Law], Przegląd Sejmowy 2001, no. 1, p.27.

28 They have been analysed in the work of M. Wiącek, Orzeczenia Trybunału Konstytucyjnego ..., *op. cit.*

judgement, also referred to as affirmative one), or – are inconsistent with the Constitution (negative interpretative judgement).

Such judgements, in particular of a negative character, raised doubts in the jurisprudence of the Supreme Court in two ways, firstly, whether the courts of the common jurisdiction and the Supreme Court are bound with the interpretation of law contained in the operative part of such judgement of the Constitutional Tribunal and, secondly, whether the negative interpretative judgement constitutes the basis for the request to reopen the court proceedings pursuant to article 401 (1) of the Civil Procedure Code.

According to the Supreme Court, the authority to interpret the legal provisions is primarily vested with the courts that adjudicate specific cases and thus the courts of common jurisdiction as well as the Supreme Court are strictly bound only with such rulings of the Constitutional Tribunal which ultimately eliminate the contested provisions from the legal system being in force in the Republic of Poland, namely they are bound only with the judgement that declares the loss of the binding power of the provision found to be inconsistent with the Constitution (article 190, paragraph 1 of the Constitution). The Supreme Court's reasoning is based on a closed catalogue of judiciary powers of the Constitutional Tribunal set forth in article 188 of the Constitution. Since this provision refers only to the power of declaring the analysed provision inconsistent with the Constitution, the international agreement or with the statute, the powers of the Constitutional Tribunal cannot be by way of a functional interpretation extended to cover the possibility of rendering interpretative judgements.

As a consequence of this view, the Supreme Court passed a resolution on 17 December 2009 of seven Supreme Court judges (case reference number III PZP 2/09) which reads as follows: "The ruling of the Constitutional Tribunal that declares the unconstitutionality of a specific interpretation of the normative act, which does not result in the loss of the binding force of a given legal provision, does not constitute the basis for the resumption of the proceedings provided for in article 401 (1) of the Civil Procedure Code." Only clearly validating judgements, in which the Constitutional Tribunal acts as so-called negative legislator, provide the basis for the resumption of the proceedings. This resolution of the Supreme Court was granted the power of the legal principle.

The above problem did not constitute the subject of direct decisions of the administrative courts. Some assumptions as to the possible standpoint of the Supreme Administrative Court can be inferred from the statement of reason of the abstract resolution of the Supreme Administrative Court of 28 June 2010, case reference number II GPS 1/10. The thesis of this resolution states that the administrative court proceedings can be resumed in any case where the decision of the Constitutional Tribunal in respect of the inconsistency of the provisions of the substantive law and the procedural provisions related to the Constitution, the international agreement or the statute, covers the normative act that the administrative court or the public authority applied or should have applied in a given case.

In its statement of reasons the Supreme Administrative Court noted that, according to the settled case law of the Constitutional Tribunal[29], article 190 paragraph 4 of the Constitution provides for the right of the individual to restore the constitutionality after the Constitutional Tribunal has declared unconstitutional the provision that constituted the basis of the adjudication. The Supreme Administrative Court referred to the judgement of 27 October 2004 (case reference number SK 1/04), in which the Constitutional Tribunal pointed out that article 190 paragraph 4 of the Constitution, while granting the individual the subjective right to have the case adjudicated as a result of the loss of power by a repealed legal norm, does not *ex lege* declare the legal power of the unconstitutional acts of law application. In accordance with the principle of legal certainty and the principle of the protection of trust (article 2 of the Constitution) it is required to resume those proceedings which were validly completed. This provision refers to the ordinary laws, thus warranting the regulation of the mode of the said procedure and determining the purpose of the "resumption". According to the Supreme Administrative Court, the achievement of the constitutional aim is therefore left to the ordinary legislator and to the adjudicating courts on the basis of the procedures set forth in the ordinary legislation.

The Supreme Administrative Court emphasised that the public personal right, under article 190 paragraph 4 of the Constitution, is closely connected with the guarantees resulting from the constitutional right to court, and the case law of the Constitutional Tribunal has established a position that the right to effectively reopen the proceedings, due to "Constitutional Tribunal's derogation", is treated as the element of the right to court, especially in terms of the possibility of initiating the resumption proceedings and their fair course.

The purpose of the statutory procedure, implementing the norm of article 190 paragraph 4 of the Constitution, must be therefore to effectively guarantee the right to have the case re-settled in the new legal order determined through the judgement of the Constitutional Tribunal. In the view expressed by the Supreme

29 Judgement of 9 June 2003, case reference number SK 5/03, OTK ZU no. 6/A/2003, item 50; the preliminary ruling (indicating the need to ultimately rule on a specific issue) of 2 March 2004, case reference number S 1/04, OTK ZU no. 3/A/2004, item 24; judgement of 27 October 2004, case reference number SK 1/04, OTK ZU no. 9/A/2004, item 96.

Administrative Court, the freedom of the legislator to shape the provisions that implement the said entitlement is narrowed in this case and its limits are determined by the fact that the "challengability" of law application acts has been already prejudged on the basis of the Constitution itself.

If so, according to the Supreme Administrative Court, the ordinary statute is to define only "the principles and procedures" for resuming the proceedings, because the Constitution determines the very fact of restoring individual legal relations, thus setting the goal of "resuming" the proceedings pursuant to the modes set forth in the statutes. Therefore, any restrictions of article 190 paragraph 4 of the Constitution are acceptable if justified by the disposition of a particular provision of the Constitution, which excludes the resumption of the proceedings as contrary to the constitutional essence of a given legal institution (this applies, for example, to the inadmissibility of resuming the proceedings after there has been issued a judgement annulling marriage or divorce, or declaring the non-existence of marriage, if even one of the parties remarried after the judgement has become final and valid – article 18 of the Constitution).

According to the Supreme Administrative Court, it is unacceptable to restrict the principle of "challengability" of law application acts resulting from article 190 paragraph 4 of the Constitution, by means of the regulations introduced in ordinary legislation, whether directly or through their interpretation.

The resolution does not therefore relate to the problem of a mere admissibility of the interpretative judgements but rather to the individual's relation to broadly understood right to court. The views expressed in the resolution of the Supreme Administrative Court, contrary to the Supreme Court's view, however, indicate that the Supreme Administrative Court very liberally and broadly interprets the basis for the resumption of the proceedings after the issuance of the Constitutional Tribunal's judgement. The cited resolution can be therefore regarded as a manifestation of extending the premises for the resumption rather than of narrowing them down. The Supreme Administrative Court is of the view that article 190 paragraph 4 of the Constitution creates the public personal right to resume the proceedings after the Constitutional Tribunal provided the answer to the question of law. According to the Supreme Administrative Court, the statute can only lay down the principles and the procedures of the resumption, since the challengability itself was regulated in the Constitution. In turn, the outcome of the resumed proceedings is not prejudged. The Constitution leaves the new settlement of the individual legal relationships to the adjudicating court.

11. The influence of the case law of the Constitutional Tribunal on the interpretation of the administrative law is also manifested in **the dispute over the**

relation of the Constitution to the EU law. Its outcome is of a particular importance in the area of the tax on goods and services that has been entirely subjected to the control of the EU directives.

In accordance with article 90 paragraph 1 of the Constitution, "The Republic of Poland may, on the basis of the international agreements, delegate to an international organization or an international body, the competence of state authorities in certain cases". The Constitutional Tribunal held that such regulation can be regarded as a manifestation of a sovereign opening of the constitutional legislator to a possible expansion of the catalogue of the legislation that is to be uniformly applicable in the territory of the Republic of Poland. When expressing the view on the relation of the Constitution to the EU law, the Constitutional Tribunal was clearly guided by the case law of the Federal Constitutional Court of Germany.

In its judgement of 11 May 2005, case reference number K 18/04, the Constitutional Tribunal took the view that neither article 90 paragraph 1, nor article 91 paragraph 3 can be the basis for transferring to the international organization (or its body) the authority to enact legislation or take decisions which would be in conflict with the Constitution of the Republic of Poland.

In the statement of reasons the Constitutional Tribunal found that the cited provisions could not be used as the foundation for delegating the competence to the extent that would prevent the Republic of Poland from functioning as a sovereign and democratic state.

In this respect the Constitutional Tribunal's view remains convergent, as a rule, with the position of the Federal Constitutional Court of Germany. Although the Constitutional Tribunal did not specify as clearly as the Federal Constitutional Court of Germany the elements of the Constitution, the violation of which by the EU law would deprive Poland of the possibility of a sovereign functioning, by referring to the preamble of the Polish Constitution, the Tribunal suggested that there are such values involved as democracy, respect for individual rights, cooperation between the authorities, social dialogue and subsidiarity. The Tribunal emphasized that these values as well as the principle of subsidiarity, can be at the same time regarded as the fundamentals of the functioning of the Communities and the European Union.

Until recently, the Tribunal examined only the constitutionality of the treaties that formed the primary EU law. Only in its judgement of 16 November 2011, case reference number SK 45/09, the Tribunal found that the EU regulations, though being secondary EU law, can be subject to their compliance with the Constitution in the proceedings initiated by a constitutional appeal. In the statement of reasons (point 2.3.), the Constitutional Tribunal stressed the need to distinguish the mere examination of the conformity of EU secondary law with the treaties, namely with the primary EU law, from the examination of their compliance with the Constitution. The body which ultimately determines the compliance of the EU regulations with the treaties is the Court of Justice of the European Union, while the examination of their compliance with the Constitution is undertaken by the Constitutional Tribunal.

The Tribunal found that the consequence of its ruling would only be that the Polish bodies would not be able to apply the EU secondary law and the latter would not exert legal effects in Poland. The judgement of the Constitutional Tribunal would therefore suspend the application of the EU norms inconsistent with the Polish Constitution in the territory of Poland (section 2.7).

It can be said that the administrative courts have already created a specific rule to solve the conflict between the EU laws and the rights of the Polish citizen, thus determining the limits of pro-EU interpretation. Its pattern was developed on the basis of tax case law, in which the Supreme Administrative Court ruled in favour of applying pro-constitutional interpretation in cases of the conflict between the outcome of pro-EU interpretation with the solutions adopted in the Polish Constitution, if the fact of adopting in such case the pro-EU interpretation would impose on the taxpayer the duties which were not directly expressed in the domestic law, since this would violate article 217 of the Constitution[30].

Similarly, like in the case law of the Constitutional Tribunal, the priority of the European order is therefore not recognized in the jurisprudence of the Supreme Administrative Court in a conventional manner, as a manifestation of the hierarchy of law. The administrative courts also define it as the most serious argument raised in the discussion on the content of the legal order.

The argumentative approach to priority means that the Community law must always be weighed in the discussion of the constitutional principles and it affects legality by means of the proportionality principle.

12. In the theory of law and in the constitutional law there is posed the question of **whether in Poland there exists a specific theory of interpreting the Constitution**. In the theory of law there seems to dominate the view that in order to undertake the examination of the constitutional interpretation it is sufficient to apply the existing theories of interpretation. Accordingly, there is no essential

30 Cf. case reference numbers: I FSK 600/07, I FSK 743/07, I FSK 922/08.

feature of the interpretation of the Constitution, for which one would require a separate model of interpretation[31].

The jurisprudence of the constitutional law also emphasizes that the interpretation of the Constitution is not a process qualitatively different from the interpretation of other normative acts[32].

On the basis of the Constitutional Tribunal's case law there arose **the concept of the autonomous interpretation of the Constitution**, which can be described as a doctrine (ideology) of interpretation. The three rulings of the Constitutional Tribunal, which are typically cited as initiating the doctrine of the autonomous interpretation, are as follows: the judgement of the Constitutional Tribunal of 14 March 2000, case reference number P 5/99, OTK ZU no. 2/2000, item 60; the judgement of the Constitutional Tribunal of 10 May 2000, case reference number K 21/99, OTK ZU no. 4/2000, item 109; and the judgement of the Constitutional Tribunal of 7 February 2001, case reference number K 27/00, OTK ZU no. 2/2001, item 29, in which the Tribunal described the said phenomenon.

It should be noted, however, that the outline of the doctrine appeared earlier in the work of J. Trzciński[33]. When referring to the ruling of the Constitutional Tribunal of 5 December 1997, case reference number Ts.14/97, J. Trzciński stressed that some concepts should be considered autonomous in the sense that they are

---

31 Cf. T. Gizbert-Studnicki: Teoria wykładni Trybunału Konstytucyjnego [The Theory of the Constitutional Tribunal's Interpretation] in: Teoria prawa, filozofia prawa, współczesne prawo i prawoznawstwo [Theory of Law, Philosophy of Law, Contemporary Law and Jurisprudence] in: Księga Jubileuszowa ku czci Profesora Wiesława Langa [The Jubilee Book in Honour of Professor Wiesław Lang], Toruń 1988, pp.75ff; S. Oliwniak, Wpływ orzecznictwa Trybunału Konstytucyjnego na system prawa [The Influence of the Constitutional Tribunal's Case Law on the Legal System], Białystok 2001, pp.142–206; such views seemed to be expressed by A. Bator, A. Kozak, Wykładnia prawa w zgodzie z Konstytucją [The Interpretation of Law in Compliance with the Constitution] in: Polska kultura prawna a proces integracji europejskiej [The Polish Legal Culture and the European Integration Process], ed. S. Wronkowska, Zakamycze 2005, p.44.

32 Cf. P. Tuleja: Podstawowe problemy związane z interpretacją Konstytucji Rzeczypospolitej Polskiej w orzecznictwie Trybunału Konstytucyjnego [The Basic Problems Associated with the Interpretation of the Constitution of the Republic of Poland in the Case Law of the Constitutional Tribunal] in: Księga XX-lecia orzecznictwa Trybunału Konstytucyjnego [The Book of the Twentieth Anniversary of the Constitutional Tribunal's Case Law], Wydawnictwo Trybunału Konstytucyjnego, Warszawa 2006, p.218.

33 It was noted by T. Stawecki, Autonomiczna wykładnia przepisów konstytucyjnych [The Autonomous Interpretation of the Constitutional Provisions], typescript, p.21.

constitutional concepts of a specific content in relation to the concepts contained in the legal acts of a lower order[34].

According to T. Stawecki, the conception of the autonomous interpretation of the concepts or of the autonomous nature of the constitutional concepts may be included in the form of several key theses, sometimes assumptions and sometimes assertions[35]:

a) the assumption of a limited scale of the conception. According to T. Stawecki, the conception of the autonomous interpretation of constitutional concepts has not been formulated as a fundamental theory (descriptive or normative) of the interpretation of the Constitution, but merely as a consistent application of the general principles concerning both the interpretation of law, as well as the role of the Constitution in the legal system;

b) the thesis of the systemic inevitability of the semantic differences. In this conception, the need for the autonomous interpretation of the constitutional concepts follows, according to T. Stawecki, from the structure of the legal system. Some issues are regulated by the Constitution and, simultaneously, by the ordinary statutes. For this reason, there may take place the differentiation of the meanings given to the specific constitutional and statutory concepts;

c) the thesis of the uniqueness of the constitutional concepts, which stems from the fact that the terminological differences between the Constitution and the ordinary statutes are not mere coincidence. Such differences give expression to the constitutional legislator's intention to apply a new (separate) concept, with possibly most general character. For this reason, "the process of interpreting the constitutional concepts" should run in the opposite direction, i.e. constitutional provisions should impose the way and the direction of the interpretation of the provisions contained in other normative acts.

The name of the autonomous interpretation of the Constitution (the autonomy of the interpretation of the constitutional concepts) has been widely accepted in the jurisprudence of the constitutional law and it is also contemporarily used[36]. In

34 J. Trzciński, Komentarz do art. 79 ust. 1 Konstytucji [The Commentary to Article 79 paragraph 1 of the Constitution], in: Konstytucja Rzeczypospolitej Polskiej. Komentarz [The Constitution of the Republic of Poland. Commentary], Warszawa 1999, p. 12.

35 T. Stawecki, *op. cit.*, pp. 17–18.

36 In the footnote 13 of the cited work, T. Stawecki indicates the following works where this name was used: P. Tuleja: Podstawowe problemy związane z interpretacją Konstytucji Rzeczypospolitej Polskiej w orzecznictwie Trybunału Konstytucyjnego [The Basic Problems Associated with the Interpretation of the Constitution of the Republic of Poland in the Case Law of the Constitutional Tribunal] in: Księga XX-lecia

the theory of law, the issue of the autonomous understanding of the concepts was undertaken in the book by J. Mikołajewicz, dedicated to the judiciary principles of the Constitutional Tribunal[37].

The principles of the autonomous interpretation of the Constitution have to this day a significant impact on the case law of the Supreme Administrative Court. An example of the presence of this doctrine in the jurisprudence of the administrative courts is the judgement of the Supreme Administrative Court of 20 May 2011, case reference number I OSK 1069/10, in which the court stated that the starting point for the interpretation of the term "judgement" within the meaning of article 190 paragraph 1 of the Constitution should be the directive of the so-called autonomous interpretation of the constitutional concepts. The Supreme Administrative Court shared the view expressed with the Constitutional Tribunal, that the meaning of particular concepts adopted in the statutes cannot determine the interpretation of the constitutional provisions, because in such case the guarantees contained therein would lose any sense. On the contrary, the constitutional norms should dictate the manner and the direction of the interpretation of the provisions of other statutes[38]. (Constitutional Tribunal's judgement of 27 April 2005, case reference number P 1/05).

13. The abovementioned overview of the issues related to the impact of the case law of the Constitutional Tribunal on the case law of the administrative courts, cannot be naturally regarded as complete. The selection criterion was

---

orzecznictwa Trybunału Konstytucyjnego [The Book of the Twentieth Anniversary of the Constitutional Tribunal's Case Law], Wydawnictwo Trybunału Konstytucyjnego, Warszawa 2006, p.213; similarly, M. Zubik: Status prawny jednostki – między statyczną a dynamiczną interpretacją Konstytucji RP [The Legal Status of the Individual – between the Static and the Dynamic Interpretation of the Constitution of the Republic of Poland] in: M. Wyrzykowski, ed.: Prawa stają się prawem. Status jednostki a tendencje rozwojowe prawa [Laws become Law. The Status of the Individual and the Developmental Tendencies of Law], Warszawa 2006, pp.31 – 37; M. Stębelski: Artykuł 77 ust. 1 Konstytucji w orzecznictwie Trybunału Konstytucyjnego. Wybrane zagadnienia [Article 77 paragraph 1 of the Constitution in the Case Law of the Constitutional Tribunal. Selected Issues], „Studia Juridica" XLVII/2007 p.278.

37 J. Mikołajewicz: Zasady orzecznicze Trybunału Konstytucyjnego. Zagadnienia teoretyczno prawne [The Judiciary Principles of the Constitutional Tribunal. Theoretical and Legal Issues], Wydawnictwo Naukowe UAM, Poznań 2008, pp.110, 111.

38 Cf. the judgement of the Constitutional Tribunal of 27 April 2005, case reference number P 1/05. A similar standpoint can be interpreted from the judgement of the Supreme Administrative Court of 17 June 2010, case reference number I OSK 1120/09.

provided by the topics encountered in the case law of the Supreme Administrative Court, which can be presented in the traditional categories of jurisprudence.

One can speak of an overall argumentative structure, emerging from the case law, in respect of the relation between the case law of the administrative courts and the case law of the Constitutional Tribunal. The latter is in fact used in the context of well-defined argumentative situations that involve the assumptions about the primacy of the Constitution, the assumptions about the possibility of inferring individual rights directly from the Constitution, as well as the assumptions about the possibility of limiting the constitutional rights and freedoms while complying with the requirements set out in the limitation clause. The argument also includes the issue of the differences between the validation and the interpretative rulings, the problem of the relation between the Constitution and the EU law as well as the conception of the autonomous interpretation of the Constitution. The identity of the administrative law manifests itself in the discourse of the case law of the administrative courts through the above-mentioned and clearly defined topics and argumentative structures.

The Polish constitutional practice still lacks the principle of the radiation of the Constitution, known in the German law. However, it is postulated to introduce this principle into the Polish conceptions of the relations between the private law and the Constitution. On the basis of the public law in Poland this concept refers to the postulate of applying the constitutional principles to the interpretation of evaluative and vague phrases as well as general clauses.

This article, in turn, left aside the issues that would require answers to questions on the border of the theory of law, the Constitution and politics, namely the disputes about the place of the Constitutional Tribunal in the horizontal structure of the state bodies and the resulting jurisdictional disputes of the constitutional courts with the legislative and the executive power, the issue of the role of the dynamism of the legal principles in the political dimension of the administrative law as well as judicial activism – in word, the issues that have their roots in the adopted political philosophy and which cannot be settled by means of purely legal instruments[39].

---

39 Marek Zirk-Sadowski prepared this article as a research project funded by the National Science Centre, No. DEC-2012/05/B/HS5/01111.

Roman Hauser
Adam Mickiewicz University, Poznań, Poland

The Place of the Case-law of the Administrative Courts in the System of the Constitutional Control of the Activities of Public Administration

Abstract: According to the Constitution, one of the standards of the rule of law is an institutionally developed system of control. The existence of the control of state activities and its bodies, is a prerequisite for the protection of the individual. In the rule of law, in addition to the institutions established specifically to exert control over the compliance with law by certain state authorities, the aspect of lawful activities is taken into account when performing other forms of parliamentary, political or social control. The article discusses a particular importance which from the perspective of the rule of law should be attached to the institution of the control of the activities of public administration, especially the control of the compliance with law. It is argued that administrative courts undoubtedly contribute to a real and effective control from the point of view of compliance with law, thus eliminating the arbitrariness of administrative settlements as well as the inaction or excessive length of administrative proceedings, while defending the interests of man and citizen.

Key Words: the rule of law, the right to court, the judicial review & the appellate review, the Polish Constitution, the Supreme Administrative Court of the Republic of Poland

According to the Constitution, one of the standards of the rule of law is an institutionally developed system of control. All postulates and prescriptions in respect of the operation of the state authorities in accordance with law would lose their meaning without the institutions and forms of control. It is indeed the constitutional catalogue of diverse and effective control institutions that determines the practical value of the rule of law. In the rule of law, in addition to the institutions established specifically to exert control over the compliance with law by certain state authorities, the aspect of lawful activities is taken into account when performing other forms of parliamentary, political or social control.

The existence of the control of state activities and its bodies, is a prerequisite for the protection of the individual. Basically, this protection is to be provided by the content of the legislation which – under the rule of law – should embody the principles of social justice and, above all, exercise the rights and freedoms of the individual, assuming the state self-restraint in setting its own goals, independent of rights and freedoms. However, the examination of the legality and transparency of the activity of public administration bodies plays an important role in the functioning of the rule of law. In this regard, the most crucial role and function is the one of the administrative judiciary, which constitutes the expression of exercising the right to court, accommodating the need to control the activity of public administration.

A closer analysis shows that in the context of the interrelations between the appellate review in the proceedings before the public administration bodies and the control exercised by the administrative court there clearly emerged two concepts of these relations. The first, aimed at a specific symbiosis between these types of control and the second, expressed by the opponents of maintaining the appellate review in administrative proceedings in connection with introducing a two-stage judicial review of the administrative actions, exercised by the Supreme Administrative Court and other administrative courts.

As a result of the reform of the administrative judiciary there has been preserved the current principle that initiating the judicial review must be preceded by the appellant using firstly the legal remedies that initiate the appellate review in the administrative proceedings. Thus, the possibility of using the right to court is conditioned by the need to make use of the right to an appellate review in the administrative proceedings. To put simply, there prevailed the view that the right to an appellate review in the administrative proceedings before public administration bodies, and the right to court are two separate, yet inherently combined, elements of a comprehensive system of the guarantees of the individual rights in a democratic rule of law.

In this model, it is essential to understand the essence of an appellate review and a judicial review. And there, I think, lies the basis of much confusion, including the one arising in the doctrine, whose essence seems to rely on the expectation that in every case the administrative court will make a statement in respect of the interpretation of the provisions of the substantive law that provide the basis of the settlement of the public administration body (including, naturally, the settlement of tax authorities).

In the light of article 10 in conjunction with article 184 of the Polish Constitution, the bodies which adjudicate in the administrative proceedings and hold the power of an appellate review in the said proceedings (appeal bodies) belong to the category of the executive branch, and as such they carry out public tasks. Administrative courts, as judiciary bodies, exercise the judicial power vested in them. In such case, the judiciary, in accordance with article 184 of the Polish Constitution, consists in controlling the activities of the public administration. The manner of exercising this control was determined by the statutes that implemented the reform of the administrative judiciary.

These two models of control serve different purposes and they have been built based on different rules. It is rightly pointed out in the doctrine that the appellate review is built on the principle of compulsory complaint procedure, relative formalism, the principle of not being bound by the limits of appeal, the extent of the proceedings to collect evidence being limited by the requirements arising from the principle of two-tier proceedings, taking into account the changes in the legal and factual state, which occurred between the decision issued by the first instance and the resolution of the appellate body as well as the aim to settle the matter as to its substance at the stage of the administrative proceedings.

Judicial control is, in turn, built on the principle of compulsory complaint procedure, the principle of the court of first instance not being bound by the limits of the complaint (yet the principle of the Supreme Administrative Court being bound by the limits of cassation appeal), the limitations of the proceedings to collect evidence, cassation nature of the regional administrative court judgments, and – as a rule – cassation nature of the judgments of the Supreme Administrative Court.

The first of these types of control, at the same time, constitutes the element of intra-administrative control and, as such, it is exercised based on the criterion of legality, fairness and expediency. The second, in turn, while constituting the element of external control, is exercised only on the basis of the criterion of legality. The fact that these elements complement each other makes the system of the control of the public administration, in respect of the operation of public administration bodies that assumes the form of individual administrative acts, a system with a closed structure. At the same time, the operation of the first of these elements (appellate review) is determined by the efficiency of the second element (judicial review).

The limits of the jurisdiction of administrative courts are set out explicitly in the Constitution. Administrative courts exercise judicial power by means of controlling the public administration, which also includes adjudicating on the legality of the decisions of local self-government bodies and the normative acts of the territorial bodies of government administration. The latter means, as already pointed out in another of my studies, that the cases in which the administration of justice is to rely on the control of the activities of public administration, are reserved to the jurisdiction of the administrative courts. This is not tantamount to the fact that the issues arising from the activities of public administration may not be covered by the jurisdiction of the common courts. Yet, the point is that the delegation of such cases to common courts consists in delegating the cases as such to their ultimate settlement, rather than in delegating the exercise of the control over the activity of public administration bodies. The issue whether the matters arising from the activities of public administration shall be settled by the administrative court or common court is determined by the fact whether the court proceedings are to rely on the control of the activities of the administration or on adjudicating the case delegated to the court for a final settlement. For example, in matters connected with social security the competent administrative bodies issue administrative decisions, but at the stage of judicial proceedings it is not just about the control of the activities of these bodies (the assessment of the legality of the decisions), but about the court adjudicating the case as such (the case "is delegated" to the jurisdiction of the court), therefore, due to this fact, the competent one is the common court rather than the administrative court. It can be said that the fact of separating the administrative courts in the Constitution (with the Supreme Administrative Court), as a separate division of the judiciary, in addition to the common courts (with the Supreme Court), has its justification in that it takes into account the specificity of the administrative justice, which lies in the fact that the administrative courts have control over the activities of public administration.

The difference between exercising the control over the activities of public administration by the administrative court and settling the case that results from the operation of public administration by common court is evident and must be noticed, because it has provided the basis of the provisions determining the structure, jurisdiction and procedure before the administrative courts.

In case of the control of the activities of the administration by court, it is important that the case, whose object is connected with the activity of a specific public administration body, does not cease to be the case which should be settled by this administrative body. In turn, the task of the administrative court consists in evaluating (controlling) this activity. This means that the administrative court, due to an appeal against the action (inaction) of the administrative body, does not take the administrative case as such for its ultimate adjudication, but it only has to control (assess) the action of the said administrative body. For this reason, the administrative court, as a rule, cannot replace the administrative authority and issue a final decision in the case. Accordingly, the rulings of the administrative court, due to their nature, in case of granting the complaint, adjudicate on revoking or annulling the contested act and they impose the obligation on the administrative body to comply with relevant indications in the course of further adjudication of the case by the administrative body. Exceptions to this kind of decisions can be encountered in the existing regulations, but only as exceptional cases and, moreover, they fall within the general formula of exerting control. The act of taking over the control of the ultimate settlement of the case by the administrative court from the administrative authority would be treated as exceeding the limits of the control of the operation of the public administration, as determined by the Constitution. The court would indeed replace the public administration body, while in fact subjecting the activities of public administration to the control of the administrative court means that in matters covered by this control we still deal with the administrative matters, and the administrative authority, being the administrating entity, continues to be responsible for the process of administration.

These factors caused that article 1 of the Law on the Administrative Courts System, which defines the basic scope of the operation of the administrative courts, states that the administrative courts exercise judicial power by means of controlling the activities of public administration bodies, which is equivalent to the control of executing public administration. This control is performed in terms of compliance with law. This rule applies to all cases under the jurisdiction of the administrative courts, namely the administrative decisions in individual cases, the resolutions of the organs of local government and the normative acts of local authorities of government administration, the acts of supervision over the activities of local government, the conflicts of jurisdiction between local government bodies and government administration as well as other cases arising from the operation of the public administration, and subjected to the jurisdiction of the administrative courts.

The problem, which has traditionally been questionable in the field of administrative judiciary, is the scope of judicial control. In particular, the point is whether the case law of the administrative court which in principle verifies the legality of the operation of the administration in fact effectively ensures the implementation of the right to court. The views presenting the problem in this way are an obvious simplification and, it seems, they do not result from an in-depth analysis of the nature of the administrative court case law and judicial practice. Accordingly, it should be emphasized that examining the legality of the operation of the public administration by the administrative courts relies not only on examining whether the decision or the operation of the administration has appropriate basis in the existing substantive law (and, sometimes, procedural law), and whether these measures are taken by the competent authorities of public administration. The administrative court considers whether the ruling or action have been issued or taken while complying with a proper procedure set forth by law. This sphere of the control over the legality of the administration allows the court to interfere in the operations of the administration to a greater extent than it would result from a simple understanding of the control of the legality of acts or other activities of the administration. The analysis of the case law of the Supreme Administrative Court shows that over 70% of the disputed decisions of the administrative bodies include the cases of violating procedural rules. In such rulings the court indicates the inaccuracies in the factual findings, the cases of the restrictions on the procedural rights of the parties and other participants in the administrative proceedings, the fact of resigning from the preliminary proceedings etc. The activity of the court in this field allows to rightly conclude that the Supreme Administrative Court is involved in the process of the administration shaping the proper conduct of the administrative proceedings which aims at rendering a proper decision in a given case. However, the latter does not lead to replacing the administration by the court and its decisions by judicial decisions. A similar view on the case law of the Supreme Administrative Court seems to be expressed by the Constitutional Tribunal, which, in its ruling of 4 February 1998 (case reference number TS 1/97) held that the proceedings before the Supreme Administrative Court provide enough opportunity of controlling the decision itself, as well as controlling the legal provision that constitutes the basis of the latter.

It is also difficult to expect from the court in the abovementioned situation the interpretation of the substantive law provisions. Such an interpretative statement, uttered on the occasion of repealing the contested administrative act due to the infringement of procedural provisions, would be at least premature. After all, only the state of facts that has been properly established in the administrative proceedings can provide the foundations of the administrative adjudication on the basis of a proper provision of the substantive law. The administrative court, when challenging the state of facts made by the public authority, is not authorised to interpret the provision of substantive law referenced in the decision rendered by the administrative body. Such a decision of the administrative court could indeed suggest to the public administration body that the proper basis for a decision in a particular case is the provision of the substantive law referred to by the public administration body. In turn, finding the proper substantive basis for the settlement of an administrative case depends, in fact, on the proper determination of the facts of the case.

As already indicated, the administrative court controls the said acts (decisions, rulings) and the activities in the field of public administration under the principle of legality. In case the complaint against a given decision or ruling is deemed justified, the administrative court repeals this act if it finds a material infringement of the substantive law, the violation of law giving rise to the resumption of the administrative proceedings or other material breach of the procedural law.

However, in case of qualified infringements, for example gross violation of law or the competence of the administrative body, the court annuls the decision or the ruling in whole or in part. Yet, if – due to procedural reasons (e.g. the lapse of time, the irreversible legal consequences) – it is not possible to deem the annulment, the court merely states that the decision or the ruling have been issued with the violation of law.

If, in turn, the complaint against the act (or activity) in respect of the powers or duties arising from the provisions of law is granted, the administrative court repeals this act or states the ineffectiveness of a given activity.

When granting the complaint against the resolution or local law act, the court states the annulment of this resolution or act in whole or in part, or states that they have been issued with violation of law, when a special provision excludes their annulment. In contrast, when granting the complaint against the act of supervision, the Supreme Administrative Court repeals this act.

There is no doubt that in the current case law of the Supreme Administrative Court and regional administrative courts, it is assumed that in the course of adjudicating the case by the administrative court and issuing the ruling, the court shall examine and evaluate all the elements of the case, namely the court hears the case as to its merits. Accordingly, it is erroneous to state that the case law of the administrative court does not address the merits of the case. The standpoint according to which the act of exerting control by the court should not take the form of substantive decisions, should be merely read that the judicial decision – in case of granting the complaint – cannot by itself be a ruling ending the administrative proceedings. In such case, the judicial settlement is defined as the adjudication of a cassation character. The judgment of the administrative court cannot be therefore treated as a substitute for the settlement of the public administration body. When speaking about the nature of the judicial decisions in cases handled by way of administrative decisions, the crucial question does not in fact concern the issue whether these judicial decisions concern the merits of the case (since they always concern the merits to the fullest extent) but rather what should be the form of the judicial adjudication in case of granting the complaint, namely whether the judicial decision can settle the administrative case as to its substance, thus replacing the administrative decision, or whether it should be limited to remove the erroneous decisions, which stands for the necessity of the public administration body to render a new decision after the judgment of the administrative court has been issued. It should be, at the same time, kept in mind that if the case is reheard after the administrative court renders a relevant judgement, the administrative body is obliged to take into account the legal assessment and the indications of the court for further proceedings. The problem is, in fact, whether, as at present, the indications as to how to settle the case, should be included in the court's statements of reason of the judgment granting the complaint against the decision, or whether in some cases there could be implemented the possibility of including already in the judgment that grants the complaint specific indications (prescriptions) on how to settle the case. The basic problem in this context is the issue of executing these types of judicial decisions. In particular, there would arise the need to create a complex system of court – administrative executive bodies. There is no doubt that these issues concerning the nature of the decisions of administrative courts may be the subject of further discussion.

Opting for a cassation nature of the case law of administrative courts also has specific consequences in terms of administrative proceedings conducted by the public administrative bodies. Due to the cassation nature of the case law of the administrative courts, there arises the need to maintain two-tier administrative proceedings (as a rule) which "precede" the initiation of the administrative court proceedings. This rule also seems to be apparent from the provisions of the Constitution. First of all, in this context there should be indicated article 78 of the Constitution, according to which each party has the right to appeal the rulings and the decisions issued in the first instance (the exceptions to this rule and the appeal procedure are specified by the statute).

The right to court and the principle of two-tier court proceedings cannot be opposed to the right of appealing the decisions issued in the first instance in the course of administrative proceedings. Moreover, due to the familiar problems of the judiciary (the length of the litigation, the costs of these proceedings) it is common in Europe to aim at expanding the pre-court proceedings. The latter is quite understandable, because the intention of the citizen is not to address the court with the case but rather to have it quickly – and possibly positively – settled.

The postulate of resigning from the second instance within the public administration and from the supervisory powers of the administrative bodies in the administrative proceedings, combined with the transfer of these functions to the administrative courts, would result in depriving the administration of the essential tools of administrative law application, in disintegrating the administration, blurring the differences between the executive and judicial power and, ultimately, in atomisation of the administrative law.

It is also worth recalling that in the course of the discussions on the constitutional drafts and during the work on the Constitution there were considered different wordings that defined the scope of the jurisdiction of the administrative courts. Article 184 of the Constitution, having an essential significance in this context, sets out the tasks of this judiciary as "the control over the activities of public administration" and "the adjudication on the compliance of the resolutions of local government bodies and the normative acts of the government administration bodies with the statutes". These terms have specific importance from the perspective of the character of the case law of the administrative courts. First of all, it should be noted that the Supreme Administrative Court and the administrative courts exercise the judicial power. Thus, they are in fact appointed to settle the conflicts of law arising out of the operation of the administration. When presuming the jurisdiction of common courts, the latter should, in principle, concern the matters related to the public administration. The issue is also to settle these conflicts by means of assessing the operations of the public administration as to their compliance with law. This is in fact in line with the understanding of the constitutional wording that the Supreme Administrative Court and other administrative courts shall exercise the control over the performance of public administration. The exercise of the control of the activities of other bodies cannot and should not take the form of substantive decisions which replace the rulings of the controlled entities. It is not the function of such control. Each control, including judicial control, should not lead to replacing the operation of the controlled entity. The implementation of the substantive case law of the administrative courts would lead directly to "administrative recourse" from settling complex cases. It would also directly lead to a change in the function of the court, which would become the administrator. These considerations also argue for the need to maintain the existing character of the case law of the administrative courts.

In other words, a particular importance from the perspective of the rule of law should be attached to the institution of the control of the activities of public administration, especially the control of the compliance with law. This aim is accomplished within the administrative structures by means of the appellate review and through the administrative courts. The appellate review allows for the change of the administrative decision issued by the lower court with violation of law. In turn, the administrative courts examine the legality of final administrative decisions, deeming them – at the request of interested parties – as complying or not complying with the applicable law. The administrative courts undoubtedly contribute to a real and effective control from the point of view of compliance with law, thus eliminating the arbitrariness of administrative settlements as well as the inaction or excessive length of administrative proceedings, while defending the interests of man and citizen.

József Benke [1]
University of Pécs, Hungary

European Constitutional Culture and Civil Procedure

Abstract: – I. Preliminary remarks. – II. The Fundamental Law of Hungary (FLH) in the common European constitutional culture and some FLH-dominated parts of civil procedural law. – III. Some constitutional influence on the new Hungarian Civil Code (HCC) and the relevant morals of its codification. – IV. The Constitutional Court of Hungary (CCH) on the Hungarian Code of Civil Procedure (HCCP) in force: A short 'historical' approach. – V. The methods and purposes of the re-codification of the HCCP and the organizational structure of its proceeding. – VI. The triangular interdependence among the FLH, the social expectations on and the characteristics of the future HCCP. (1) The major questions and correlations. (2) The rules of the FLH, which define the designation of the civil process. (3) The FLH-based, profound demands of the society on the civil process. (4) The designation (purpose, goal) of the civil process. – VII. The duties of courts determined by the constitutionally defined designation of the civil process. (1) The questions of double-codification along with the FLH: its redundant and its necessary ways. (2) The settlement of disputes and its manner as the duty of court based on the constitutional purpose of the civil process. – VIII. Some remarks on the court system and on the legal remedies. (1) A preliminary aperçu on the work performed. (2) (a) The court system of four levels. (b) The relocation (transfer) of cases of highest priority by designation of the court in charge. (c) The constitutional questions of joint adjudication.

Key Words: the Fundamental Law of Hungary (FLH), the Hungarian Code of Civil Procedure (HCCP), the cultural and legal Hungarian legacy, the common European legal heritage, the European Union

Some Observations on the Constitutional Orientations of the Actual Re-codification of the Hungarian Code of Civil Procedure (HCCP)[2]

Contents: – I. Preliminary remarks. – II. The Fundamental Law of Hungary (FLH) in the common European constitutional culture and some FLH-dominated parts of civil procedural law. – III. Some constitutional influence on the new Hungarian Civil Code

---

1 The author obtained PhD (Pécs, 2011) in Roman Law, Comparative Law and Private Law. Serves as judicial secretary at the High Court of Appeal of Pécs and as assistant professor at the Department of Private Law, Faculty of Law, University of Pécs.

2 The Hungarian Code of Civil Procedure in force is the Act III of 1952 [='HCCP']

(HCC) and the relevant morals of its codification. – IV. The Constitutional Court of Hungary (CCH) on the Hungarian Code of Civil Procedure (HCCP) in force: A short 'historical' approach. – V. The methods and purposes of the re-codification of the HCCP and the organizational structure of its proceeding. – VI. The triangular interdependence among the FLH, the social expectations on and the characteristics of the future HCCP. (1) The major questions and correlations. (2) The rules of the FLH, which define the designation of the civil process. (3) The FLH-based, profound demands of the society on the civil process. (4) The designation (purpose, goal) of the civil process. – VII. The duties of courts determined by the constitutionally defined designation of the civil process. (1) The questions of double-codification along with the FLH: its redundant and its necessary ways. (2) The settlement of disputes and its manner as the duty of court based on the constitutional purpose of the civil process. – VIII. Some remarks on the court system and on the legal remedies. (1) A preliminary aperçu on the work performed. (2) (a) The court system of four levels. (b) The relocation (transfer) of cases of highest priority by designation of the court in charge. (c) The constitutional questions of joint adjudication.

I. Preliminary remarks

As an introductory summary of this paper, which is a synthesizing report and nonetheless an independent commentary, we can state the followings.

(1) The common modern constitutional tradition of the European democracies or Member States of the European Union is the basis also of the new Fundamental Law of Hungary (*FLH*, 2011[3]).

(2) We shall in advance sum up that the common European constitutional tradition is both theoretically and practically the legal, political and moral fundament of the forthcoming Hungarian Code of Civil Procedure (*HCCP*) and its just begun proceeding of re-codification as well.

(3) The proofs of this statement are, on the one hand, the provisions of the new FLH accentuated in this paper and, on the other hand, the brief analysis of the organizational structure, the leading methods and the first outcomes of the re-codification's process.

(4) We are now barely at the 'daybreak' of this long time period of codification, but even its first steps show us that each participant of its organizational units is aware of the great importance of the common European constitutional culture and tradition.

3 In Hungarian i.e. 'Alaptörvény' (2011).

(5) The fundamental – but not the sole – sources of this paper are: the synthetic, final Proposals of two Panels[4] (out of the eight so-called 'Work-Panels for Subject-Matters'[5]) and four preliminary, interim proposals[6] elaborated in the bosom of one of these Panels. The more traceable is the authorship and the more improvable is the documentary value of this paper, the more effective is to cite the interim proposals – instead of the citation of the final Proposals themselves.

(6) Accordingly, this paper has more or less to ignore the elucidation of the jurisprudence's preceding literary sources, the so-called 'legal authorities'. The reasons are quite obvious:

(a) the majority of the papers on the HCCP-reform were published before the new FLH (2011), which cardinally and essentially defines the route and the proceeding of the re-codification (some of those papers, which were published right after the new FLH's entry into force, ignore the new constitution, because of their methods – e.g. of their historical approach[7]);
(b) the great part of the 'flowers' of the Hungarian civil procedural law's authorities is involved and takes part in the various units of the organizational structure ('framework') established for governing the re-codification's proceeding;
(c) the quantitative limits of this paper do not allow to be long-winded.

---

4 Each so-called 'Work-Panel for Subject-Matters' is signed with letters in alphabetical order. The two panels, the Proposals of which were analyzed, are: Panel 'A' on the organizational structure of Judiciary and on legal remedies and Panel 'B' dealing with the duties of court and the rights of parties.

5 These are: Panel 'C' on the parties and their (legal) representatives; Panel 'D' on costs of trials; Panel 'E' on orders of proceedings (litigious and non-litigious processes); Panel 'F' on probation and evidence; Panel 'G' on the applicability of modern technologies; and Panel 'H' dealing with international and European subject matters and nonetheless on ADR (i.e. alternative dispute resolution).

6 These were composed by four Hungarian judges appointed to courts of appellatory instance and assigned to a preparatory unit and sub-unit of the codification's framework, the task of which was drafting and outlining the conception of the future Code in accordance with the rights and obligations of the courts and that of the parties and other participants.

7 See most recently e.g. CZOBOLY, Gergely: Civil Procedure Reforms in Central and Eastern Europe. Preclusion in the Post-Socialist Countries. In: Aspects of Local and Regional Development. Drinóczi, Tímea / Legčević, Jelena (eds.). Pécs / Osijek, Faculties of Law (Publishers), 2013. 147–160.

However, we shall not neglect to refer those parts of the legal and codificatory questions, which are preliminarily exposed in the – contemporaneous – literary sources (see e.g. the widely known problems of group litigation[8]).

(7) We shall stressfully underline that the process of the re-codification has not been closed yet. According to this, the conclusions of the paper represent momentarily neither the consummative point-of-view of the so-called Main Commission, nor – even less – the official position of the Government.

(8) Although this paper deals tangentially even with some other questions in connection with constitutionality and constitutional tradition, it focuses on two major subject matters: on the purpose and the goal of the civil procedure, nonetheless that of the coming HCCP, and on the duties of the courts. Both topics show us the way how 'Common European Constitutional Culture' influences and how it has effects on the nascent codification process of an EU–Member State's Code of Civil Procedure.

II. The Fundamental Law of Hungary (FLH) in the common European constitutional culture and some FLH-dominated parts of civil procedural law

The FLH (Hung. 'Alaptörvény') is deeply enrooted in the common heritage of our European culture and history, as well as the common European constitutional culture.

The traces of this profound connection appear in three ways:

(1) the one is the multitudinous declaration of the reminiscences of cultural and historical legacy;

(2) the other is the composite presence of the common European legal heritage of the Greek–Roman Antiquity and of the Modern Democracies and so also the Rule of Law;

(3) lastly, the third conjunction is the conglomerate of rules inspired by the legal co-existence of the European Union and Hungary as its Member State.

8 Most recently see NAGY, Csongor István: Javaslat a csoportper honi szabályozására az új Polgári Perrendtartás kodifikációjának apropóján. [Proposal on the Regulation of the Group Litigation à propos the Codification of the New Code of Civil Procedure in Hungary.] In: Magyar Jog 61/4 (2014) 203–213.

The National Avowal[9] expresses e.g. that (i) the Hungarian Nation is "proud that our king Saint Stephen [...] made our country a part of Christian Europe one thousand years ago" and that (ii) "our people has over the centuries defended Europe in a series of struggles and enriched Europe's common values with its talent and diligence"[10]. (iii) The Members of the Hungarian Nation believe that their "national culture is a rich contribution to the diversity of European unity"[11]. (iv) The FLH declares that "[...] in order to enhance the liberty, well-being and security of the people of Europe, Hungary shall contribute to the creation of European unity"[12]. (v) The FLH proclaimed that the "form of government based on the rule of law, and the previous communist dictatorship are incompatible. [The leaders of the] Hungarian Socialist Workers' Party and its legal predecessors and the other political organisations established to serve them in the spirit of communist ideology [...] have responsibility without statute of limitations for [...] systematically devastating the traditional values of European civilisation"[13].

This time ignoring the thirdly mentioned group of rules of the FLH, which regulates the legal relationships between EU and Hungary as its Member State, there is much evidence proving the tight contacts of Hungarian and European – historical or contemporary – constitutional and legal culture. Among these multiple rules of the FLH there are a few related to *en general* the 'law' as such and to the HCCP in force – the Act III of 1952 – and to the coming Code as well.[14]

Some of these essential aspects are (i) the purpose of the civil procedure and the duty of court, (ii) some principles of the civil procedural law and some general

9 The National Avowal [according to an unofficial transl.: 'National Avowal of Faith'] is the first substantive, preamble-like unit of the FLH, which stands after the legal title and the opening oration or prayer: 'God bless the Hungarians' [according to an unofficial transl.: 'O Lord, blessed be the Hungarian nation'].

10 The quotations are extracted from the official English version of the 'Alaptörvény'. See: http://www.kormany.hu/download/2/ab/30000/Alap_angol.pdf [13.01.2014]

11 The sentence stands likewise in the National Avowal.

12 Cf. FLH Art. 'E' § (1).

13 Cf. FLH Art. 'U' § (1) section f). Supplemented by Article 3 of the Fourth Amendment to the Fundamental Law (25 March 2013).

14 Cf. FLH Art. XV § (1); Art. XXIV § (1), Art. XXV, Art. XXVIII § (1) and (7) and Artt. 25–28. Some of these provisions are enacted by the Fourth and the Fifth Amendment to Hungary's Fundamental Law.

provisions of the future HCCP[15], and nonetheless (iii) the court system and the system of legal remedies[16].

Although this paper focuses on the first of the previously enumerated items, so the purpose of civil procedure and the duty of court, it does not ignore some constitutionally relevant questions have already emerged in the final Proposal on the court system and on the system of legal remedies.

Beforehand – for the better appreciation – we shall *per tangentem* examine two connected circles of questions: on the one hand, the relevant morals of the codification of civil *substantial* law and, on the other hand, the civil procedural law or HCCP (1952) related practice of the Constitutional Court of Hungary (*CCH*) in the past decades.

III. Some constitutional influence on the new Hungarian Civil Code (HCC) and the relevant morals of its codification

The new Hungarian Civil Code (*HCC*, Act V of 2013) came into effect 15th March 2014. The Official Motives of its Final Draft stated that the Code does not choose any foreign civil code as model, but pays deep regard to numerous foreigner Civil Codes' methods and institutes.

One of the important legislative morals of the substantive law's re-codification was the method of finding those constitutional provisions, the re-codification of which into the new HCC would be redundant. So the one moral of the HCC's re-codification was the technique of avoiding superfluous double-codification and that of preventing the need for precocious deregulation. *Au contraire*, this means a development of the legislator's capability of finding those rules, which need to be codified into the HCC, although their constitutional parallels has already been legislated as a provision of the FLH as well.

The following three – apparently illustrative – questions of the Civil Law have partly fundamental significance in their very essence according to the common European constitutional culture, partly great importance in the problem of codificational technique of avoiding the redundant double-codification. I shall well in

15 Most recently s. LUGOSI, József: A hatályos polgári perrendtartás általános rendelkezéseinek reformja Magyarországon. [The Reform of the General Provisions of the Hungarian Code of Civil Procedure in force] In: Jogtudományi Közlöny 69/6 (2014) 285–295.

16 See e.g. HARSÁGI, Viktória: Development of the System of Legal Remedies in Hungarian Civil Procedure Law after the Democratic Transformation. In: Iustum Aequum Salutare 3/3 (2007) 45–56.

advance emphasize that this paper does not target the analysis of these questions in their firstly mentioned very essence, because these lines concentrate on the secondly referred morals of the substantial law's re-codification. The reason is that '*omne nimium vertitur in vitium*'[17].

(1) The one is the principle of the *protection of property*. The principle is expressed in the FLH as the indigenous right to property, which "shall entail social responsibility"[18]. According to the new HCC's official Motives, this constitutional right is to be made effective among others through the single rules of the Code, and the right does not need to be simultaneously double-codified as a principle of the civil law.[19]
(2) By the same token, the other is that the HCC does not express distinctively the *protection of persons* as a principle. The FLH declares on top-level that: "The inviolable and inalienable fundamental rights of MAN shall be respected and defended by the State as a primary obligation."[20] Accordingly the Official Motives, the repetition of the constitutional principle in the HCC is not the appropriate way of making the provision effective in civil matters. The proper and adequate manner of the effectuation of this principle of law is the legislation or the codification of some coherent single, special rules, the so-called *leges speciales*, which are convenient to protect the inherent rights in general and also in special levels.
(3) Lastly, as the third illustration is the principle of *protection of marriage and family*. The top-ranked regulation belongs naturally to the FLH. It sounds: "Hungary shall protect the institution of marriage as the union of a man and a woman established by voluntary decision, and the family as the basis of the nation's survival."[21] It does not mean that the HCC protects through its special rules only the marriage and the other family relationships (the consanguinity

17 I use the proverb in the sense of 'grasp all, lose all'. Originally see by Seneca Minor's "On Tranquillity of Mind" [de tranquillitate animi], IX.6: "Vitiosum est ubique quod nimium est".
18 Cf. FLH Art. XIII § (1).
19 See Official Motives of the Draft of the new Hungarian Civil Code, i.e. the No. T/7971 Bill of the Civil Code, 374. [page].
20 "MAN" means "a human being" or "a (natural) person". Cf. FLH Art. I (i.e. 1 as Roman numeral) § (1).
21 Cf. FLH Art. L § (1).

based on descent,[22] the adoption[23] and the guardianship[24]). But the law in Code and other special laws also protect evidently the other forms of co-existence guaranteed by the practice of the *Cour Européenne des Droits de l'Homme*, like the unmarried partnerships and the registered partnerships (for same-sex couples)[25], the cohabitation[26] or the step- and foster parental relationships[27].

IV. The Constitutional Court of Hungary (CCH) on the HCCP in force: A short 'historical' approach

The CCH passed more than 300[28] conclusions (i.e. decisions[29] and orders[30]) on the HCCP in force (1952) between 1990 and 2014.

These conclusions consist of 180 decisions – out of which cca. 20 pcs. were published in the Hungarian Official Gazette – and some 130 orders as well. The conclusions decided partly the *annulment of regulations* or *provisions* of the HCCP in force, partly the *declaration of omission on the part of the law-maker* that results in violating mainly the former Constitution (1949[31]) and in two cases in 2013[32] the FLH.

22 See the new HCC Artt. 4:98–118.

23 See the new HCC Artt. 4:119–145.

24 See the new HCC Artt. 4:223–244.

25 See the Act XXIX of 2009.

26 See the new HCC Artt. 6:514–517.

27 Cf. the new HCC e.g. Artt. 4:198–200.

28 Source: www.mkab.hu [20.05.2014].

29 Cf. Act CLI of 2011 on the Constitutional Court: Section 63 (1) The Constitutional Court shall pass decisions on the merit of cases and on the temporary measures specified in Section 61 (2), and shall pass orders on all other issues that come up in the course of the proceedings.

30 According to the former Constitutional Court Act (i.e. Act XXXII of 1989) the Court passed exclusively decisions, however its practice from the very beginning (i.e. 1990) also knew the form of order: if the actual question to be decided was not about the merit of the case.

31 Sc. Act XX of 1949.

32 Cf. 36/2013. (XII. 5.) AB határozat and 2/2013. (I. 23.) AB. határozat. Some explanations on this notation of decisions are the followings. E.g. "36/2013" means that the current decision is the 36th in the year of 2013; "határozat" means decision; "(XII. 5.)" is the date of promulgation of the decision in the Gazette – i.e. December 5 in this case; and at last "AB" is the abbreviation of the Hungarian term for CCH, i.e. "Alkotmánybíróság". Further on I am using the English way of notation of decisions. All of the decisions assigned with this kind of notation are published in the Hungarian Official Gazette.

The 'topics' of the CCH's decisions can be enumerated as follows:

(1) the annulment of some provisions on the way of procedure without a trial;[33]
(2) the annulment of an extraordinary legal remedy – the so-called 'protest for legality'[34] – leading in some cases to the annulment or the cassation of a final court judgement;[35]
(3) the annulment of the provision, which made possible the rejection of the obviously bad (groundless) or evidently impossible claims without examining its merits;[36]
(4) the annulment of the overall right of the prosecutor in civil procedures for sue (bringing an action), intervention (a party-like participant in civil procedure), appellation (ordinary legal remedy against non-final court judgements) and revision (extraordinary legal remedy against final court judgements);[37]
(5) the annulment of the provision, which made the court possible to oblige a party to forbear blood-taking if the court ordered medical examination of e.g. blood-type or in other physiology question;[38]
(6) the declaration of unconstitutional omission on the part of the law-maker, because the Parliament omitted to make a law on the right to refute the presumption of postal service of documents in civil procedure;[39]
(7) the annulment of the provisions of the Code in force, which narrowed the right of the parties, other participants and touched persons for revision of the final court judgments in case of such violation by court, which influenced the merit of the case;[40]
(8) the annulment of the provision of the HCCP in force, which excluded the forfeit (fine) against pecuniary offence committed during civil trial by military or law enforcement personnel, because the named persons were impeached disciplinarily.[41]

If the notation is like "Decision 672/B/1990. AB", that means that the current decision should not have published in the Gazette.

33 Cf. Decision 26/1990. (XI. 8.) AB.
34 The remedy could be caveated ex officio by the President of the former Supreme Court or the Supreme Prosecutor.
35 Cf. Decision 9/1992. (I. 30.) AB.
36 Cf. Decision 59/1993. (XI. 29.) AB.
37 Cf. Decision 1/1994. (I. 7.) AB.
38 Cf. Decision 75/1995. (XII. 21.) AB.
39 Cf. Decision 46/2003. (X. 16.) AB.
40 Cf. Decision 42/2004. (XI. 9.) AB.
41 Cf. Decision 21/2007. (III. 29.) AB.

(9) The most recent, hereafter (2014–2015) realizable question in this topic is the annulment of the laws (§§ 62–63 of AOAC[42]) establishing right for the President of the National Office for the Judiciary (*NOJ*) to relocate (transfer) cases of highest priority and that of special gravity by a designation to courts, which are not so busy[43] as the court in charge, so as the 'original' court with legally grounded general or special cognizance or territorial competence, and which the action or motion was originally brought to.[44]

The constitutional base of this right of the President of the NOJ is the right for settlement of dispute within a reasonable period of time.[45] This right seems to be in collision with the right to a lawful judge.[46] The CCH has already stated that the parallel legal provision of the Code of Penal Procedure – although the law-maker has already repealed it[47] – violated the FLH and were contrary to an international treaty.[48]

The same decision about the analogous – also repealed[49] – regulation of the HCCP[50] is just provoked by the High Court of Appeal of Pécs.[51] (The CCH may declare that a repealed legal regulation is contrary to the FLH, should the given legal regulation still be applicable in a concrete case.[52])

(10) The CCH rejected the petitions on annulment of each regulation of the HCCP in force by the other dozen of published decisions examining the merits of the cases.[53]

---

42 Sc. Act CLXI of 2011 on the Organisation and Administration of Courts.

43 HCCP in force, i.e. Act III of 1952 § 47 (1).

44 Cf. infra VIII. 3.

45 Cf. with the so-called Recommendation of the President of NOJ No. 3/2012. (II. 20.) OBH on the designation of the court in charge for the purpose of providing for judging upon cases within a reasonable time. See: http://www.birosag.hu/en/information/recommendation-president-noj [03.07.2014].

46 Cf. Opinion no. 683 / 2012 of the European Commission for Democracy through Law (Venice Commission) Points No. 60–74. Source: www.venice.coe.int [20.05.2014].

47 Act CXXXI of 2013 § 2.

48 Cf. Decision 36/2013. (XII. 5.) AB.

49 Act CXXXI of 2013 § 1.

50 Cf. s. 47 s-s. (1).

51 No. of judicial order: Gf.IV.30.403/2013/6.

52 See Act CLI of 2011 on the Constitutional Court s. 41 s-s. (3) [i.e. § 41 (3)].

53 Cf. e.g. (only the published ones) Decision 13/1991. (IV. 13.) AB; Decision 38/1991. (VII. 3.) AB; Decision 57/1991. (XI. 8) AB; Decision 5/1996. (II. 23.) AB; Decision 8/2003. (III. 14.) AB; Decision 70/2006. (XII. 13.) AB; Decision 74/2009. (VII. 10.)

This complete enumeration of cases show us the problems of unconstitutionality – violations against mainly the former Constitution[54] and in two, above mentioned cases against the FLH and in some cases against international treaties as well – emerged in the last two and a half decades about the HCCP in force in Hungary.

It seems quite obvious that – among many others – these topics will orientate all members of each organizational units of the framework for the HCCP re-codification's proceeding. The reason for this fairly complete – though slightly brief – analysis lays just in this foreseeable circumstance.

V. The methods and purposes of the re-codification of the HCCP and the organizational structure of its proceeding

The Hungarian Government ordered the extensive modernization of Civil Procedural Law inclusive the HCCP and other special laws in 2013.[55]

The declared goal of the re-codification proceeding is to achieve: (i) an up-to-date Code, which (ii) fits for international standards and praxis, and which (iii) is leaning on the achievements of jurisprudence, legal practice and on the acquisitions of technology, and which (iv) is as well as capable of the more effective prevalence of new substantive law codified in the new HCC (in force since 15 March 2014).

The organizational structure established for the process of the re-codification stands on a tripedial framework executing a trifurcated system of tasks and duties. All units of the organization were founded by September 2013.

(1) The so-called *'Work-Panels for Subject-Matters'* (hereinafter called: Panels) are settled to the lowest level of this layout, and these are responsible for elaboration of proposals for each of the rules and institutions of civil procedural law. The *eight* Panels – officially signed with letters in alphabetical order – dealt with: (A) the organizational structure of Judiciary and the legal remedies; (B) the duties of courts and the rights of parties; (C) the parties and their representation; (D) the costs of processes; (E) the litigious and non-litigious orders of proceedings; (F) the probation and the evidence; (G) the applicability of modern technologies; (H) and the international aspects, EU–belonging

AB; Decision 21/2010. (II. 25.) AB; Decision 23/2010. (III. 4.) AB; Decision 180/2010. (X. 20.) AB; Decision 2/2013. (I. 23.) AB.

54 Sc. Act XX of 1949.

55 Government Decision No. 1267/2013. (17 May) on the Codification of Civil Procedural Law.

subject matters and ADR[56]. The Panels completed their work on the final Proposals in Spring of 2014.

(2) Then the *'Drafting Committee'* – as the middle rank of the scale – conducts and co-ordinates the activities of the Work-Panels, whenceafter submits the drafts for the 'Main Commission' bestowed to the top of the organizational structure of the re-codification.

(3) The *'Main Commission'* settles the conceptional disputes and decides the fundamental questions emerged by the proposals and drafts of the above mentioned subdivisions of the framework, after which evolves the Conception of the new Code.

(4) Then the *political debate of professionals' and laymen's* about the Conception (envisaged the first quarter of 2015) will be followed by the final part of the procedure, which is the *formulation of the legislative text* of the new Code by the Drafting Committee regarding the outcomes and the issues of the previous segments of the codification process (in the fourth quarter of 2016).

VI. The triangular interdependence among the FLH,the social expectations on and the characteristics of the future HCCP

This paper examines merely those topics of the final proposals of Panel 'A' and 'B', which are related – through some questions of constitutionality – to the main theme: the common European constitutional culture. The goal of these two Panels was to elaborate proposals for each of the rules and institutions of the organizational structure of Judiciary and the legal remedies, nonetheless the duties and rights of courts and parties. It is seemingly obvious that these themata are very near to the major topic of this paper.

(1) So far as the FLH grounds – declares or constitutes – the expectations of society among others on civil procedure, its nature's fundaments are even these social demands.

What is the 21st century physiognomy of characteristics and that of nature of the evolving Hungarian law of civil procedure? What does the forthcoming new civil process look like? The proposals of Panel 'B' agree that the lawsuit, the action, the process is the *Privity* (i.e. *'Interessengemeinschaft'*) of court and parties, which requires the expressive codification of their obligation to co-operate in favour of the effective execution of the purpose or the goal of the civil process.

---

56 Sc. Alternative Dispute Resolution.

The Proposal of Panel 'B' declares in its Thesis No. 2.1 that the purpose of civil process can be deducted from the rules of the FLH and that the constitutional purpose of civil procedure has the greatest significance in the re-codification. The Proposal emphasizes that – according to the tool- or instrumental-like character of the institution of civil process[57] – the civil process has preferably a designation or a function than a goal, an aim or a purpose. This designation of the institution is the satisfaction of the needs, demands and expectations of the society. The paramount expression of these demands appears in the rules of the FLH.

(2) The final Proposal[58] of the Panel 'B' (on the rights and duties of courts and parties) recites the rules of the FLH, which are highly influential on the designation and nature of the civil process, as follows.
  (a) "We, the Members of the Hungarian Nation" [...] "hold that the common goal of citizens and the State is to achieve the highest possible measure of [...] justice and liberty" [... and] "that democracy is only possible where the State serves its citizens and administers their affairs in an equitable manner, without prejudice or abuse."[59]
  (b) Then: "Everyone shall be responsible for him- or herself [...]".[60]
  (c) "Everyone shall be equal before the law."[61]
  (d) "Everyone shall have the right to have his or her affairs handled impartially, fairly and within a reasonable time by the authorities. Authorities shall be obliged to give reasons for their decisions, as provided for by an Act."[62]

---

57 The reasons for that lay also in the legal and juridical characteristics of the civil process, which locates it onto the borderline of civil and public law. This fact shows us, that the legal relationships in the civil procedural law lack that kind of subjectivity, which appears so clearly in the legal relationships of substantial law. Cf. the Final Proposal of Panel 'B' 5. [hereinafter: page].

58 This Panel is presided by T. Éless (attorney, honorary professor of School of Law of the Eötvös Loránd University, 'ELTE', Budapest). The members were Judge G. Kiss (assigned to the Curia [Kúria], i.e. the supreme court), Judge A. Döme (assigned to the High Court of Appeal of Pécs), Judge V. Ébner and Judge M. Parlagi (appointed to various Courts of Justice) and L. Wallacher (attorney).
The interim résumé of the voluminous proposals and the 'aperçu des propositions' was elaborated by Judge Döme – his work was apparently the pith and apex (i.e. main source) of the Panel's final Proposal.

59 See both in the National Avowal.

60 Cf. FLH Art. 'O'.

61 Cf. FLH Art. XV. § (1).

62 Cf. FLH Art. XXIV. § (1).

(e) "Everyone shall have the right to submit, either individually or jointly with others, written applications, complaints or proposals to any organ exercising public power."[63]
(f) "Everyone shall have the right to have any charge against him or her, or his or her rights and obligations in any litigation, adjudicated within a reasonable time in a fair and public trial by an independent and impartial court established by an Act."[64]
(g) "Everyone shall have the right to seek legal remedy against any court [...] decision which violates his or her rights or legitimate interests."[65]
(h) "Courts shall administer justice."[66]
(i) "Courts shall decide on [...] civil disputes and on other matters specified in an Act."[67]
(j) "In the course of the application of law, courts shall interpret the text of legal regulations primarily in accordance with their purposes and with the Fundamental Law. When interpreting the Fundamental Law or legal regulations, it shall be presumed that they serve moral and economical purposes which are in accordance with common sense and the public good."[68]

(3) The profound demands of the society on the civil process, which find their basis in the stressed provisions of the FLH, are named in the final Proposal of the Panel 'B' as follows.[69]
(a) The purpose of the state and that of the people shall be common.
(b) This common purpose of state and citizen shall be the highest possible rank of achievement of Justice.
(c) The civil process shall serve the citizens.
(d) The principle requirements and claims on trial courts shall be the Equity, the Rule of Law, the impartiality, the equal and fair treatment and the prudent manner of process.
(e) These requisites shall dominate the decisions on the civil dispute.

---

63 Cf. FLH Art. XXV.
64 Cf. FLH Art. XXVIII. § (1).
65 Cf. FLH Art. XXVIII. § (7).
66 Cf. FLH Art. 25. § (1) See the proposal of Judge Döme, of Judge Ébner and of Judge Parlagi.
67 Cf. FLH Art. 25. § (2) section a) Cf. The proposal of Judge Ébner's and that of Judge Parlagi also.
68 Cf. FLH Art. 28. Referred by the proposal of Judge Virág.
69 See the proposal of Judge Döme.

(f) Each party and other participant and also every subjective of the procedure shall be expected to be responsible for their facts and conducts according to their particular capabilities and possibilities.

(4) What is then the goal of the civil procedure? How is the purpose of civil process to be formulated then? Initially, in connection with the definition of the procedure's purpose, there was a perceivable dislocation of accents among the interim proposals elaborated in Panel 'B'.[70]

According to this diversity, the conceivable goals of the civil process can be construed within two different paradigms: as the purpose of the *civil procedure* or as that of the *Code*. The fact, that this bifurcate method produces a partial coincidence between the goals of process and the duty of courts, will clearly appear below. The evident – though in regard to the various proposals also inhomogeneous – goals of the procedure are first to be enlightened as follows.

(a) The purpose of the forthcoming civil procedure is the protection and the execution of the Due Process of Law as well as in an individual and in a social perspective. Even this goal of procedure grounds the very responsibility of courts.[71]

(b) The goal of the coming civil procedure is the settlement of individual civil disputes, which stands in the common interest, so in the Privity of the parties. The role of the court is the facilitation or as an *ultima ratio* the complementation or substitution of the capability of the parties to settle their dispute voluntarily on their own.[72]

(c) According to a supplemental point of view[73] annexed to the previous statements, this duty of the court cannot be interpreted as if the court would be legally responsible for the eventual and full, utter and complete settlement of the dispute of the individuals.

(d) The following statement appeared as *communis opinio* among the proposals: Justice as such or as a Substantive–Objective cannot be interpreted as the normative, i.e. legally accountable purpose of the civil process,

70 NB! I believe that it was much effective to cite the interim – the final Proposal establishing – proposals than the Proposal itself, because the authorship is much more traceable there, the documentary value of this paper is therefore also much more improvable.

71 See the proposal of Judge Ébner.

72 See the proposal of Judge Döme.

73 See the proposal of Judge Parlagi.

because normatively expectable is solely the *effort* to fulfil the postulate of Justice.[74]

(e) As the long and the short of it, according to the interim proposals[75]: the normative, constitutionally based, legally accountable purpose of the civil procedure is (i) the fair, (ii) in a reasonable period of time (iii) with the co-operation of parties and court realizable settlement of disputes (iv) arising from the parties' legal or legally relevant relationship, (v) which materializes the palpable fruits of the effort to fulfil the postulate of Justice.

The final Proposal compressed this into the following definition: The constitutional purpose – then not the designation (!) – of civil process is the responsible settlement of private law disputes in contribution of the court.[76]

(f) One of the proposals[77] states the goals of the procedure from the angle of the forthcoming Code, i.e. it defines the purpose of the *Code* and not that of the *procedure*. However, it does mean that the *purposes* of the Code determinate even its *principles* and through this the purposes of the process as well.

(g) The outcomes of this approach are still common. As the ground of the future HCCP some principles subsist from the Code in force: the principle of fair trial, and the principle of the reasonable period of time realizable settlement of dispute. These are even the duties of the courts, which are in a measure enrooted into the one testifier of the common European constitutional culture: the judicial practice of the *Cour Européenne des Droits de l'Homme* (Strasbourg).

In lack of a similar high ranked (in an Act) regulation, those constitutional principles – being in connection with the purpose of the civil process – must appear in the new HCCP, which can not prevail between the subjects of the process through

74 The reason for this is that the FLH does not define the conception or the notion of 'Justice'. The CCH layed down in 1992 [Decision 9/1992. (I. 30.) AB] that a right to enforce substantive Justice or to ensure every court sentence to be lawful can not be guaranteed constitutionally. The purpose or the goal of the state can only be the pursuit or the effort to try to realize these aims through elaborating legal institutes and appropriate processual warranties. The substantive Justice as an ideal differs from the real. Cf. Final Proposal of Panel 'B' 7.

75 Synthesized by Judge Döme.

76 Cf. Final Proposal of Panel 'B' 10.

77 See the proposal of Judge Parlagi.

a direct reference to the FLH. These principles are – according to the final Proposal of Panel 'B'[78] – the principle of *co-operation*, of *disposition*, of *settlement of dispute* and that of *responsibility*.

(h) The explicit codification of the purpose of civil process, which is enrooted into the FLH and into the common European constitutional traditions, is truly questionable. Its codification requires two attributes: its autonomous normative power and its efficiency to avoid the harm of the procedural Prohibition of Chicane.[79]

(i) If it can have normative power, it should be codified into the HCCP. Its autonomous normative power lays in its capability to dissolve the collisions emerged between the principles of civil procedural law or between the general provisions of the forthcoming HCCP.

(ii) If the expressive codification of the purpose of civil process has a positive effect on the avoidance and prevention of the harm of the procedural Prohibition of Chicane, the codification is proper.

Sometimes the process or the trial itself becomes the instrument of unlawful harms and injuries (scil. gain of time, persecution, harassment, blackmail, industrial espionage, fraud against creditors etc.).

The legal, codified definition of the purpose of civil process can make the judge capable to apply the Prohibition of Chicane not only at the end of the proceeding, but already at the beginning of it (with certain procedural law guaranties) in these unwished situations.[80]

VII. The duties of courts determined by the constitutionally defined designation of the civil process

So far as the FLH-based social expectations on civil process define its designation (or goal, purpose), that of the process lays down the fundaments of the duties of courts, because the essential duty of court consists in the effort to realize and materialize the designation (goal, purpose) of the civil procedure.

(1) Some of these provisions regulating the duty of courts had already been codified appropriately and practicably into the FLH: (i) the achievement the

78 Cf. Final Proposal of Panel 'B' 10.

79 To the point (h) see the final Proposal of Panel 'B' 12–13.

80 Cf. Final Proposal of Panel 'B' 12–13.

highest possible measure of Justice;[81] (ii) the State serves its citizens and administers their affairs in an equitable manner, without prejudice or abuse;[82] (iii) Equality before the Law;[83] (iv) Fair Trial;[84] (v) Adjudication within a Reasonable Period of Time;[85] (vi) Independency and Impartiality of Courts;[86] (vii) Publicity.[87]

(a) In some cases it would therefore be inappropriate to codify them into the new Code also, as long as causeless duplicated regulations are superfluous and are to be deregulated as such.

(b) Although there is *no need* to double-codify the principle of the *settlement of dispute within a reasonable period of time*, which is a part not only of the FLH but also the public international law,[88] every single relevant rule of the coming HCCP is for the realization of this postulate.

According to the realization of this task, the final Proposal's Thesis No. 6[89] suggests the elaboration of a more clear way of the so-called *caesura of process*, which firmly divides the previously more or less homogeneous process into two parts: the part of the so-called *Appearance* (i.e. *'Klageeinlassung'* under German law) with the possibility of *preclusion* and the part of the *settlement of dispute by decision on its merits.*

(c) Compared with the previous principle, the postulate of and the right to a *fair trial is to be* codified into the new HCCP but exclusively in accordance with the constitutional purpose of the civil procedure. This means that the postulate is to be regulated as the *common responsibility* of every single subject of the procedure: so the court and *also the parties and the other participants*! Each interim[90] and also the final[91] proposal accorded.

---

81 Cf. FLH – the National Avowal [of Faith].

82 Cf. FLH – in the National Avowal [of Faith].

83 The next four principles are among the regulations of the "Freedom and Responsibility" – scil. FLH Artt. I–XXXI. – cf. Art. XV.

84 Cf. FLH Artt. XXVIII. § (1).

85 Cf. FLH Artt. XXVIII. § (1).

86 Cf. FLH Artt. XXVIII. § (1).

87 Cf. FLH Artt. XXVIII. § (1).

88 Cf. European Convention on Human Rights Art. 6. and the Charter of Fundamental Rights of the European Union Art. 47.

89 Cf. Final Proposal of Panel 'B' 41–56.

90 See especially the proposals of Judge Döme and that of Judge Parlagi.

91 Cf. Final Proposal of Panel 'B' 17.

(d) Hereby shall be emphasized that the question of superfluous double-codification emerges not only in connection with the FLH, but with regard to the Act CLXI of 2011 on the Organisation and Administration of Courts (hereinafter *AOAC*) as well. The Postulate and the Principle of the Independency of Courts has obviously an overriding importance in the common European constitutional culture.

The whole Act (AOAC) – according to its Preamble – is scil. adopted in favour of (i) the legal effectivity of highest possible measures in the practice of courts' competences on the top level of the Rule of Law, (ii) the Independency of Courts and (iii) the unity of the judicial practice. All the special rules of the extensive[92] AOAC is so adopted for the fulfilment of these constitutional goals in their highest possible rank. The double-codification of these rules into the new HCCP seems therefore superfluous.

(e) The final Proposal of Panel 'B' also admits under its Theses No. 3.1–5 that:
(i) the duties of courts, the re-codification of which is reasonable and current, are the instruments of the realization of the civil process' purpose;
(ii) also the rights and obligations of parties have to serve the purpose of the process, and they are to be codified reasonably altogether with the duties of courts;
(iii) although it is not necessary to double-codify the duties of courts having been ruled already in the FLH, the postulate of and the right to a fair trial is to be codified in the new HCCP as the common responsibility of all subjects of the civil process, i.e. every kind of participants inclusive the courts.[93]

(2) One of the very duties of courts, which is based also in the FLH, is the realization of the civil right *to settle a* legally relevant, civil *dispute*: "Courts shall decide on [...] civil disputes, other matters defined by laws [...]."[94]

As the *duty* of the court, this *right* is rather about the *'what'* – so about the fact of the litigious or non-litigious process aiming the examination of the petitioned decision –, than about the *'how'* – so the impartial, fair etc. *manner* of the decision and that of the trial and that of the process as a whole as well. This does not mean however, that this rule, which appeared already in the FLH, should remain uncodified in the future HCCP. The reason for that is the

92 Almost 200 pieces of Artt. in force.
93 Cf. Final Proposal of Panel 'B' 14.
94 Cf. FLH Art. 25. § (2) section a).

function of this provision: determining the whole character of procedure and its each particular rule.

The situation is very similar to the constitutional principle, according to what: "Courts shall administer justice."[95] It does not need to be expressively 'echoed' or repeated in the new Code, but in fact this constitutional provision for the courts is at the same time an implicit principle of the forthcoming HCCP, which determines and pervades also the whole Code and its every single rule as well. This topic with all of its detailed rules belongs however both to the theme of the *'art of jurisdiction'* as one of the central questions of legal theory and to the practical problems of probation, evidence and proof. Because of this it – as such – cannot be further dissected in this paper.

VIII. Some remarks on the court system and on the legal remedies

(1) The final Proposal[96] of the Panel 'A' synthesized the work performed to eleven theses, which can thematically be collocated (grouped) as follows.

(a) The System of Forum in the renewed civil procedural law shall adapt itself to the already existing four levels model of Judiciary.[97]

(b) (i) The civil jurisdiction of first instance shall remain divided between the local (i.e. district courts[98]) and the first instance jurisdiction of the courts of justice (i.e. quasi county courts[99]).[100] (ii) The structural renovation of the local courts' system directly defines the according questions of the re-codification.[101] (iii) The question of the judicial panels' personal composition by the courts of justice at first instance needs to be further investigated.[102]

---

95 Cf. FLH Art. 25. § (1).

96 This is titled originally as "Synthetic Report", but the lawful title is (final) Proposal.

97 Cf. Thesis No. 1. in the final Proposal of Panel 'A'.

98 I.e. the so-called „járásbíróság" in Hungarian, which means, that the court's territorial competence is more or less adapted to the smallest local administrative unit between the municipalities and the counties, the so-called „járás".

99 I.e. the so-called „törvényszék" in Hungarian, which means, that the court's territorial competence is more or less adapted to the administrative unit of the counties. These courts have competence for first and also for second instance, i.e. revisionary jurisdiction (against district court's decisions).

100 Cf. Thesis No. 2. in the final Proposal of Panel 'A'.

101 Cf. Thesis No. 7. ibid.

102 Cf. Thesis No. 9. ibid.

(c) (i) The regulation of the division of competences shall be realized through the partition of two groups of cases: the general group of cases and the taxatively enumerated items of cases taken out from the general group of cases.[103] (ii) There is no need to modify the existing model.[104]
(d) The modification of the territorial competence or cognizance rules seems to be reasonable to a narrower extent.[105]
(e) The relocation or transfer of cases of highest priority by the designation of the court in charge is not unconstitutional (cf. *supra* IV.9).[106]
(f) The integration of labour jurisdiction into the general civil jurisdiction shall be the object of further investigations.[107]
(g) The re-introduction of the new-old institution of sub-judges shall be deeply investigated through the clarification of the so-called judicial secretaries' (cca. law clerks', professional judicial assistants') legal position, fungibility and civil procedural operability.[108]
(h) The modification of legal remedies' system is not acute at this time.[109]

(2) The questions of highest constitutional relevance are enumerated under points (a), (b/iii) and (e) above.
(a) The Judiciary system of the renewed civil procedure shall accord to the existent court system of four levels, there is no need for its paradigmatic modification.

Modern societies use different techniques of dispute settlement: the ADRs (alternative dispute resolutions), the mediation, the arbitration and obviously mainly the jurisdiction by the state's Judiciary system.[110] According to the FLH, the organisation of the Judiciary shall have multiple levels.[111] The detailed rules for the organisation and administration of courts shall be laid down[112]

---

103 Cf. Thesis No. 3. ibid.
104 Cf. Thesis No. 4. ibid.
105 Cf. Thesis No. 5. ibid.
106 Cf. Thesis No. 6. ibid.
107 Cf. Thesis No. 8. ibid.
108 Cf. Thesis No. 10. ibid.
109 Cf. Thesis No. 11. ibid.
110 Sc. courts shall administer justice; cf. FLH Art. 25 § (1).
111 Cf. FLH Art. 25 § (4).
112 Cf. FLH Art. 25 § (8).

in a so-called Cardinal Act[113], which is the AOAC[114]. Its second Chapter defines the system of Judiciary, its levels, instances, and the basic characteristics of the division of competences. The cardinality of the AOAC has a high relevance in the definition of the direction of HCCP's re-codification, because the HCCP in force is not and likewise the new HCCP will presumably not be a Cardinal Act, so the HCCP shall be adapted also to the AOAC.

Hereby we shall repeatedly remind that the whole AOAC[115] is adopted in favour of the legal effectivity of courts' competences at its highest possible measure, that of the realization of the Rule of Law, the Independency of Courts and the unity of the judicial practice. The double-codification of the single rules (cca. 200 Artt.) of the AOAC – which is adopted for the fulfilment of these constitutional goals – into the new HCCP would seem therefore redundant.

(b) According to the final Proposal, the relocation (transfer) of cases of highest priority and that of greatest gravity by the designation of the court in charge has no constitutional hindrance (cf. *supra* IV.9 and VIII.1.e).

While the social and economical circumstances change, new types of disputes emerge and the judicial statistics of cases vary. The legal regulations on cognizance and competence can respond only to persistent and perdurable changes of types of civil law disputes.

Au contraire, if the fluctuation is only temporal and provisional, the frequent amendment of law is less appropriate, than the introduction of flexible rules on administrative rights (authorities) to relocate and transfer cases by e.g. designation of the court in charge.[116]

The constitutional goal is the homogeneous allocation of cases, because it has direct effect e.g. on the right for settlement of dispute within a reasonable period of time. This constitutional postulate underlines however the *exceptional* character of the legal instrument of relocating cases by the designation the court in charge, and that its every relevant circumstance and condition shall be regulated in an Act, so the own discretion of the authorized designator shall be

113 According to FLH Art. T § (4): Cardinal Acts shall be Acts, for the adoption or amendment of which the votes of two-thirds of the Members of the National Assembly present shall be required.

114 Sc. the Act CLXI of 2011 on the Organisation and Administration of Courts.

115 Sc. according to its Preamble.

116 Cf. the final Proposal of Panel 'A' 7.

minimal. Some other constitutional guarantee shall also be introduced,[117] such as: the legal remedies against the decision of the designator, and that the right for designation shall remain in the bosom of the independent and impartial system of courts, and automatic mechanisms in the choice of the newly appointed (signed) court.[118]

(c) According to the FLH,[119] unless otherwise provided in an Act, courts shall adjudicate in chambers. The final Proposal of Panel 'A' showed some constitutional and nonetheless practical problems about the lack of the general rule on joint jurisdiction in adjudication of *first instance* either in the district courts or in the courts of justice (the former county courts). The sum up of the investigations was that the judicial panels' personal composition by the different levels of courts of first instance needs to be further researched.[120]

The constitutional side of the emerged problem is the seeming collision between the constitutional principle of joint jurisdiction (i.e. the adjudication in chambers composed either of a single professional judge and two assessor laymen or of three professional judges) and some general rules of HCCP in force on single judge jurisdiction of first instance.[121] The court of appellatory instance adjudicates scil. generally in chambers composed of three professional judges.[122]

The joint jurisdiction is on the other hand a constitutional principle,[123] likewise the rule on the possibility of participation of non-professional judges (assessor laymen) in the administration of justice: "Non-professional judges shall *also* participate in the administration of justice in the cases and ways specified in an Act."[124]

Accordingly: (a) the single judge jurisdiction is only the exceptional case of adjudication, so the joint one shall be the general rule irrespectively the level or the instance of the adjudication; (b) the principle of joint jurisdiction shall not be applied to the chambers composed also of laymen assessors.

117 Cf. Opinion no. 683 / 2012 of the European Commission for Democracy through Law (Venice Commission) Points No. 60–74. Source: www.venice.coe.int [20.05.2014].

118 Cf. the final Proposal of Panel 'A' 7.

119 Cf. FLH Art. 27 § (1).

120 Cf. Thesis No. 9. ibid.

121 Cf. HCCP in force § 11 (1).

122 Cf. HCCP in force § 11 (4).

123 Cf. FLH Art. 27 § (1).

124 Cf. FLH Art. 27 § (2).

This modification would realize an enormous change in the Hungarian court system, therefore the final Proposal suggests further prudent researches.

Although the FLH ordered the detailed rules for the organisation and administration of courts to a cardinal Act[125] (thus ignored the regulation of these question in itself), the Official Motives of the FLH do not give us any lucid reason of elevating the rule of joint jurisdiction to the very high rank of the constitutional postulates.

The final Proposal of Panel 'A' stated therefore that under these circumstances the Motives would have clarified some problems. Furthermore, neither the Motives of the FLH, nor the AOAC and its Motives contain any guideline for the legislator, how and under which conditions it can *abstain* the application of joint jurisdiction. The joint jurisdiction, so the adjudication in chambers composed of three professional judges in the courts of *first* instance would enormously increase the *functional* effectivity of the Judiciary, but analogically decrease its *cost* effectivity. However the first one has constitutionally a superior importance – states the Proposal.

Not besides, it is a great public interest, that disputes shall be settled as low instance of jurisdiction as possible. According to the Proposal, the question of cost ineffectivity can be reposed by connecting this problem to the regulations of competences' division. If the joint jurisdiction of first instance would be realized only in cases before the courts of justice (the former county courts), the relative cost ineffectivity would also be justifiable.[126]

---

125 Cf. FLH Art. 25 § (8).

126 The Proposal suggests – cf. Page 15 – that the refilling of staff shall be executed partially through the application of the personnel of sub-judges. See supra VIII.1.g.

DIA-LOGOS
Schriften zu Philosophie und Sozialwissenschaften
Studies in Philosophy and Social Sciences

Herausgegeben von
Edited by
Tadeusz Buksiński & Piotr W. Juchacz

"*Dia-Logos. Studies in Philosophy and Social Sciences* is a peer-reviewed book series publishing valuable monographs and edited volumes on various aspects of philosophy and social sciences. The series is intended to be an interdisciplinary forum of deliberation according to our firm belief that challenges of the contemporary world require common and multilevel research. The *Dia-Logos* series does not represent a single ideology or school of thought, but it is open to different trends and various styles of reflection, trying to understand better the contemporary world. We invite the submission of manuscripts of monographs and edited volumes from academic philosophers and social scientists."

Bd. / Vol. 1 Piotr W. Juchacz / Roman Kozłowski (Hrsg.): Freiheit und Verantwortung. Moral, Recht und Politik. 2002.

Bd. / Vol. 2 Norbert Leśniewski / Ewa Nowak-Juchacz (Hrsg.): Die Zeit Heideggers. 2002.

Bd. / Vol. 3 Marek Kwiek (ed.): The University, Globalization, Central Europe. 2003.

Bd. / Vol. 4 Ewa Czerwińska-Schupp (Hrsg.): Philosophie an der Schwelle des 21. Jahrhunderts. Geschichte der Philosophie, Philosophische Anthropologie, Ethik, Wissenschaftstheorie, Politische Philosophie. 2003.

Bd. / Vol. 5 Danuta Sobczyńska / Pawel Zeidler / Ewa Zielonacka-Lis (eds.): Chemistry in the Philosophical Melting Pot. 2004.

Bd. / Vol. 6 Marek Kwiek: Intellectuals, Power, and Knowledge. Studies in the Philosophy of Culture and Education. 2004.

Bd. / Vol. 7 Marek Kwiek: The University and the State. A Study into Global Transformations. 2006.

Bd. / Vol. 8 Andrzej Przylebski (Hrsg.): Das Erbe Gadamers. 2006.

Bd. / Vol. 9 Ewa Czerwińska-Schupp (ed.): Values and Norms in the Age of Globalization. 2007.

Bd. / Vol. 10 Tadeusz Buksiński (ed.): Democracy in Western and Post-Communist Countries. Twenty Years after the Fall of Communism. 2009.

Bd. / Vol. 11 Marek Zirk-Sadowski / Mariusz Golecki / Bartosz Wojciechowski (eds.): Multicentrism as an Emerging Paradigm in Legal Theory. 2009.

Bd. / Vol. 12 Bartosz Wojciechowski: Philosophical Approach to the Interculturality of Criminal Law. 2010.

Bd. / Vol. 13 Marek Nowak / Michał Nowosielski (eds.): (Post)transformational Migration. Inequalities, Welfare State, and Horizontal Mobility. 2011.

Bd. / Vol. 14 Tadeusz Buksiński (ed.): Religions in the Public Spheres. 2011.

Bd. / Vol. 15 Bartosz Wojciechowski / Piotr W. Juchacz / Karolina M. Cern (eds.): Legal Rules, Moral Norms and Democratic Principles. 2013.

Bd. / Vol. 16 Ewa Nowak / Dawn E. Schrader / Boris Zizek (eds.): Educating Competencies for Democracy. 2013.

Bd. / Vol. 17 Tadeusz Buksiński (ed.): Identities and Modernizations. 2013.

Bd. / Vol. 18 Karolina M. Cern: The Counterfactual Yardstick. Normativity, Self-Constitutionalisation and the Public Sphere. 2014.

Bd. / Vol. 19 Vito Breda / Lidia Rodak (eds.). Diverse Narratives of Legal Objectivity. An Interdisciplinary Perspective. 2016.

Bd. / Vol. 20 Marek Woszczek: Platonic Wholes and Quantum Ontology. Translated by Katarzyna Kretkowska. 2015.

Bd./Vol. 21 Roman Hauser / Marek Zirk-Sadowski / Bartosz Wojciechowski (eds.): The Common European Constitutional Culture. Its Sources, Limits and Identity. 2016.

www.peterlang.com

www.ingramcontent.com/pod-product-compliance
Ingram Content Group UK Ltd.
Pitfield, Milton Keynes, MK11 3LW, UK
UKHW041828100926
8556IPUK00002B/73

9 783631 659915